THE BiBLe ALMANAC FOR KiDS

Copyright © 2004 by Educational Publishing Concepts, Inc.
Wheaton, IL 60189

Published in Lakeland, Florida, by White Stone Books.

Scripture quotations noted KJV are from the KING JAMES VERSION.

Scripture quotations noted NIV are from the HOLY BIBLE: NEW INTERNATIONAL VERSION®. Copyright © 1973, 1978, 1984 by International Bible Society. Used by permission of Zondervan Publishing House. All rights reserved.

Scripture quotations noted NLT are from the Holy Bible, New Living Translation, copyright © 1996. Used by permission of Tyndale House Publishers, Inc., Wheaton, Illinois 60189. All rights reserved.

Managing Editor: Carolyn Larsen
Manuscript written and prepared by Terry Hall
Design: Diane Bay, Bay Design, Wheaton, Illinois

ISBN: 1-59379-018-X

Printed in the United States of America

04 05 06 07 08   5 4 3 2

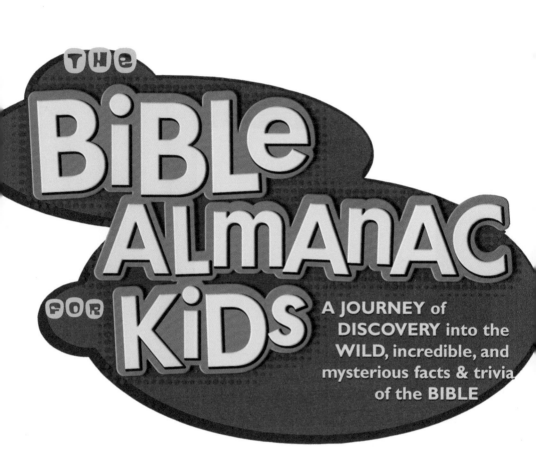

THE BiBLE ALMANAC FOR KIDS

A JOURNEY of DISCOVERY into the WILD, incredible, and mysterious facts & trivia of the BIBLE

Terry Hall

WHITE STONE BOOKS
LAKELAND, FLORIDA

TABLE OF CONTENTS

INTRODUCTION

WELCOME TO THE GREAT BIBLE ALMANAC ADVENTURE!

PREPARE TO EMBARK ON A JOURNEY FILLED WITH IN-TERESTING FACTS ABOUT THE BIBLE, ITS PEOPLE, PLACES AND WHAT LIFE WAS REALLY LIKE IN BIBLE TIMES.

YOU WILL ALSO DISCOVER LOADS OF INFORMATION ABOUT LIFE TODAY, SUCH AS STORIES ABOUT FAMOUS CHILDREN AUTHORS, TOP TEN LISTS, TV SHOWS, MOVIES AND SO MUCH MORE.

BE SURE TO CHECK OUT THE INDEX IN THE BACK OF THE BOOK TO LOOK UP SPECIFIC THINGS THAT INTEREST YOU.

WE KNOW YOU WILL ENJOY EACH AND EVERY PAGE IN THIS EXCITING BOOK. AND, ALONG THE WAY YOU MAY JUST DISCOVER SOME NEW INTERESTS, HOBBIES, AND WAYS YOU CAN USE THE GIFTS AND TALENTS THAT GOD HAS GIVEN YOU!

LET THE JOURNEY BEGIN!

Angels

What's a Real Angel Like?

Angels are God's spirit messengers (Hebrews 1:14). Everyone has at least one guardian angel (Matthew 18:10).

Angels are special creations. The number of the angels always remains the same. The Bible says there are tens of thousands (Daniel 7:10).

Angels are spirits. They are invisible. However, there have been times when God has allowed people to see angels.

Angels are powerful creatures (2 Thessalonians 1:7). But they are not all-powerful like God. They do only what God tells them to.

Angels were once allowed to choose whether or not to love and obey God. At one time Lucifer, a top-ranking angel, led a rebellion against God. He and his followers were cast out of Heaven. Lucifer became Satan. His followers became demons. They are in the world today, but God limits their powers. Someday all the evil angels will be cast into Hell forever.

Angelic Activities

Angels keep busy. It's good they don't have to take time to sleep.

Angels: * Praise God (Isaiah 6:1-4)
* Deliver God's messages to people (Matthew 1:20)
* Help God's people (Psalm 91:11)
* Punish God's enemies (Acts 12:21-23)
* Explain God's plans (Daniel 10:13, 14)
* Bring answers to prayer (Luke 1:13)
* Rejoice over people who turn from their sins to God (Luke 15:7, 10)
* Lead God's people (Exodus 23:20, 21)

The angel Gabriel told Mary that Jesus was going to be born. The archangel Michael is the commander in chief of God's army of angels. The angel of the Lord is God himself. He spoke to Moses out of a burning bush.

Angels may be disguised as ordinary people. Abraham entertained three visitors and later realized they were angels (Genesis 18:1, 2; 19:1).

Did You Know?

Amazon.com lists 781 books for kids about angels or that have angel in the title.

Billy Graham, the famous evangelist, wrote a best-seller about angels, *Angels: God's Secret Agents* (Word). You might also enjoy *Flights of Angels* by Joni Eareckson Tada and others (Dimensions for Living).

Big Screen Angels

It's a Wonderful Life (Liberty Films, 1946)
Clarence the clockmaker AS2 (angel second class) "earns his wings" by showing George Bailey (Jimmy Stewart) what life would have been like if he had never been born. One of the greatest classic films of all time. www.geocities.com/Hollywood/Makeup/8156

Angels in the Outfield (Disney, 1951)
When a young boy prays for a father and a struggling baseball team prays for a pennant, angels are assigned to make that possible. http://disneyvideos.disney.go.com/moviefinder

The Bishop's Wife (RKO Radio, 1947)
When a bishop trying to build a new cathedral prays for guidance, an angel named Dudley (Cary Grant) arrives. www.carygrant.net/reviews/bishop.html

TV Angels

Touched by an Angel (CBS)
For nine years, Monica, Tess, Andrew, Gloria and many popular guest stars brought a message of God's love to weekly prime-time TV. Nielsen found over 16 million households tuned in to one episode. The program moved to the Hallmark Channel in September 2003. Meet the cast and go behind the scenes at http://www.touched.com.

7th Heaven (WB)
This award-winning family drama about a minister and his wife sharing love, laughter and life with their seven children has been Warner Brothers' highest-rated series for the past four seasons. Link to the whole family, including Happy the dog at www.thewb.com/Shows/Show/0,7353,||152,00.html

Did You Know?

The Internet Movie Database lists 114 films, videos and TV series with angel themes. It lists 641 titles containing the word "angel" as well as 532 actors and 147 actresses by that name. http://www.imdb.com

Touched by an Angel has been nominated for 11 Emmy Awards, two Golden Globe Awards and numerous Image, TV Guide, Screen Actors Guild and other awards.

They Saw Angels

Angels are usually invisible. But dozens of real people in the Bible saw angels and interacted with them. They believe angels are real. Read their fascinating stories for yourself.

Abraham (Genesis 22:11, 12)
Apostles (Acts 1:10, 11)
Balaam (Numbers 22:21-35)
Cornelius (Acts 10:1-8)
Daniel (Daniel 6:21, 22)
David (2 Samuel 24:17)
Donkey (Numbers 22:22-35)
Elijah (I Kings 19:5)
Elisha's servant (2 Kings 6:15-17)
Gideon (Judges 6:11-22)
Hagar (Genesis 21:17)
Isaiah (Isaiah 6:1-7)
Jacob (Genesis 28:10-19)
Jesus (Matthew 4:11)
John (Revelation 1:1, 5:2-7)
Joseph (Matthew 1:20, 21; 2:13)
Joshua (Joshua 5:13,14)
Lot, his wife and daughters (Genesis 19:1-22)
Manoah and his wife (Judges 13:1-20)
Mary (Luke 1:26-38)
Moses (Exodus 3:2)
Nebuchadnezzar (Daniel 3:25)
Paul (Acts 27:23)
Peter (Acts 12:7-10)
Peter and John (Acts 5:19)
Philip (Acts 8:26)
Shadrach, Meshach and Abednego (Daniel 3:25-28)
Shepherds (Luke 2:8-14)
Women at Jesus' tomb (Matthew 28:2-6)
Zacharias (Luke 1:5-25)
Zechariah (Zechariah 1-6)

Look for Angels

In these accounts, look for angels who:

* ate meals with people
* tapped a preacher in prison
* delivered warnings
* announced births
* were seen by a donkey and its rider
* rescued people
* startled shepherds
* wrestled with a man all night
* climbed a stairway to heaven
* cooked a meal
* rode in chariots of fire
* shut lions' mouths

For Fun

How many uses of the word "angel" can you think of in three minutes? (Starter hints: baseball, food, city. Some answers on page 332)

Angels Around School

Rebels advanced on a school in the Congo where 200 missionary children lived. "They planned to kill the children and teachers," Corrie ten Boom writes. "Those inside the school prayed for protection.

"The rebels came close but suddenly ran away! The same thing happened on the second and third day. One of the rebels was wounded and brought to the hospital. The doctor asked, 'Why didn't you attack the school as you planned?'

"We couldn't," the soldier said. "We saw hundreds of soldiers in white uniforms, and we were scared."

"In Africa," Corrie explains, "soldiers never wear white uniforms. So it must have been angels."

Angels in Church

After her 11-year-old nephew, Brian, was killed by a bus, Zena Marie Anagnostou went to church. A young boy stepped aside to let her be seated. Zena slumped into the pew. Some elderly ladies sat behind her and the boy.

Zena noticed the young boy recited the prayers perfectly. Not only did he say the people's responses, he also murmured the priest's part. "He glowed with peace. He sang all the songs in a beautiful voice, without using the songbook," Zena says. Her sorrowing spirit began to lift. She decided she would compliment him when the service was over.

When they recited the Lord's Prayer, the boy took Zena's hand, and she felt a serenity seeping into her. But after Communion, the boy suddenly disappeared.

When the service ended, Zena asked the ladies behind her, "Did you happen to notice where that boy who sat in front of you went?"

The ladies looked at each other, puzzled. "There was no boy in front of us, dear," one told her gently. "You were alone in the pew."

Surely Brian's guardian angel sent Zena a signal that all is well.

Did You Know?

In her book, *The Hiding Place*, Corrie ten Boom tells how angels protected her in a concentration camp. http://www.billygraham.org/ourMinistries/WorldWidePictures/theHidingPlace

Joan Wester Anderson's book, *Where Angels Walk*, records 50 true stories of heavenly visitors. http://joanwanderson.com/where_angels_walk.htm

Do you have an angel story you'd like to share? See page 350.

Angel Tree

When Sam was 5 and Alex was 2 their parents went to prison and the boys went to live with their grandparents. Two years later they were contacted by Angel Tree.

"For five years now, Angel Tree has provided gifts for my grandsons and paid their way to camp," says their grandmother.

Sam has accepted Christ and faithfully reads his Bible and attends the church youth group. His grandparents are now involved in a Bible study there. Sam and Alex also try to reach out to others. Sam helps a disabled student at his school, and Alex serves as an interpreter for a deaf girl.

Angel Tree staff encourages inmates to sign up their children to receive Christmas gifts from volunteers (on behalf of the incarcerated parent). "Look Mom! I told you Daddy wouldn't forget me" was Amanda's reaction when she received her Angel Tree Christmas gift.

Angel Tree started in Birmingham, Alabama, in 1982 by Mary Kay Beard, an ex-prisoner who once was on the FBI's "Most Wanted" list. She received permission to put Christmas trees in shopping malls to recruit shoppers to purchase presents for prisoners' children. Angel tags on the tree bore a child's name and desired gift. When Mary Kay saw women inmates gather soap and shampoo to give to their kids as gifts, she realized "children don't care as much about things as they do about being loved."

Did You Know?

Children of prisoners are five times more likely to end up in prison.

Nearly two million children have an incarcerated parent. An estimated 10 million kids nationwide have had one or both parents behind bars at some time.

In 2001, Angel Tree Christmas volunteers reached out to 612,000 children across the United States. Over 4.5 million prisoners' children have received 8.5 million Angel Christmas Tree gifts since 1982.

In 2002, 6,500 children attended Christian camps through Angel Tree Camping.

More than 14,500 churches in all 50 states participate in Angel Tree.

Find out more at www.angeltree.org or call 800-55-ANGEL.

Angel Awareness

1. At an angel's direction, he joined the treasurer of Ethiopia in his chariot.

2. Cast out of her home twice by Sarah, this servant girl was encouraged by an angel both times.

3. Because he would not give glory to God, this proud New Testament king was killed by an angel.

4. His donkey got his attention so an angel could address him.

5. An angel appeared to this priest by an altar prior to his son's birth.

6. An angel called this person from threshing wheat to defeat the Midianites.

7. After sinfully numbering his subjects, this king saw an angel kill seventy thousand people.

8. Though this man was on trial for his life, his face looked like an angel's.

9. He saw an angel holding a little scroll.

10. This archangel disputed with the devil over Moses' body.

11. An angel shut lions' mouths to protect him.

12. In a great sea storm on his way to Rome, an angel encouraged him.

13. As he was about to kill his son, he was stopped by an angel.

14. Two angels rescued him from the destruction of Sodom.

15. He was encouraged by an angel to continue with his wedding plans.

16. Angels ministered to him after forty days of fasting and temptation in the wilderness.

17. In his dream he saw angels going up and down a stairway to Heaven.

18. He saw an angel in flames of fire from within a bush.

19. After Jesus' birth good news of great joy was announced to this group by an angel.

20. This place has been prepared for the devil and his angels.

ANIMALS

"**Creature**" means a created being something God gave life. God made all the animals, birds, insects and fish. The Bible mentions 108 different creatures, starting with every letter of the alphabet except one. They are all pictured on these two pages. How many can you name?

(Answers are on page 332)

Record Holders

Many records are held among the 108 different animals and creatures mentioned in the Bible.

Fastest
Nine of the 10 fastest animals in the world are mentioned in the Bible. They are (speed in miles per hour clocked for a quarter mile): cheetah (65), pronghorn antelope (55), Mongolian gazelle (50), springbok (50), Grant's gazelle (47), brown hare (45), horse (43), greyhound (42), red deer (42).
Peregrine falcons can fly as fast as 217 miles per hour.

Sleepiest
The sloth sleeps an average of 20 hours per day. Only the koala sleeps longer (22). In the Bible opossums (19), squirrels (14), cats (13) and pigs (13) are also among the sleepyheads.

Heaviest
An African elephant is the heaviest terrestrial mammal, topping the scale at 7 tons (14,432 pounds). At 24 feet it was also the longest in this category. African elephants also hold the longest gestation record: 660 days to produce a baby.
Whales take the top 7 spots for heaviest marine mammals.
Blue whales can grow to 110 feet and weigh 143 tons.
(They also have gullets large enough to swallow a prophet.)

Largest
The ostrich is the largest flightless bird, growing to 108 inches tall. Storks have wingspans up to 13 feet across.

Smallest
Jesus used the gnat as an object lesson in a message (Matthew 23:24).

Did You Know?

Camels don't store water in their humps. Extra water is stored in their stomachs. A camel can live off the fat in its humps on long trips.

Elephants are only hinted at in the Bible. King Solomon imported ivory from elephants' tusks. (1 Kings 10:18)

A great fish swallowed Jonah the prophet and spit him out unharmed three days later. (Jonah 1:17)

Jesus fed five thousand people with two fishes from a kid's lunch. (John 6:9-12)

Pigs and people have something in common. They are the only mammals that can get sunburned. Can you guess why? (Hint: It has to do with how much hair they have.)

Dinosaur bones have been found on every continent, even in Antarctica.

A chameleon can move its eyes in two directions at the same time.

Some male songbirds sing more than 2,000 times each day.

Pet Profiles

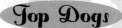
Top Ten Pets

Dogs and cats are by far the favorite pets for USA families.

Top Dogs

Breeds: Labrador retrievers outnumber the next most common breed 3 to 1. The top 10: Labrador retriever, golden retriever, German shepherd, rottweiler, dachshund, beagle, poodle, Chihuahua, Yorkshire terrier, pomeranian.

Names: American Pet Classics analyzed 140,000 I.D. tags and found the top 10 dogs' names to be: Max, Molly, Buddy, Maggie, Bailey, Jake, Lucy, Sam, Sadie and Shadow.

Top Cats

Breeds: Persian cats outnumber all other feline pets combined by 3 to 1 with 35,400 registered in the USA. The other most common breeds are: Maine coon, Siamese, exotic, Abyssinian, Oriental.

Names: Five of the top 10 names for cat pets start with the letter S: Tiger, Sam, Max, Tigger, Smokey, Shadow, Sammy, Simba, Lucky and Misty.

Did You Know?

Border collies and poodles tested highest on dog IQ tests. Rotweilers and Australian cattle dogs received the lowest scores.

Three out of every four dogs can perform at least one trick.

The top goldfish name is Jaws! Other top fish names in order: Goldie, Fred, Tom, Bubbles, George, Flipper, Ben, Jerry and Sam. Interesting: More fish are given common kids' names than cats receive.

Greyhounds are the fastest breed of dogs. They have been clocked at speeds of 40 miles per hour and are used in races.

How many motion pictures can you think of which feature dog stars? (For starters: 101 Dalmatians, Lady and the Tramp, Oliver & Company, Turner and Hooch, The Fox and the Hound, Beethoven, Homeward Bound and K-9).

To explore more about animals in the Bible, read *Bible Animals* by Bruce Barton and others (Tyndale).

8 Ways to Protect Wildlife

Here's a few things you can do to protect animals:

1. Look around you and list all the animals, insects, trees and plants in your neighborhood. Then go to the nearest park, woods or any natural setting and record what you see. Compare the two lists.

2. Ask your teacher to contact Project Wild at www.projectwild.org. for info on things to do.

3. Write to your state's senators, representatives, and the mayor of your own town and explain why you think that they should also be concerned. (Find your representative at www.house.gov/writerep and your senator at www.senate.gov.)

4. Volunteer your services at a park or wildlife refuge. You can help by cleaning up litter, maintaining trails, or teaching visitors about the importance of respecting wildlife. (A national wildlife refuge locator is at www.enature.com.)

5. Ask the owner of a nearby pet store not to sell animals that have been taken from the wild. Many of these animals die from stress or disease soon after they are captured. Ask an adult to go with you. Starting a petition is also a good idea.

6. Get your friends involved by throwing a costume party. Ask everyone to come dressed as a plant or animal and to explain who they are and what they need.

7. Write an article for your school newspaper about some of the things you have learned about wildlife.

8. Read the science section of your newspaper to learn about the wildlife issues in your area.

MISSING CREATURES

Adam was the first zoologist. He named all the animals God made. (Genesis 2:19, 20)

A lamb once had seven horns and seven eyes. John the apostle saw this in a vision. (Revelation 5:6)

A fish paid taxes for Jesus and Peter. His disciple caught a fish with the right amount of money in its mouth. (Matthew 17:27)

1. Christ, righteous people, the devil and wicked men are all compared to a _____.

2. Jesus referred to King Herod as "that _____."

3. On the night the Hebrews left Egypt, they painted the blood of a _____ on their doorposts.

4. False teachers in religion are likened to _____ in _____'s clothing.

5. John the Baptist's diet included wild honey and _____.

6. A good example of industry, planning ahead, and personal responsibility is the _____.

7. As a shepherd, David had killed both a lion and a _____.

8. Jesus told His disciples to be as shrewd as _____ and innocent as _____.

9. As Jesus mourned over Jerusalem, He likened Himself to a _____.

10. One of the ten plagues in Egypt was upon the _____.

11. If the Lord is our Shepherd, we are His _____.

12. Satan appeared to Eve in the form of a _____.

13. God gave the Israelites _____ for their meat in the desert.

14. It's impossible for a _____ to go through the eye of a needle.

Answers are on page 333

Donkeys and serpents can talk. A donkey talked to the prophet Balaam, and Eve conversed with a serpent. And neither of them seemed surprised! (Numbers 22:28; Genesis 3:1-15.)

29

Digging Up Dirt

Imagine this: 300 years from now no one believes there is a place called California and no one has heard of Walt Disney! Let's say just one book talks about California. Because there's so little evidence people don't believe the writer. Then someone starts digging and finds Magic Mountain! They find other books about California and pictures of Walt Disney. Now they believe the writer and they take her seriously.

That's what happened with the Bible. For a long time, it was the only book that talked about certain places and people, so scholars didn't believe that those people or places ever existed. Then along came archaeologists who study anything old to learn about the past. In the last eighty years, they have found other writings mentioning the same things as the Bible. They have also dug up ancient ruins that confirm what the Bible says.

Wherever people live they leave things behind—clay pots, weapons, writing and buildings. Some of these things are kept safe in the ground for thousands of years. By studying these ancient things, archaeologists learn about their owners.

They might study a hill. Long before it was a hill, people built a town there. Over time, dirt, garbage and new building projects added layers. Maybe the town was destroyed by enemies. Another town was built on the ruins. Archaeologists dig down through the hill's layers, often finding several towns built on top of each other. Archaeologists compare what they find with things from other places. They discover when the things were made, who lived there and for how long, who they did business with, and so on.

Thousands of sites have been excavated all over Bible lands. And guess what! Nothing has been found to prove the Bible wrong! Nada! Zilch! Zero!

Did You Know?

Some people think an archaeologist's work is dry as dust.

*Arch*aeology is not just the study of Noah's *ark* or the Hebrews' *ark* of the covenant.

How is a kid in a big hurry like an Egyptian mummy? (Both are pressed for time.)

If you're into archaeology, you'll dig this cool site: http://digonsite.com/.

Bones and Stones

Some people have found bones to pick (found fault) with the Bible for various reasons. Most objections were to people, places or events not found outside the Bible. But what archaeologists have found among the stones proves the Bible right in every case.

Bones: The Hittite race, mentioned 40 times in the Bible (Genesis 10:15), was then unknown to secular history.

Stones: William Wright found the first Hittite inscriptions and relics in 1872. By 1900 so much had been uncovered that scholars admitted that this ancient empire was once as powerful as the Egyptians and Assyrians.

Bones: Sodom and Gomorrah weren't real cities.

Stones: The Ebla Tablets mention the same cities in the same order as Genesis 14. And ruins of more than 70 towns and cities from Abraham's time and older have been found there.

Bones: Moses didn't write Scripture as he claimed (Exodus 24:4) because writing wasn't developed yet.

Stones: The Moabite Stone, Ras Shamra Tablets and Siloam Inscriptions proved writing was common in Moses' time. Libraries of thousands of clay tablets with writing have been found in the Tigris Valley from Old Testament times.

Bones: Joshua didn't really conquer Canaan (Joshua 10-11). The Hebrews simply made treaties with the Canaanites.

Stones: Clay writing tablets were discovered on which kings of Canaan asked Egypt for help against the Habiru (Hebrew) invaders.

Bones: King David was only a legend, not an historical person.

Stones: An inscription from David's time was unearthed that refers to the "House of David" and the "King of Israel."

Bones: Jonah's ride inside a great fish or sea monster (Jonah 1:17) was impossible because whales don't have gullets big enough to swallow a man whole and unharmed.

Stones: The current *Encyclopedia Britannica* describes sperm whales with 20-foot gullets.

There are many other examples of things being found that agree with what the Bible says. The Bible has withstood every attack put upon it for over 2,000 years. Everything archaeologists have found agrees with the Bible.

31

Boy Discovers Dead Sea Scrolls

Mohammed was a shepherd boy who took care of goats in the valley of the Dead Sea. By chance he discovered a number of clay jars in one of the many caves in the area. Inside the jars were wads of cloth covered with pitch (a tarlike substance). These cloths were wrapped around manuscripts. This discovery was made in 1947.

Not knowing what the scrolls were, the boy sold them for next to nothing. Several years later, the true value of the discovery was realized. Archaeologists and shepherds searched the almost inaccessible caves. By the time they were finished, they had discovered more than 400 scrolls or books.

The books, mostly written in Hebrew or Aramaic, include copies of all Old Testament books (except Esther). The Isaiah scroll—dating from about 100 B.C.—was 1,000 years older than any other known manuscript of the Old Testament.

The scrolls belonged to the library of a strict Jewish religious sect called the Essenes at Qumran on the edge of the Dead Sea. The owners had placed their valuable manuscripts in jars and hidden them in caves when the Roman army invaded the area in A.D. 68. Fortunately, the dry heat of that location preserved the historic collection.

These important copies of the Scriptures provide valuable information concerning the accuracy of the Bible text. The scrolls also tell us a lot about Jewish religious and political life in the New Testament period.

Before 1947, there were only four handwritten copies (called manuscripts) of the Old Testament in Hebrew, produced about A.D. 900. Now there are thousands of fragments and copies of whole books dating from at least a century before Christ. Seeing the similarity of these 1,100-year-apart copies gives us assurance that copies of the Bible were made accurately.

Did You Know?

A mysterious treasure map launches the Odyssey gang on a perilous journey leading to the Caves of Qumran in Palestine and the hope of discovering riches in *The Caves of Qumran* (book or video from Tyndale).

*Take a virtual tour of the Dead Sea scroll caves at **www.digbible.org/tour/index.html.***

10 Places to See a T. Rex

There are 22 known Tyrannosaurus rex fossils in North America, but not one complete skeleton. Nearly all the fossils are in museums. Here's the top 10.

1. "Sue," a 90% complete skeleton, is the largest, most complete and best preserved Tyrannosaurus rex. She was discovered in 1990 in the badlands of South Dakota by Sue Hendrickson. Hence, the dino's nickname. She is on display at the Field Museum of Natural History in Chicago.

2. An 85% complete skeleton was discovered in Montana in 1988. A cast of the skeleton is on temporary exhibition at the Museum of the Rockies in Bozeman, Montana.

3. "Scottie" was discovered in Saskatchewan, Canada, in 1994. It is 60% to 70% complete. Scottie is not on exhibition yet, but its preparation can be seen at the Royal Saskatchewan Museum in Regina.

4. "Stan" was discovered in South Dakota in 1987 and is a 65% complete skeleton. Stan is on exhibition at Black Hills Institute of Geological Research in Hill City, South Dakota.

5. "Black Beauty" was discovered in Alberta, Canada in 1981. It has a complete skull and is 50% complete. Black Beauty is on traveling exhibition.

6. A 50% complete skeleton found in Montana in 1902, has a full skull, jaws and pelvis. The skeleton is on display at the Carnegie Museum, Pittsburgh.

7. "Z. rex" was discovered in South Dakota in 1992 and is estimated to be 50% complete. Privately owned, Kansas.

8. A 45% complete specimen was discovered in Montana in 1907. The skeleton is on exhibition at the American Museum of Natural History in New York.

9. The "Huxley T. rex" was discovered in central Alberta, Canada, in 1946. This 25% to 30% complete skeleton is on permanent display at Royal Tyrrell Museum of Paleontology, Drumheller, Alberta.

10. A 25% to 30% complete skeleton was discovered in Montana in 1994. It is at the University of Wisconsin at Madison Museum, but currently is not on display.

Did You Know?

"Sue" has her own web site: www.fmnh.org/sue. The Field Museum purchased Sue for 8.3 million dollars.

Check out fun dinosaur stuff at http://dsc. discovery.com/guides/dinosaur/dinosaur.html

CLAY CREATOR

How about this – a kid who is a best-selling artist? You'd never guess that several years ago Joshua Burkhardt thought he didn't have any artistic ability. "I didn't think I was an artist, because I couldn't paint or draw anything," Joshua says.

Then in September 1998, at age 9, Joshua sat down with his mom when she was making tiny clay mice for a craft show. He made a few mice and discovered it was fun. Plus, he was good at it!

Within months Joshua had come up with his own polymer clay designs and was selling them at craft shows and on the web. "The first thing I sold was a nativity scene," Joshua explains. "Most of the stuff I do is based on the Bible. I know my talent is from God. I couldn't have done any of this without Him." His best-selling sculpture is still the Nativity scene with Mary, Joseph and shepherd kneeling beside Baby Jesus.

Radio, TV, newspapers and magazines quickly spread the news of Joshua's art, bringing custom orders from far and wide.

Joshua even published a book about his clay art, Hangin' Around with Noah. Joshua and his family worked for nine months on it. He is homeschooled, so Joshua is able to work an hour or two a day on his art—including teaching other people how to sculpt.

Did You Know?

Try your hand at Joshua's free clay projects, too. He hopes you will be inspired to find your own creative abilities. Enjoy and Happy Crafting! www.joshclay.com

To find out how you can create Noah and 10 critters with only three simple tools (a craft knife, a needle tool and a paintbrush handle), see how to get Joshua's book at his site.

Joshua's 10-year-old brother Jonathan likes to paint with watercolors. The lion is his creation. He is also a talented candle crafter. See his work at Joshua's site.

Mouth Painter

Joni Eareckson Tada was a typical teenager who loved having fun and hanging out with her friends. But in 1967 a diving accident left her a quadriplegic, unable to use her hands or legs. Joni was devastated. Her future seemed doomed. She struggled with finding where God was in her situation.

But God used Joni's injury to teach her many things. He developed her patience, tolerance, love and joy. The things that didn't matter so much when Joni was on her feet started to really matter when she was in a wheelchair. She came back to God and has spent her life serving Him.

After her accident, Joni spent long hours in rehabilitation learning how to paint by holding a paintbrush in her teeth. She learned well and her paintings are very popular.

Joni founded her ministry, Joni and Friends, in 1979. It seeks to help disabled people all around the world. Her autobiography, *Joni*, was a best-seller and was made into a feature-length movie with the same title. It's been translated into 15 languages.

Joni has traveled to 35 countries sharing the message of hope in God's love. She has a daily 5 minute radio program that is carried on 850 radio stations. It has been honored as "Radio Program of the Year" by the National Religious Broadcasters.

In a recent year, Joni and Friends hosted 500 special needs families at retreats. Through Wheels for the World, over 14,000 wheelchairs have been shipped to developing nations. Physical therapists fit each chair to a disabled child or adult.

Joni was given a presidential appointment to the National Council on Disability. During the time she served on the Council the Americans with Disabilities Act became law.

Joni and Ken Tada have been married since 1982. Ken taught school for 32 years and now works full-time with Joni and Friends.

No doubt living in a wheelchair brings a lot of limitations. However, as a Christian, Joni says she has found "limitless joy and peace" because she knows the Lord Jesus.

Did You Know?

Joni has written 30 books, some of them for kids. *Tell Me The Promises* and *Tell Me The Truth* both received the Evangelical Publishers' Gold Medallion award.

Joni's web site is **www.joniandfriends.org**.

Top 10 Online Art Museums for Kids

Some art museums devote entire sections of their websites to kids. They offer interactive fun for kids. Here are the top 10.

1. The National Gallery of Art - Kids Site www.nga.gov/kids

2. The Minneapolis Institute of Arts web presentation ***Restoring a Masterwork*** www.artsmia.org/restoration-online

3. The deYoung Museum - Ghosts of the DeYoung www.thinker.org/fam/education/publications/ghost

4. The Exploratorium Museum's Learning Studio www.exploratorium.edu/explore/online.html

5. Metropolitan Museum of Art - Explore & Learn www.metmuseum.org/explore

6. Seattle Art Museum - Activities for Kids www.seattleartmuseum.org/Teach/learnOnline.asp

7. The Berkeley Art Museum - Online Guide for Kids www.bampfa.berkeley.edu/education/kidsguide/welcome/welcomekids.html

8. MOMA - Art Safari from the Museum of Modern Art www.artsafari.moma.org

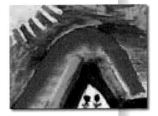

9. The Childrens Museum of Indianapolis - Fun On Line page www.childrensmuseum.org/kids/games.htm

10. The Cleveland Museum of Art - Rosetta Stone, tour guide www.clevelandart.org/archive/pharaoh/rosetta/index.html

Did You Know?

Don't miss the KidsArt Gallery site. It's art by kids, and you can send in your own art! It has lots of "Top 10" lists, too. www.kidsart.com/Gallery

Other sites which accept and display your creations are www.kidstalkaboutgod.com and www.mgfx.com/kidlit/kids/artlit.

The Caldecott Medal honors the artist of the best picture book. Recent winners are for young children, but the 2001 winner was *So You Want to Be President?* illustrated by David Small and text by Judith St. George (Philomel Books). Funny stories show that anyone can be president: a fat man or a tiny man, a relative youngster or oldster. www.ala.org/ALSC (click on "Awards")

Art Works!

Andy Holmes of Allen, Texas, was no normal toddler. When he was just a little guy, he could draw. "I guess it's a part of me that God made," he says, "kind of like having red hair and blue eyes.

"I wasn't even 2 yet when I drew a picture of an Easter bunny for a friend. It was fun! Then I'd just spend an afternoon drawing a whole page of arms and legs, then a whole page of dolphins or owls or whatever."

When he was 6 years old he was disqualified from a school art contest because the judges didn't believe he drew his own picture. Of course, he had.

When he was 8 years old he won first in a national art contest, and his whole family got a trip to Disneyland. *National Geographic World* magazine printed his art when he was 8 years old. He was interviewed on CNN and he taught Rosie O'Donnell how to draw on her television show!

Andy says he gets his character ideas when he's doodling. "I'll invent a rough version of some character. Then if I like it, I'll work with it. Right now I really like drawing cartoony kids."

Andy's prize-winning animation, "Rocket Guy"!

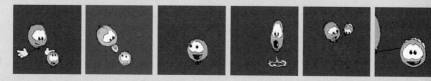

(http://www.amazing-kids.org/ani-ah.htm#top)

He knows that his talent is a gift from God. "Ever since I can remember, I could draw. It's weird because people are always like, 'Wow.' And I'm like, 'I was going to throw that away. Do you want it?'"

"When I was 7, I accepted Jesus as my Savior. A week or two later I was baptized. Up until a couple years ago I mainly drew for fun. Now I'm trying to use my talent for God."

Andy says that if you like to draw the secret is, "Practice, practice, practice. Whatever you're good at, just keep doing it over and over. Everybody has a talent. Just use whatever God gives you."

Andy thinks he has a fun life. He's homeschooled and is glad that he and his sister don't fight much.

"Snowflake" Bentley

Willie Bentley discovered something very unusual.

He lived in Vermont about a hundred years ago and was curious about just about everything in the world. He was a natural scientist. Willie got a microscope when he was a teenager and soon discovered that snowflakes are crystals and . . . most amazingly—no two snowflakes are exactly alike!

Willie set up a little lab in a barn where he could have the same temperature inside as outside and he sketched snowflakes. Willie drew more than 300 snowflakes. Why would he spend so much time doing that? "Because no two are alike," he explained, "so when one melts, its beautiful design is gone forever."

But sketching each flake took him forever. Then Willie saw something in a catalog that changed everything—a camera that photographed into a microscope. His family helped him buy the special camera. On January 15, 1885, Bentley wrote this in his journal: "First snow crystals ever photomicrographed."

Willie caught the flakes on a small tray covered with black velvet that he held out the door. Then he took pictures of the snowflakes.

It wasn't long before Bentley became known throughout the U.S. Weather Bureau. He was the first scientist to accurately measure raindrops and determine how and why they were the size they were.

Between the ages of 19 and 66, Snowflake Bentley made some 5,381 photomicrographs! He never got tired of studying snowflakes. His pictures have become very famous and have even been used on wrapping paper.

Bentley wanted to record God's creativity that was shown in each individual snowflake.

"If you have a dream
and a talent,"
Bentley told young people
before he died,
"Make the most of it.
The whole world is there
for you to discover."

Did You Know?

2453 of W. A. Bentley's photographs can be seen in his book *Snow Crystals* (Dover; available at www.amazon.com). To view some go to www.snowflakebentley.com.

Click here to view a TV video clip about "The Snowflake Man:" http://snowflakebentley.com/vid.htm

Bible

The Strangest
Publishing Project *of All Time!*

The Bible was written over 1,600 years by 40 different authors, of 20 occupations. They wrote in 3 languages. There are 2,930 characters in the 66 books which has 1,189 chapters, 31,173 verses, 774,746 words, and 3,567,180 letters.

There is no doubt that God was involved in writing the Bible. Just look at its unity despite having so many different authors.

Did You Know?

Moses began writing the Bible about 1,500 years before Jesus was born. His first five books (Genesis, Exodus, Leviticus, Numbers and Deuteronomy) make up about one-fourth of the Old Testament. These five books are known by different names such as the Law, Pentateuch (Greek for "five books") or Torah (Hebrew for "law").

Jews read their Bible from the back to the front. Hebrew, the original language of the Old Testament, is written from right to left.

The Bible prophets claimed nearly 3,800 times to be writing God's words when they wrote: "The Lord says..." or "Hear the word of the Lord."

The earliest Bibles were written on scrolls and kept in a box. Each book was written on a separate roll of parchment (animal skins) or papyrus (ancient form of paper).

Just the book of Matthew took about 30 feet of papyrus. In the second century, bound volumes of cut sheets (like modern books) replaced the scroll.

The New Testament books were written as letters to churches or individuals. Each was hand carried by a messenger.

The Bible is the best-selling book of all time. Over 7 billion copies have been printed in more than 2,000 languages. That equals more than one copy for every person alive in the world today!

Ahead of Its Time

600 YEARS before Christ, the Bible stated that the stars could not be numbered (Jeremiah 33:22). Later Greek astronomer Hipparchus counted 1,056 stars, which Ptolemy verified long after. Then Galileo invented his telescope in 1610. Now astronomers estimate there are over 100 billion stars in our galaxy and countless more beyond.

The Bible declares that each star is different (1 Corinthians 15:41), a fact verified by astronomers. Of the millions of stars photographed to date, no two have been found to be alike.

When the ancients thought the earth was flat, the Bible declared it was a circle hung in space (Isaiah 40:22; Job 26:7). The old theory began to crumble with the voyages of Columbus and Magellan, but one photograph taken from the moon shows it all.

How Accurate Are the Copies?

The Bible is more accurate and reliable than any other ancient document. That's a strong statement. What backs it up?

The Bible has the most original handwritten copies to compare with each other. There are about 750 manuscript copies of the Old Testament in Hebrew and over 5,000 of the New Testament in Greek. The next closest are Homer's *Iliad* with 643 copies and Sophocles' 100.

The Bible has the least differences among all its handwritten copies. Computer analysis of all the New Testament manuscripts found 99.9 percent perfect agreement. And most differences are in spelling ("honour" versus "honor") or word order ("Paul the apostle" versus "the apostle Paul"). The *Iliad,* the next closest, has 50 times more differences.

How Good a Scribe Are You?

Long before computers, photocopiers or printing presses, each new copy of the Bible had to be hand copied by scribes. The Old Testament copies were in Hebrew, which reads from right to left without vowels.

Try copying this line a few times and check your accuracy:

HTRHTDNSNVHHTDTRCDGGNNNGBHTN
TDNSNVHHTDTRCDGGNNNGBHTN

Or, just copy this simple English sentence:

It's fun to be in
in Paris in the
the spring.

Compare your copy with the above. Did you correctly copy the two duplicated words?

41

What KIDS say About the Bible

Ten thousand Christian kids — 60% were girls, 40% guys from every denomination — were surveyed about their beliefs.

65% believe the Bible is totally accurate in everything it teaches.

63% said Satan is a living spiritual being, but more than a third said he's only a symbol of evil.

36% said a good person can earn salvation through good deeds.

93% considered themselves Christian.

70% said they attend church once or twice a week, **25%** said they're "absolutely committed" to their Christian faith.

54% said they're "mostly committed."

94% said they're "very familiar" or "somewhat familiar" with the Christian faith.

What the BIBLE Says About Itself

"All Scripture is inspired by God and is useful to teach us what is true and to make us realize what is wrong in our lives. It straightens us out and teaches us to do what is right. It is God's way of preparing us in every way, fully equipped for every good thing God wants us to do. Preach the word of God."
(2 Timothy 3:16-17, 4:2 NLT)

"Above all, you must understand that no prophecy in Scripture ever came from the prophets themselves or because they wanted to prophesy. It was the Holy Spirit who moved the prophets to speak from God."
(2 Peter 1:20-21 NLT)

"You have been born again. Your new life did not come from your earthly parents because the life they gave you will end in death. But this new life will last forever because it comes from the eternal, living word of God. 'The grass withers, and the flowers fall away. But the word of the Lord will last forever.' And that word is the Good News that was preached to you." (1 Peter 1:23-25 NLT)

"Heaven and earth will disappear, but my words will remain forever." (Mark 13:31 NLT)

Something to Think About
Over 4,000 times the Bible itself claims to be a record of what God says.

The Homespun Bible That Became a Runaway

"But Daddy, if that's what it means, why doesn't it say so?" asked eight-year-old Janet. Dr. Ken Taylor had just explained a verse from the *King James Bible* during family devotions.

Dr. Taylor prayed, "Lord, how can our family devotions become more interesting to my children?" Then he had an idea, "Why not restate each verse to make it more understandable?" He says, "I opened the Bible to 2 Timothy, chapter 2. I read the first several verses, thought about them and analyzed them word by word. Then I wrote down their meaning in everyday language. Here's how I rewrote verse 4:"

King James Version: "No man that warreth entangleth himself with the affairs of this life; that he may please him who hath chosen him to be a soldier."

My rewrite: "As Christ's soldier do not let yourself become tied up in worldly affairs, for then you cannot satisfy the One who has enlisted you in His army."

"That night I read my version of the chapter to the family and questioned the children to see if they understood. I was elated when they understood! I prepared other chapters for family devotions . . . with the same positive response. I knew that God wanted me to translate the New Testament Epistles into words that anyone could understand."

Over the next six years Dr. Taylor rewrote the 21 letters of the New Testament—Romans through Jude. He titled this section of the Bible, *The Living Letters*.

He couldn't find a publisher so Dr. Taylor printed the book himself. Then Billy Graham offered it on nationwide TV and it became a best-seller. In 1971, 16 years after Dr. Taylor started, *The Living Bible* was complete. More than 45 million copies have been distributed throughout the English-speaking world.

Did You Know?

All or portions of *The Living Bible* have been translated into 100 languages.

In 1996 Dr. Taylor and 90 scholars launched the *Holy Bible, New Living Translation* (NLT). To learn more, go to: www.newlivingtranslation.com. Read Mark Taylor's comment about being Ken Taylor's son in this autobiography, *My Life: A Guided Tour* (Tyndale).

The Kids' Life Application Bible (Tyndale) has the New Living Translation (NLT) combined with memory verses, interesting facts, timelines, maps, and photos. "Sticky Situations" help you learn to choose between right and wrong. "Do the Right Thing" helps in learning godly character. "Life Then, Life Now" shows the differences between life today and Bible times. "I Wonder" notes help answer questions about things in the Bible.

Develop the habit of regular Bible reading with **The One Year Bible for Kids** (NLT; Tyndale). Each selection ends with how to apply it to your life today. (This is not a complete Bible.)

More than two million kids have **The NIV Adventure Bible** (ZonderKidz). "Life in Bible Times" and "People in Bible Times" describes life in Bible times. "Words to Treasure" offers Bible verses to memorize. "Did You Know?" fills your factoid/trivia needs.

The New Explorer's Study Bible for Kids (Nelson Word) makes Bible study an adventure. "Digging in" goes behind the scenes of familiar Bible stories and how the people lived. "Word finders" explains hard-to-understand names and words. In "Cameos" Bible people "tell" their own stories. "News Stories" in newspaper headline format recounts exciting stories..

The NIrV Kids' Quest Study Bible (Zondervan) weaves in 500 illustrated questions and answers about the Bible, your world and God (from the popular Questions Kids Ask series).

In **The Treasure Study Bible** (Kirkbride) you can go on 500 different Treasure Hunts that explore topics chosen by kids like you, such as Bad Habits, Making Wise Decisions, Feeling Guilty, and Pleasing God. Clues lead you from one Bible passage to another and finally to a Treasure Gem that wraps things up and explains how it applies to your life.

Unusual Bibles

Several editions of the Bible received nicknames due to printers' errors.
- The "Wicked Bible" left "not" out of the seventh commandment.
- The "Murderer's Bible" misspelled "filled" as "killed" in Mark 7:27.
- The "Vinegar Bible" substituted "vinegar" for "vineyard" in Luke 20:15.
- The "Bug Bible" printed Psalm 91:5 as, "Thou shalt not be afraid of any bugges by night."

THE ACROSTIC BIBLE

Read this list: onions, watermelon, soup, flour, relish, eggs, lettuce. Now look away from the page and recite the seven items. Now look at the same list rearranged on the acrostic FLOWERS:

F lour
L ettuce
O nions
W atermelon
E ggs
R elish
S oup

Notice how much easier it became to recall the seven items. An acrostic is a word or phrase written vertically so each letter can begin another word.

Barry Huddleston summarized each chapter of the Bible in a four-word title while he was a student. Then he arranged them so the first letters of each title spell out the theme of that Bible book. This is his acrostic summary of the book of Zechariah in the Old Testament. Messiah is a Hebrew name for Jesus, the coming Savior. (Number = chapter.)

ZECHARIAH

M eaning of Zechariah's vision (1)
E xamination with measuring line (2)
S atan and the Branch (3)
S even lampstands of gold (4)
I nterpreting the flying scroll (5)
A ct of crowning Joshua (6)
H earts become like flint (7)
S ecurity comes to Jerusalem (8)

R eturn of the Messiah (9)
E phraim and Judah restored (10)
T eaching about wicked shepherds (11)
U nderstanding whom they pierced (12)
R efining of God's remnant (13)
N ew kingdom ushered in (14)

(The complete *Acrostic Bible,* including a cartoon-style graphic depicting the theme of each Bible book, is available. Contact Media Ministries. See page 350.)

Bible in Life

The Name Says It

Jeremy was packing his suitcase for a trip and wanted to take along the following items: a book, cleanser, a companion, a lot of gold, a hammer, honey, a lamp, medicine, milk, meat, a mirror, seeds, a song, a sword, and lots of water. The problem is he only had room for one of those things. Jeremy figured out how to bring all those items by putting in just one thing. What is the thing he packed? *(The Bible.)*

The Bible uses many names and symbols to describe itself. Each reveals either something the Bible does for us or that we are to do with the Bible.

Commandments - to obey (Psalm 119:6)
Fire - to warm us (Jeremiah 23:29; 20:9)
Food - to nourish (1 Peter 2:2; Hebrews 5:12-14)
Gold - to treasure (Psalm 19:9-10)
Hammer - to break bad habits (Jeremiah 23:29)
Holy Scriptures - to give God's perfections (Romans 1:2)
Honey - to delight in (Psalm 19:9-10)
Judgments - to accept (Psalm 119:7)
Lamp - to guide (Psalm 119:105)
Law book - to legislate (Psalm 119:1)
Light - to illumine our path (Psalm 119:105,130; Proverbs 6:23)
Meat - to invigorate (Hebrews 5:14)
Medicine - to strengthen (Psalm 119:28)
Milk - to nourish (1 Peter 2:2)
Mirror - to reveal (James 1:23-25)
Oracles of God - to give us God's thoughts (Romans 3:2)
Priceless possession - to cherish (Psalm 19:7-10; 119:72)
Rain - to produce fruit (Isaiah 55:10-11)
Sayings - to hear and heed (Rev. 22:6-10)
Scalpel - to cut (Hebrews 4:12)
Seed - to grow (Matthew 13:23)
Soap - to remove sin (Psalm 119:9-11)
Song - to sing (Psalm 119:54)
Statutes - to heed (Psalm 119:12)
Sword of the Spirit - to fight (Ephesians 6:17)
Testimonies - to declare (Psalm 119:1-2)
Treasure - to value (Psalm 119:14,72,127)
Water - to wash (Titus 3:5)
Way - to walk in (Psalm 119:30)
Word of God - to reveal God's thoughts (Hebrews 4:12)
Word of life - to bring us eternal life (Philippians 2:16)

Listening to God

If you regularly attend church you spend up to 121 hours a year listening to sermons or lessons. But how much do you get out of them? Can you remember the title or any of the points from last week's sermon?

You remember only 20 percent of what you heard 3 days ago. Part of the problem is that you can think five to seven times faster than people can talk.

To get more out of hearing God's Word, **jot down the highlights** of what you hear —you'll more than double what you retain. Notes may be short and simple—the main points of a message, or three or four ideas you want to remember. Write down the Bible reference for each point. You'll retain the message longer because more of your five senses have been involved in the process.

Following along with an open Bible during the message helps, too, looking up any references that are used.

Listening ability is greatly enhanced by a good night's sleep, getting up in time to get ready without being rushed, eating a healthy breakfast and preparing your heart by confessing your sins and asking God to speak to you.

After the message or lesson, **ask the Lord** to show you one thing you can do today to put His Word to work in your life.

Maximize your profit by **reading over your notes** later. Everything you heard is part of "a pie." Put the letters **A, P, I** or **E** in the margin for any note that is:

- **A**pplication—something to be or do
- **P**roof—why you should believe something is true
- **I**llustration—an example of the topic
- **E**xplanation—more about what the subject is or means

Keep your notes in a notebook. Current church programs, handouts, missionary newsletters, prayer lists and such could also be included. Personalize your notebook with photos or drawings. Be sure to include your name and phone number in case your personal guide to growth gets lost.

Off the Shelf and Into Yourself

Just as physical babies need milk to grow, spiritual babies need the nourishment of God's Word (1 Peter 2:2).
It's impossible to outgrow the Bible, just as it's impossible to grow without it!

The Bible has many benefits for us. All Scripture is inspired by God and is useful to:
- Teach us what is true
- Make us realize what is wrong in our lives
- Straighten us out
- Teach us to do what is right

"It is God's way of preparing us in every way, fully equipped for every good thing God wants us to do" (2 Timothy 3:16, 17).

There are several ways we can get the Bible off the shelf and into ourselves.

- **Hear.** Our faith grows as we hear someone teach us the Bible (Romans 10:17).
- **Read.** The average reader can complete the Bible in a year by reading just 12.8 minutes a day (Revelation 1:3).
- **Study.** This is digging deeper — making some notes, looking up unfamiliar words and asking questions (Joshua 1:8).
- **Memorize.** As a kid, King David memorized and meditated on the Scripture as he tended his flock of sheep (Psalm 119:11).
- **Apply.** The Bible was given to change our lives, not just satisfy our curiosity. Pray this about a Bible passage: Lord, what do You want me to *know?* What do You want me to *feel?* What do You want me to *do?*

The Bible can become like good salty pretzels — you just can't stop eating 'em. And through the power of God and His Word in us, we can be winners in life!

Did You Know?

12 percent of kids who say they believe the Bible actually read it every day.
34 percent read it only once a week
42 percent hardly ever read it.
12 percent never read it!

Three interesting, well-illustrated books can help you understand the Bible (New Kids Media/Baker):
The Children's Bible Encyclopedia by Mark Water
The Baker Bible Handbook for Kids
The Baker Book of Bible People for Kids by Terry Jean Day

Who's Responsible?

It's never fun to be blamed for something that's not even our responsibility. God understands that. He gets blamed all the time for things that aren't His fault! Living in God's family is a shared responsibility. God has His jobs, and we have ours. A meaningful way to apply God's Word to our lives is to sort out who's responsible for what.

To begin, label a sheet of paper like this:

Verse	My Responsibility	Results	God's Responsibility

As you read a Bible passage, ask, "What is here for God to do? What is here for me to do? Are there any results of either God or me doing our part?" Write what you discover in the appropriate column. Not every Bible verse has something for each column. And some data doesn't fit any column.

Here's how a familiar verse might look. "For God so loved the world that he gave his only Son, so that everyone who believes in him will not perish but have eternal life." (John 3:16)

Verse	My Responsibility	Results	God's Responsibility
John 3:16	Believe in God's Son	I'll not perish I'll have eternal life	Love the world Give His only Son

Practice sorting out Psalm 1, Philippians 4:4-9 or Titus 2:12-13 this way. This method works well in Psalms, Proverbs and the New Testament letters (Romans-Philemon).

Use what you've written as a prayer list. Thank the Lord for what He has done or will do, ask His help in doing our part, and thank Him for the results that will follow.

GOD'S PART   OUR PART

GARBAGE IN - GARBAGE OUT!

"Garbage in — Garbage out!" is true of your mind. What goes in is what comes out. Your mind needs to be continually cleansed.

The best "brain cleanser" is the Bible (Hebrews 4:12). But we have to plug God's words into our minds.

Here's how to "SWAP" for Scripture verses in your mind:

Say It Aloud

Recite a verse out loud, emphasizing one key word at a time. For example: "I can do everything with the help of Christ who gives me the strength I need." "I *can* do everything. . . ." and so on. (Philippians 4:13)

Write It Down

Write a verse on one side of a card and the reference on the other side. To review a verse, write just the first letter of each word. For example, Zephaniah 3:17 would be:

T L Y G I W Y	"The LORD your God is with you,
H I M T S	He is mighty to save.
H W T G D I Y	He will take great delight in you,
H W Q Y W H L	He will quiet you with his love,
H W R O Y W S	He will rejoice over you with singing" (NIV).

Act It Out

Create your own hand motions to a verse. Here are some suggestions for Zephaniah 3:17. "The Lord (make a triangle representing the Trinity by touching your thumbs and two index fingers) your (point to person) God (point upward) is with you (point to person), He is mighty (flex biceps) to save" (cross arms in a figure of the cross). Finish the verse on your own.

Picture with Sketches

Doodle each word or phrase in the memory verse. Here's an example of Zephaniah 3:17. "The Lord your God (triangle labeled T.L.Y.G.) is with you (stick figures around triangle), He is mighty (man's flexed biceps) to save" (cross)....

TIDBITS

Suggested passages to memorize:
- Fact of sin—Romans 3:23
- Salvation a free gift—Ephesians 2:8-9
- Christ's payment—Romans 5:8
- Penalty of sin—Romans 6:23
- Receiving Christ personally—John 1:12

Matching Truth to Life

Choose the person whose life or writings is the best example of each statement. (Not all names are used)

_____ 1. The people made their houses nicer but left God's temple in ruins.

_____ 2. Someone not out to gain a personal following can lead people to Jesus.

_____ 3. Israel's defeat at Ai shows how one person's sin affects others.

_____ 4. His love for his wife is a picture of God's love for His children.

_____ 5. Jesus didn't give up on the follower who denied Him.

_____ 6. He believed he could destroy his younger rival, but jealousy destroyed him.

_____ 7. God forgave him, but his illegitimate son died.

_____ 8. In spite of what his friends said, sickness is not always caused by sin.

_____ 9. He cheated his brother and father, then was cheated by his uncle.

_____ 10. He wept over the sins and judgment of his nation.

A. Achan	F. Hosea	K. Judas
B. Amos	G. Jacob	L. King Saul
C. David	H. Jeremiah	M. Noah
D. Ezekiel	I. Job	N. Peter
E. Haggai	J. John the Baptist	

Answers are on page 334.

Does the Bible Really Say That?

Which of the following statements are actually in the Bible?

1. God helps those who help themselves.
2. Be sure your sin will find you out.
3. The lion will lay down with the lamb.
4. God is love.
5. To the victor go the spoils.
6. Can the blind lead the blind?
7. Money is the root of all evil.
8. A house divided against itself cannot stand.
9. A heart of gold.

Answers are on page 334.

The Bible in Threes

The Bible has two parts: Old and New Testament. "Testament" means a will. The Bible reveals God's will for us.

There are **3** letters in the word "old" and 9 letters in "testament". These two numbers show there are 39 books in the Old Testament. The words "New Testament" has **3** and 9 letters. Multiply 3 X 9 to get 27, the number of books in the New Testament. Subtract the **3** from the 9 for each testament, and the two remaining 6's reminds us of 66 books in the whole Bible.

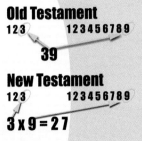

Old Testament

1 2 3   1 2 3 4 5 6 7 8 9

39

New Testament

1 2 3   1 2 3 4 5 6 7 8 9

3 x 9 = 27

The word **hep,** sometimes used by drill sergeants to keep their marching troops in step, reminds us of the three topics in the Bible:

O.T.   **History**   **N.T.**
17   5
5   **Experience**
17   21
           Prophecy   1

History (about the past)
Experience (about the present)
Prophecy (about the future)

The history begins each testament with the story of how God has worked in His world. The experience books in the middle of each testament tell how God wants to work in our lives now. Both testaments end with prophecy — how God will do things in the future. The Bible is about **3** things: what God has done, is doing and will do.

Dividing the Bible's 66 books by **3** gives 22. There are 22 history books in the Bible (the first 17 books in the Old Testament and the first five in the New). In both testaments there are 22 supplements. (The supplements are the experience and prophecy books.)

In the Old Testament, God emphasized the past (1) and the future (2); in the New Testament, our present (**3**) experience with Him and His Word is emphasized.

Did You Know?

The Bible contains 66 books, 1189 chapters, 31,173 verses, 773,692 words, and 3,567,180 letters!

The Old Testament history books begin in Genesis and end in Esther. The first two letters of GEnesis, the first Bible book, remind us of this. The first two letters of MAtthew indicate the New Testament history books are from Matthew to Acts.

The Bible in 12 Symbols

God's work from Creation to Completion can be told in 12 Cs.

1
Creation
God makes everything . . .
from scratch!
6 days, God's time
Genesis 1-11

2
Clan
God's people – the
Hebrew nation begins
350 years
Genesis 12-50; Job

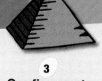

3
Confinement
Hebrews are kept as
slaves; then freed
400 years
Exodus 1—19

4
Covenant
The Hebrews make an
agreement with God
40 years
Exodus 20—Deuteronomy 34

5
Conquest
Hebrews take the
Promised Land — Canaan
7 years
Joshua 1—24

6
Court
Hebrews are governed by
judges
350 years
Judges 1—1 Samuel 8

7
Crowns
Hebrews insist on a king,
then are ruled by kings
450 years
1 Samuel 9—2 Kings 16
1 Chronicles—2 Chronicles 28
Psalms—Song of Solomon
Isaiah—Lamentations
Hosea—Zephaniah

8
Captivities
Hebrews are conquered
and scattered
70 years
2 Kings 17-25
2 Chronicles 29-36

9
Construction
Hebrews return to
Jerusalem and rebuild
the temple
120 years
Ezra—Esther
Haggai—Malachi

10
Christ
Jesus comes to earth to be
our Teacher and Savior
33 years
Matthew 1—Acts 1

11
Church
Jesus' disciples spread
the Gospel and establish
His Church
70 years
Acts 2-28, Romans—
Jude, Revelation 1-3

12
Completion
The end times
1,000+ years
Revelation 4-22

53

God placed Adam and Eve in the Garden of Eden (1 — symbol of world.) When people became very wicked, God sent a great flood and later scattered people around the world from the Tower of Babel. God called Abraham and Sarah from Ur to Haran and later to Canaan. They were the first Hebrews. (Most of the Bible was written by Hebrews and Jesus was a Jew which was another name for Hebrew.) The rest of Genesis records the lives of Abraham, Isaac, Jacob, and Joseph (2 — symbol of four men).

The Hebrews became a great nation in Egypt (3 — symbol of pyramid) but then became slaves. God used 10 plagues to deliver them. Moses led them through the Red Sea to Mount Sinai (4 —symbol of stone tablets). They crossed the Jordan River into Canaan. Three symbols characterize their lives there: a sword (5) for Joshua's conquest of the land, a gavel (6) for the judges, and a crown (7) for the kings.

After King Solomon's reign, the Jewish kingdom split, with the northern section called Israel and the southern called Judah.

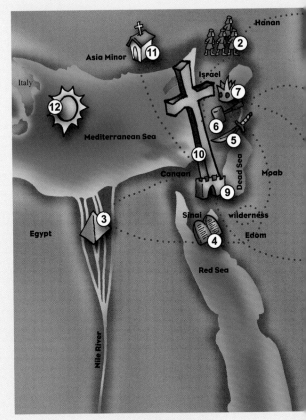

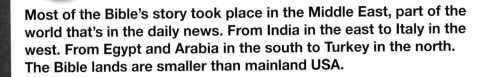

Most of the Bible's story took place in the Middle East, part of the world that's in the daily news. From India in the east to Italy in the west. From Egypt and Arabia in the south to Turkey in the north. The Bible lands are smaller than mainland USA.

THE MAIN STORYLINE OF THE BIBLE CAN BE SUMMARIZED WITH A MAP AND 12 SYMBOLS.

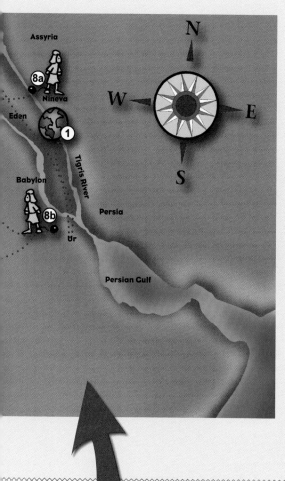

Israel was conquered and scattered by Assyria (8A — symbol of captive). Later Judah was captured by Babylon (8B — symbol of captive). Seventy years later Persia conquered Babylon and allowed the Jews to go home (9 — symbol of rebuilt city walls).

After 400 silent years, when no prophets spoke for God, Jesus came as the God-man to die on a cross for our sins (10), rise from the dead and return to heaven.

After receiving the power of the Holy Spirit, Jesus' disciples spread the good news of salvation. The apostle Paul carried the gospel to the Gentiles (non-Jews) (11 — symbol of a church). He wrote at least 13 of the New Testament letters.

The apostle John wrote the book of Revelation in exile on the island of Patmos, foretelling God's plans for the world. God will make a new heaven and earth (12 — sun). The Bible ends in Revelation as it began in Genesis — with God completely in charge of His creation.

Making Ends Meet

The first book of the Bible, Genesis, was written 1600 years before the last book, Revelation. But the Bible ends as it begins, with a perfect world directly controlled by God. Compare the first four chapters of the Bible with the last four.

GENESIS

GENESIS	REVELATION
God created the heavens and earth (1:1)	God creates a new heaven and earth (21:1)
Light is created (1:3)	The Lamb is the light (21:23)
Darkness and night created (1:5)	No darkness or night there (22:5)
Waters gathered into seas (1:10)	No more seas (21:1)
God made the sun and the moon (1:16)	No need of the sun or the moon (21:23)
Creation pronounced done (2:1)	New creation pronounced done (21:6)
Man's first home by a river (2:10)	Man's eternal home by a river (22:1)
Death for eating from a tree (2:17)	Life for eating from a tree (22:2)
Marriage of Adam (2:18-23)	Marriage of the Lamb (19:6-9)
Eve, the wife of Adam (2:22-25)	New Jerusalem, wife of Christ (21:9-10)
Serpent deceives Eve (3:1, 13)	Serpent is banned from deceiving (20:3)
Satan's first attack on man (3:1ff)	Satan's final attack (20:7-10)
Satan appears in garden (3:1)	Satan disappears in lake of fire (20:10)
A garden which became defiled (3:6-7)	A city that can't be defiled (21:27)
Fellowship with God broken (3:8-10)	Face-to-face fellowship with God (21:3)
Initial triumph of the serpent (3:13)	Ultimate triumph of the Lamb (20:10)
Savior's first coming promised (3:15)	Savior's second coming promised (22:20)
Pain greatly multiplied (3:16)	No more mourning, crying or pain (21:4)
Curse on man and nature (3:14-17)	No more curse (22:3)
Serpent's doom promised (3:15)	Serpent's doom accomplished (20:10)
Curse imposed on nature (3:17)	Curse removed from nature (22:3)
Man's rule over nature is lost (3:19)	Man's dominion restored (22:5)
First death (3:21; 4:8)	No more death (21:4)
First paradise closed (3:23)	New paradise opened (21:25)
Angel keeps people from garden (3:23)	Angel welcomes people to city (21:9-10)
Man driven from God's presence (3:24)	Believers in God shall see his face (22:4)
Tree of life taken from mankind (3:24)	Tree of life open to people (22:14)
God's mark on Cain (4:15)	God's name on peoples' foreheads (22:4)
First city built by Cain (4:17)	Holy city comes from God (20:3)

Did You Know?

If you read 5 chapters from the New Testament each Sunday and 3 chapters from the Old Testament each weekday, you would read through the entire Bible in less than a year!

What the Bible Is All About for Young Explorers by Frances Blankenbaker (Regal) is one of the all-time best summaries of the Bible for kids. www.gospellight.com/wtbiaa.html

The longest word in the Bible is Maher-shalal-hash-baz—a kid's name! (18 letters; Isaiah 8:1)

What's the Big Idea?

The Bible has one main plot that develops from beginning to end. The holy and loving God is challenged by a wicked opponent who spoils the perfect setting in Eden. Good and evil clash with such force that it sometimes appears evil will triumph. Hopes keep mounting for a conquering Hero, who will triumph over evil. The Hero promises to return on a great white horse to finish the war permanently. After more spiritual warfare God wins, with those on His side living happily ever after in a perfect place.

From book 1 to 66 the Bible library consistently pictures:

- One true eternal God, the source of all life and good

- Mankind's unwillingness to remain faithful to God, even under ideal conditions

- God always seeking to draw people into relationship

- One evil leader of the forces of darkness

- Salvation from sin and death, a gift from God received by faith

- A central focus on Jesus Christ. The Old Testament looks forward to Christ's coming. The New Testament reports on Christ's life, death and resurrection and predicts His second coming.

God gave us the Bible to reveal Himself and His way of salvation.

How do people get to Heaven? Any answer that gives people credit (do good, keep the Ten Commandments, obey the Golden Rule) misses the boat. The major message of the Bible is that God offers salvation to people who are helpless to earn it on their own.

"But these are written so that you may believe that Jesus is the Messiah, the Son of God, and that by believing in him you will have life ... For God so loved the world that he gave his only Son, so that everyone who believes in him will not perish but have eternal life." (John 20:31 and 3:16 NLT).

Salvation is trusting Jesus to do something for us we could never do for ourselves: forgive our sins and give us everlasting life.

If you'd like to talk to someone about having a personal relationship with God, you can call toll-free 24 hours a day from North America to 1-888-NEED-HIM (1-888-633-3446) or 1-866-321-SEEK (1-866-321-7335). (You may wish to ask a parent first if it's okay to make this call.)

Where Did We Come From?

Are we here accidentally or on purpose? Are we crafted by an all-powerful Creator, or is there an evolutionary explanation? Don't answer yet. Let these pages help you decide.•

Your Portable Personal Computer

How many neurons does an earthworm have?

Which has more neurons: an ant or a bee?

What's your name, address and telephone number? When were you born? Can you quote John 3:16 from memory?

All this information is stored in your brain, a control center that is constantly receiving and sending messages. The brain contains about 10 billion nerve cells called neurons. Each neuron can store about 10,000 bits of information. In all, your three-pound brain can store 100,000,000,000,000 (one hundred trillion) bits of information in a lifetime. An advanced computer would need more than 20,000 pounds of equipment to store that much data.

Your portable computer is like a three-story house. The upper story, called the cerebrum, thinks, learns, solves problems and remembers.

The middle story, the cerebellum, makes your muscles work together so you can walk, talk, and draw. Each side of your brain controls the opposite side of your body.

Think how busy you would be if you had to tell your heart to beat about 70 times every minute, and remind your lungs to inhale and exhale about every three seconds. Your amazing brain does all this and more automatically so you can think about a million other things!

The bottom story of your brain, especially the medulla, controls all the things you do without consciously thinking.

If you feed wrong information into a computer, it will give wrong answers. In the same way, what we think about comes from what we have put into our brains.

Did You Know?

An earthworm has about 20 neurons, an ant has 250 and a bee has over 900 neurons.

A brainteaser: Without lifting your pencil from the paper, can you connect all these dots with four straight lines?

```
0       0       0

0       0       0

0       0       0
```

(Answer is on page 334)

Ben Saunders contributed to all the articles in this section when he was age 12.

Your Wonderful Wrapper

It's water-repellent, tough, elastic and easy to clean. It keeps you cool in summer and warm in winter. It repairs itself. It holds your insides in and protects you from germs. What is it?

It's your "wonderful wrapper," your skin. One square inch of skin contains 20 million cells, 645 sweat glands, 1,000 nerve endings, 77 feet of nerves, 65 hairs with muscles attached to each, 97 oil glands, 19 feet of blood vessels. Skin keeps the bacteria from attacking your inner organs. You have about nine square feet of skin, weighing nearly five pounds.

Skin replaces itself totally every month. About half a million particles of skin flake off every hour. By the time you're 70, you will have lost 105 pounds of skin! Sometimes skin shows your feelings. When you're embarrassed tiny vessels in the skin expand allowing more blood to the surface, causing you to "blush."

Nerves in skin are sensitive to pain, pressure, heat and cold, sending messages to the brain as fast as 300 miles per hour.

Your skin's built-in thermometer knows when you are too warm. On a hot day, you're wet because sweat glands release water through your skin to evaporate and make you feel cooler. Every day you secrete at least a pint of sweat — even when you're not exercising.

Fingernails, toenails, and hair are a special, hardened kind of skin. Hairs grow over most of your body, but they're almost invisible, except on your head. Your hair grows about five inches a year. That's almost 30 feet in a lifetime!

You have over 125,000 hairs, about 45 of them are replaced every day. Over a lifetime you'll lose 1.5 million hairs. Your wonderful Creator even keeps count of all the hairs on your head! (Luke 12:7)

Did You Know?

Eyelids have the thinnest skin, and the sole of the foot has the thickest (30 times thicker than eyelid skin).

Fingertips and lips are the skin's two most sensitive places; the back is the least sensitive. One fingertip has 100 touch receptors, but on the back they are two inches apart.

Your Tremendous Tunnels

A network of tunnels weaves its way through your body. It carries food and air to your 60 trillion energy factories (cells). In fact, no cell in your body is more than a hair's width away from one of these tunnels.

Your blood stream tunnels contain 18 billion red blood cells. Arteries, the largest blood tubes, are an inch thick near your heart. They carry oxygen-filled blood cells to your body. When you inhale, each red blood cell picks up one molecule of oxygen from your lungs.

Capillaries, tubes smaller than a strand of hair, force blood cells to squeeze through them single file. After they deliver oxygen to your body in exchange for carbon dioxide, the blood cells are shuttled back to your lungs.

Every four months red blood cells make 250,000 round trips through your body! Two million new ones are manufactured every second inside your arm and leg bones.

Your body's strongest muscle is your fist-sized heart that pushes blood throughout your body. To see how your heart pumps, clasp your palms together in a partly filled sink and watch the water squirt as you squeeze your hands together. Repeat this every second for a minute, and imagine how much work your heart does. As a muscle, your heart gets stronger when you exercise.

You can feel your heartbeat (your pulse) by gently pressing two fingers against your wrist below your thumb. Using a watch with a second hand, how many beats do you count in one minute? What happens to your pulse after three minutes of jumping jacks?

Think of your heart as two pumps working side by side. The right side pumps blood to your lungs, where it picks up oxygen. The left pump pushes the oxygen-rich blood throughout your body.

Did You Know?

The body's strongest muscle is the heart. The heart gets its only rest between beats.

Babies and most pets have a higher pulse rate than yours.

Someone spilled his blood in your place. Read about it in 1 Peter 1:18-21.

Your Superhighway

Your throat is a busy superhighway — 18,000 words travel it daily. That's enough to fill a 66-page book!

In addition, 75 million gallons of air travel that same highway in a lifetime. Another "lane" carries 40 tons of food.

The windpipe contains your noisemaker. All sounds come from vibrations against air. Tip your head back and feel your throat with your fingertips as you talk. Can you feel the place where the sound is made? Your "voice box" (the larynx) part of your windpipe contains two elastic bands called vocal cords. Air from your lungs passes through the opening between them, making the cords vibrate.

Try this experiment: Blow up a balloon and stretch the opening to a narrow slit. That's a picture of how your lungs and vocal cords work together to make sound. Notice that the escaping air makes different sounds depending on how tightly the opening is stretched. In the same way, the tighter your vocal cords, the higher your voice.

The sounds from your vocal cords also vibrate in your nose, mouth, and chest, which make sounds louder and gives them a unique quality. No one else has a voice exactly like yours.

What sounds can you make with your mouth open and your tongue held down with your fingers? You really need your tongue, teeth, and lips to form words. Look closely in a mirror as you say, "The boy ran home." Then try reading another person's lips as he silently forms words.

What kind of words does God want us to speak? "Do not let any unwholesome talk come out of your mouths, but only what is helpful for building others up according to their needs, that it may benefit those who listen" (Ephesians 4:29 NIV).

Did You Know?

An average kid's voice in still air can be heard 600 feet away.

President John F. Kennedy set a world record by speaking 327 words per minute!

Every person's voiceprint is as unique as their fingerprints or footprints. There are over six billion different patterns!

Your Ground Contacts

Walking seems so simple . . . until you watch a baby trying to learn!

"Going on foot" makes us *pedestrians.* You take about 20,000 steps every day. In a year, most people walk the width of the United States (about 3,000 miles). A lifetime of walking takes you around the earth about six times!

For each step we take, 20 muscles move 26 bones in each foot at 33 joints formed by 114 bands of elastic material (ligaments). About one-fourth of our body's 206 bones are in our feet.

When we walk, our heel and ankle (seven tarsal bones) come down first, bearing three times our body's weight because of the force of gravity. The spike of a woman's high-heeled shoe can dent a hard floor because it exerts over a ton of pressure per square inch! Yet the foot's heel, our body's strongest bone, isn't hurt.

Shaped like an upside-down bowl, our foot's arch (five metatarsal bones) acts as a shock absorber and can hold up anyone, even a nine-foot, six-inch giant Goliath or a 1,200-pound circus fatman. Our toes (14 phalanx bones) spread out our weight and help us keep our balance. Surprisingly, a big toe has only two bones while the other four toes have three bones each.

The pattern of ridges on the soles of our feet — our footprint — make a unique impression. No two are alike, just as no two fingerprints are alike. Except for size, our footprints stay the same as long as we live.

Every footprint is a reminder that we are "creatures" (created beings).

Did You Know?

One ancient giant had six toes on each foot (2 Samuel 21:20).

The largest pair of shoes ever made for a "regular" foot were size 42!

Robert Wadlow of Alton, Illinois, was nearly seven feet tall by age 12. At age 21 he stood almost nine feet, weighed 491 pounds, and wore size 37 shoes (18.5 inches long!).

Your Private Detective

A private detective works for you 24 hours a day. What's cooking in the kitchen? What flavor of gum is your brother chewing? Your super sleuth knows! It protects you, too, alerting you to smoke before you see fire or spoiled food before you swallow it. You get early warning of a gas leak or an approaching skunk. Hooray for your nimble nose!

Most healthy people can identify about 4,000 scents. But when your nose is stuffy, you miss out on more than smell. Things like chicken soup and beef broth taste the same. That's because we smell some foods more than we taste them.

At the inside top of your nose are olfactory membranes packed with 100 million smell receptors. Unless air reaches this tissue, you can't smell anything. But how the nose distinguishes aromas is a mystery even to scientists.

Here's a "best smellers" fact: Trained dogs can sniff out skiers buried under 15 feet of snow! That's because everybody has unique odors. But even the best bloodhound can't sniff the difference between identical twins. Smelling signals from the nose pass through the part of your brain that controls memories so the smell of pine brings up thoughts of Christmas.

Your nose is also an air conditioner. Tiny blood vessels warm the incoming air, which continues down your windpipe (trachea) to your lungs. Your lungs exchange oxygen for carbon dioxide, which is carried out each time you exhale. On a cold day you can "see your breath" because moisture in your warm exhaled air changes to water droplets in the cold air.

A sneeze blasts an irritant out of your nostrils at speeds up to 100 miles per hour! When your brain starts a sneeze reflex, you take a deep breath for extra air power. That's the "ah ... ah ... ah" before the "choo!"

Did You Know?

The "best smellers," in order, are rabbit, shark, hunting dog and people.

For fun: Blindfold yourself, hold your nose, and try to identify foods someone touches to your tongue. Can you tell raw potato pieces from apple chunks?

63

Your Handy-Dandy Handles

What do you use to make a snowball, write a word or pet a cat?

Your hands.

Do an experiment to see how well they work. Try to snap your fingers, throw a ball or pick up a dime without using your hand. Hard, isn't it?

Your four fingers help you grab things, too. Their different sizes help you grab things of different sizes and shapes. Make a fist, and see that your fingers all reach the same place. This lets you hold a stick or a pencil.

Your hand has three main parts: the carpus (wrist), metacarpus (palm) and digits (the four fingers and thumb). There are 27 bones in each hand; the wrist has eight bones, the palm five, each finger four, and two in the thumb. Your middle finger has the longest and strongest hand bones. Thirty-five powerful muscles acting like cables move each bone "lever." Nerves from the brain tell the muscles whether to expand or contract.

Hands are also sensitive feelers. Blind people can "read" with their fingers, running them over the raised letters of Braille print. Hearing-impaired people "talk" with their hands, too, using sign language.

Even if you don't know sign language, you can communicate anger with hands as clenched fists; friendship with an outstretched hand; disapproval by thumbs turned down or victory by putting two fingers in the shape of a "V."

Look at the pattern of fine lines that form your unique fingerprints. Compare your prints with someone else's. No one among the world's six billion people has fingerprints exactly like yours.

Your handy-dandy handles are God's handiwork! (Isaiah 64:8)

Did You Know?

Try spelling your name with your hands, using sign language for the deaf pictured here:

When muscles on the palm side contract, the fingers close.

You can make a unique set of fingerprints by pressing each finger of one hand against an ink pad, then firmly onto a piece of plain paper. But you'll need an alcohol pad to clean your fingers.

Good question: How can you use your hands to help others today?

Your Two Cameras

Two cameras in your head? Where?
Hint: You're using them to read these words.

A camera is a box that keeps out light to protect the film inside. Your eye camera "box" is the white part of the eyeball, and the film is the light-sensitive cells (the retina) at its back. Light reflected from what you're aiming at is focused by a curved glass (lens) on a camera, just as your eye's cornea takes in light and your lens focuses it. You control how much light shines on the film by the shutter on the camera, just as the colored part of your eye changes the size of your eye's opening (the black pupil).

Your God-created eyes are superior to man-made cameras. Eyes automatically focus where aimed, whether at a speck of dust inches away or starlight many miles distant. With 20/20 perfect vision, everything is in focus. Each retina has over 100 million rod cells to register black and white images and about 10 million cone cells for color processing. Eyes can distinguish hundreds of shades of colors — far more than the best films can record.

No camera-computer combination can respond as quickly as your miraculous eye-brain team. Each second your eyes can create 10 new images and send 1 billion bits of information to the brain over tens of millions of nerve connections. It takes 1/500 second for the brain to recognize an object.

The muscles in your eyes make over 200,000 coordinated movements daily. Eyes are self-cleaning. The blinking eyelids spread tear fluid like a car's windshield washer and wiper.

But does seeing always mean believing? God sent Jesus to earth so we could clearly see what God is like (John 1:14). Someday believers in Jesus will see God face to face! (Revelation 22:4)

For Fun

In drawing #1, which vertical line is longer? In #2, which horizontal line is longer? In #3, do the two darkest lines bow in the middle? (See answers on page 334)

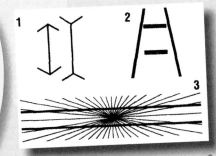

Your Two Antennas

Hammers, drums, stirrups, anvils, canals, obstacle courses, and keyboards — they're all in your body. Where? On the sides of your head! Without your two antennas to receive sound signals, you'd live in a silent world.

Any noise creates sound waves that travel as molecules bump against one another, like a row of dominoes being knocked over.

Your outer ear is shaped to collect sound waves. Cupping your hand around your ear helps you hear better by increasing the collection area. The collected sound waves reach your eardrum through an inch-long obstacle course of hairs and 4,000 wax-making glands designed to keep stuff out. Your eardrum is so delicate that an insect walking on it would make a deafening noise. Thinner than paper and about half an inch in diameter, your eardrum vibrates on only two-billionths of an inch.

Behind your vibrating eardrum is a chain of three bones arranged to amplify sound: the hammer, the anvil, and the stirrup. Sound reaches your brain in the form of electrical signals, much like those of modern computers. As the stirrup vibrates a small amount of liquid, 20,000 tiny hairs work like a piano keyboard to convert the waves to electrical signals, or nerve impulses.

A nerve strand the size of a pencil lead has 30,000 circuits, each able to fire messages about a 1,000 times a second.
Only God understands how the brain decodes the impulses to reproduce all the sounds you hear. New sounds are sorted out and compared with your mind's sound library.

Your ears also help you keep your balance. Inside each ear are three half-circle canals, filled with liquid. Hair cells sense the liquid moving and use nerves to tell your brain which way your head is moving. This system also tells you which way is up so you can come to the water's surface after a dive. After spinning around quickly, you feel dizzy because the fluid in the canals is still moving.

Did You Know?

An average adult can recognize about 500,000 different sounds.

The smallest bone in your body is the stirrup behind the eardrum.

HOW MUCH IS YOUR BODY WORTH?

The human body is composed of:
65% Oxygen
18% Carbon
10% Hydrogen
3% Nitrogen
1.5% Calcium
1% Phosphorous
0.35% Potassium
0.25% Sulfur
0.15% Sodium
0.15% Chlorine
0.05% Magnesium
0.0004% Iron
0.00004% Iodine
Traces:
fluorine
silicon
manganese
zinc
copper
aluminum
arsenic

Added together, all of the above is worth less than one dollar!

A person's most valuable asset is his or her skin, which the Imperial State Institute for Nutrition at Tokyo meticulously measured. They applied a strong, thin paper to every surface of some naked people. After the paper dried, they carefully removed it, cut it into small pieces and painstakingly totaled the person's measurements. Cut and dried, the average person is the proud owner of 14 to 18 square feet of skin. Basing the skin's value on the selling price of cowhide (25 cents per square foot), the value of your skin is about $3.50.

So adding the value of your skin and your body's elements, you are worth about $4.50! That doesn't sound like much, does it?

"But God showed his great love for us by sending Christ to die for us while we were still sinners" (Romans 5:8 NLT). Jesus said, "The greatest love is shown when people lay down their lives for their friends" (John 15:13 NLT).

YOU'RE WORTH MORE THAN YOU THINK!

Books

AUTHOR KIDS

Writing books isn't just for grown-ups! Eight-year-old Francis Hawkins wrote a book of manners called Youth Behavior. You can get the books of all the following author kids at Amazon.com or in your local library.

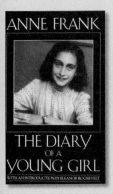

KATHARINE HULL, 15, and **PAMELA WHITLOCK,** 16, wrote a book by children, about children, and for children, *The Far-Distant Oxus.*

ANNE FRANK. *The Diary of Anne Frank* describes Anne's Jewish family's life in hiding and then in a concentration camp during World War II. Only her father survived and published her diary in 1947. http://www.annefrank.nl/ned/default2.html

DOROTHY STRAIGHT of Washington, D.C. was only 4 when she wrote How the World Began. S. E. (Susan Eloise) Hinton started her writing career in high school, beginning the first draft of *The Outsiders* at the age of 15; it took her a year and a half to complete it. This book about gangs was published in 1967. It has sold more than a million copies.

MANGHANITA KEMPADOO wrote *Letters of Thanks,* which was published in 1969 when she was 12. It is a series of thank-you notes that match the gifts in the carol, "The Twelve Days of Christmas."

ALLY SHEEDY published *She Was Nice to Mice* in 1975 when she was 12. It's about a mouse who is taken back in time to the days of Queen Elizabeth I and William Shakespeare.

A group of young Native American children in Arizona told their stories in the 1976 book, *And It Is Still That Way.*

ALEXANDRA SHEEDY became a published author at 13. Her first book, She Was Nice to Mice, describes the life of Queen Elizabeth I of England. Now 14, the young New Yorker is working on a second book.

JAMIE DEWITT was 12 when he wrote "Jamie's Turn" for the 1984 Raintree Publish-a-Book Contest. His story describes an accident on his family's farm in Wisconsin.

When **JASON GAES** was stricken with Burkitt's lymphoma, a rare form of cancer, at age 7, he decided to write *My Book for Kids with Cansur.* His twin brother, Tim, and 10-year-old brother, Adam, illustrated the book.

DAVID KLEIN was 9 when he wrote "Irwin the Sock" for a school assignment. The story of 2 argyle socks, Irwin and Irina, won the Raintree Publish-a-Book Contest in 1988.

GORDON KORMAN wrote his first book, *This Can't Be Happening at MacDonald Hall,* as a seventh-grade English project. http://

Meet Mattie

Matthew J.T. Stepanek, best known as "Mattie," started writing poetry and short stories at age three. By age five Mattie had written several hundred poems. Now that he's 12, he has written thousands of poems and published several books. Mattie is a *New York Times* best-selling author of four books, each illustrated with his own artwork: *Heartsongs, Journey Through Heartsongs, Hope Through Heartsongs* and *Celebrate Through Heartsongs* (vsp Books/Hyperion). Some of his poems have been printed in magazines and newspapers worldwide.

BOOKS

Mattie was born with a rare form of muscular dystrophy, a disease that steadily weakens one's muscles. Even though he has lost four siblings, Mattie conveys the message that there is always a reason for happiness, no matter what the circumstances. To live life fully, we must "celebrate life, every day, in some way."

Mattie is a frequent public speaker who has appeared on *Oprah, Good Morning America* and *Larry King Live.* In 2002 he was awarded the Children's Hope Medal of Honor, the Verizon Courage Award, and the Humanitarian Award from the Pediatric Nursing Society of America. Mattie serves as the Maryland State Goodwill Ambassador for the Muscular Dystrophy Association as well as the National Goodwill Ambassador for 2002. He is also a representative of Children's Hospice International, speaking on behalf of sick children and their families about the ways the government can make it easier for them to get the health care they need.

He lives in Maryland with his mother, Jeni, whom he refers to as "my mom and 'grown-old' best friend." Mattie is homeschooled.

MATTIE'S POETRY

THE LANGUAGE OF GOD

Do you know what
Language God speaks?
God speaks Every-Language.
That's because God made
Everyone and Gave
Everyone different Languages.
And God understands all of them.
And do you know what is God's
Favorite Language?
God's favorite language is
Not grown-ups's language,
But the Language of Children.
That's because children
Are special to God.
Children know how to share,
And they never lose
Their Heart-Songs.

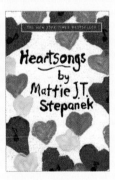

ON BEING A CHAMPION

A Champion is a winner,
A hero...
Someone who never gives up
Even when the going gets rough.
A champion is a member of
A winning team...
Someone who overcomes challenges
Even when it requires creative solutions.
A champion is an optimist,
A hopeful spirit...
Someone who plays the game,
Even when the game is called life.
There can be a champion in each of us,
If we live as a winner,
If we live as a member of the team,
If we live with a hopeful spirit,
For Life.

For more about Mattie, get his books and visit these sites:
http://myhero.com/hero.asp?hero=mattieStepanek
http://www.timeforkids.com/TFK/specials/story/0,6079,194483,00.html
http://www.washingtonpost.com/ac2/wp-dyn?pagename=article&node=&contentId=A49082-2001Jun26&notFound=true
http://www.booktv.org/ram/feature/0801/btv081101_4b.ram

The Envelope Please

The Association for Library Service to Children, a division of the American Library Association, has created many awards to recognize the best in children's literature. Read about them all at http://www.ala.org/alsc.

The Newbery Medal is the highest honor for a childrens' book.

The 2003 winner is **Crispin: The Cross of Lead** by Avi (Hyperion). In an action-filled page-turner set in 14th-century England, 13-year-old Crispin is suddenly orphaned and falls in with a juggler who becomes his protector and teacher. Pursued by Crispin's enemies, the pair races to solve the mystery of his identity.

The 2003 Newbery Honor Books winners:

The House of the Scorpion by Nancy Farmer (Atheneum). Farmer tackles the topics of cloning, the value of life, illegal immigration and the drug trade in a coming-of-age novel set in a futuristic desert.

Pictures of Hollis Woods by Patricia Reilly Giff (Random House). The 12-year-old title character unfolds her story of foster care and a search for family in images from her sketchbook, which reveal both her memories and her artistic spirit.

The Batchelder Award recognizes the most outstanding book originally published in a foreign language in a foreign country. The 2003 winner is **The Thief Lord** by Cornelia Funke (Scholastic). Two orphaned brothers come to Venice on the run from relatives who intend to separate them. A band of street kids, a mysterious Thief Lord, a nosy detective and a magical carousel are all part of the adventure.

The Belpre Medals honor a Latino writer and illustrator. The 2002 winner is Pam Munoz Ryan for **Esperanza Rising** (Scholastic). A pampered 13-year-old and her mother are forced to flee Mexico to a California migrant-worker camp.

The Sibert Medal selects the best informational book. The 2002 winner is **Black Potatoes: The Story of the Great Irish Famine,** 1845-1850 by Susan Campbell Bartoletti (Houghton Mifflin).

The Coretta Scott King Award is for authors and illustrators of African descent. One 2003 Honor Book won for both categories: **Talkin' About Bessie: The Story of Aviator Elizabeth Coleman** by Nikki Grimes, illustrated by E.B. Lewis. The fascinating story of the first black female licensed pilot in the world.

Children's Crown and Lamplighter

The Children's Crown (grades 3-6) and the Lamplighter Awards (grades 6-8) encourage students to read wholesome books by providing lists of the best literature. Students vote on their favorite books in the spring. Sandra Morrow, librarian at Brentwood Christian School in Austin, Texas, developed this world-renowned program in 1992. Learn more about it at: http://www.childrenscrownaward.org

2003 Children's Crown Winners

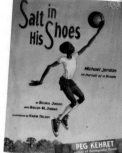

Salt in His Shoes by Deloris Jordan (Simon & Schuster). When Michael was ready to give up his basketball dreams because he is the shortest boy on his team, Mrs. Jordan told him to put some salt in his shoes and say a prayer every night.

Runners-up were:

Star in The Storm by Joan Harlow (Simon & Schuster)
Janitor's Boy by Andrew Clements (Simon & Schuster)

2003 Lamplighter Winners

I'M Not Who You Think I Am by Peg Kehret (Dutton). Ginger Shaw first senses she is being watched at her 13th birthday party in a restaurant. During the next several days (while her parents are out of town), Ginger sees the stranger wherever she goes.

Runner-up: the *Barn Burner* by Patricia Willis (Clarion)

Gold Medallion

Gold Medallion Book Awards have recognized the finest examples of evangelical publishing since 1978. See: http://www.ecpa.org/ECPA/Gawards.html

2002 Gold Medallion winner for preteens:

Window on the World by Daphne Spraggett (Paternoster). See how children all around the world live and how God is changing their lives through prayer.

2002 Gold Medallion winner for teens:

The Narrow Road by Brother Andrew with John and Elizabeth Sherrill (Revell). Follow a young Dutch Bible college student's incredible efforts to transport Bibles across closed borders in numerous near escapes. Grammy Award winning band Jars of Clay (http://www.christianitytoday.com/music/artists/jarsofclay.html) is featured on the included multimedia CD.

BOOKS

71

Top 20 Best-Sellers

Check out this list of 20 best-selling books for Christian kids. The top 2 titles sold more than 100,000 each; most of the others sold more than 50,000. (Publisher is in parentheses.)

1   **Hermie: a Common Caterpillar** (board edition) by Max Lucado (Tommy Nelson)

2   **Girls of Grace: Faith, Family, Friends, & Boys** by Point of Grace (Howard)

3   **God Made You Special** by Eric Metaxas (Zonderkidz)

4   **Hermie: a Common Caterpillar** by Max Lucado (Tommy Nelson)

5   **My Final Answer for Kids** by Paul Kent (Barbour)

6   **You Are Special** by Max Lucado (Crossway)

7   **In God We Trust** by Larry Burkett (Standard)

8   **The Prayer of Jabez for Kids** by Bruce Wilkinson & Melody Carlson (Tommy Nelson)

9   **One Year Book of Devotions for Girls** by Debbie Bible & Betty Free, eds. (Tyndale Kids)

10 **Here's Lily!** By Nancy Rue (Zonderkidz)

11 **The Little Engine That Could** by Watty Piper (Barbour)

12 **How You Are Changing** by Jane Graver (Concordia)

13 **Secrets of the Vine for Kids** by Bruce Wilkinson & Melody Carlson (Tommy Nelson)

14 **One Year Book of Devotions for Girls 2** (Tyndale Kids)

15 **Even Fish Slappers Need a Second Chance** by Eric Metaxas (Zonderkidz)

16 **You Are Special** (board ed.) by Max Lucado (Crossway)

17 **One Year Book of Devotions for Boys** by Debbie Bible & Betty Free, eds. (Tyndale Kids)

18 **The Prayer of Jabez for Little Ones** by Bruce Wilkinson & Melody Carlson (Tommy Nelson)

19 **The Body Book: It's a God Thing** by Nancy Rue (Zonderkidz)

20 **Larryboy and the Emperor of Envy** by Sean Gaffney (Zonderkidz)

The Story Behind WWJD

What would happen if a big-city newspaper, instead of reporting the usual crime and violence, emphasized the good news and instituted a policy following the teachings of Jesus Christ? It happened once, with surprising results, when a Kansas daily took up a popular clergyman's challenge and appointed him editor in chief for one week in March 1900.

The clergyman was Dr. Charles M. Sheldon, a Congregational minister who published a novel in 1896 titled In His Steps or What Would Jesus Do? The book sold 30 million copies, making it one of history's leading best-sellers.

It was a news event in itself when Dr. Sheldon moved into the hard-boiled city room of the Topeka Daily Capital to run the newspaper according to the dictates of Christ. Signed editorials became front-page items, while crime, society events and theatrical notices were played down. A page one story about a famine in India included an appeal for contributions; the paper collected more than $1 million in aid to send to Bombay.

As a result of the experiment, daily circulation jumped from 15,000 to 367,000. It proved how much people crave the inspiration of good news.

The question, "What would Jesus do?" is still popular. Sheldon's book remains a top seller over 100 years later. And the letters WWJD are worn by many kids. Visit the official web site at http://www.wwjd.com.

A story is circulating about a kid who asked a bookstore clerk about the meaning of the letters "WWJD" on a cap. The clerk responded that they stood for "What Would Jesus Do?" He explained it was to remind you before you do anything to always first stop and consider what Jesus would do in the same situation. The kid thought about it for a moment and then told the clerk, "Well, Jesus wouldn't pay 20 bucks for this hat!"

Did You Know?

In an average week, 6-to-11-year-olds spend about 74 hours sleeping; 19 hours playing indoors; 8 hours eating; 14 hours watching TV; and almost 1 hour reading (U.S. Census Bureau).

The absolutely coolest site on the whole worldwide web for kids and books is at http://www.cool2read.com/kids/homepage.html. Read sample chapters from kids' best-sellers, enter contests, play games, learn to write from the pros — it's all here — and more!

To locate a Christian bookstore near you, go to http://cba.know-where.com/cba. To find out more about any book or to order it online, go to http://www.amazon.com.

Read reviews by kids of books for kids at the KidLit site http://mgfx.com/kidlit. You can submit your own reviews and writings, too.

The Topical Bible

HISTORY	EXPERIENCE	PROPHECY
Past	**Present**	**Future**

The Topical Old Testament

of Law	Poetry	Major Prophets
Genesis	Job	Isaiah
Exodus	Psalms	Jeremiah
Leviticus	Proverbs	Lamentations
Numbers	Ecclesiastes	Ezekiel
Deuteronomy	Song of Solomon	Daniel

of Israel		**Minor Prophets**
Joshua		Hosea
Judges		Joel
Ruth		Amos
1 Samuel		Obadiah
2 Samuel	*Before* **Babylonian**	Jonah
1 Kings	**Exile of Judah**	Micah
2 Kings		Nahum
1 Chronicles		Habakkuk
2 Chronicles		Zephaniah
		Haggai
Ezra	*After* **Babylonian**	Zechariah
Nehemiah	**Exile of Judah**	Malachi
Esther		

The Topical New Testament

of Christ	**Letters from Paul**	
Matthew	Romans	Revelation
Mark	1 Corinthians	
Luke	2 Corinthians	
John	Galatians	
of Church	Ephesians	
Acts	Philippians	
	Colossians	
	1 Thessalonians	
	2 Thessalonians	
	1 Timothy	
	2 Timothy	
	Titus	
	Philemon	
	Letters from Others	
	Hebrews	
	James	
	1 Peter	
	2 Peter	
	1 John	
	2 John	
	3 John	
	Jude	

SEARCH 66

Hidden in the block of letters below are the names of all sixty-six books of the Bible. Names may be found forwards or backwards, horizontally, vertically or diagonally, but always in a straight line. The words First, Second, and Third have been omitted.

```
S T C E N S I S N A M O R E T H C L O U J D B V
N N J F Y E R A G S S I W Q K U T E B O Z O N M
A H O M S E F E I G L P C U H X E I H A J O H D
I B S I B T D W V O N S N A I H T N I R O C K N
N E H M T E X U D E M O I G H Q U A O N P W A Y
O F U S R A S E J U L M M O P P E D O Y E C L H
L N A W E S T H E R E A B E H T C M G A X O O T
A R O U N M C N O R L Y T A Q Z O X F H O P I O
S H A M O C A J E A S E I I W L L A B S D T C M
S D E A E E S J C M R D Y M O N O R E T U E D I
E Z E K I E L H C Y A L K S O N S T A S S E H T
H M U N S P I L K B Z L F A E R S H D U V I N N
T L E U M A S S O L T O B C H A I A S I J W M O
O N A H L U T P I N G S N A I T A L A G X O W M
Z E C H A R T P H N G N U S A G N E I C I C E E
E E B M S B V T O I R Z E P H E S I A N S I H L
P O C U P L A S T C L L D U S N J O N A G O T I
H M L H J E S K S U C I T I V E L H A B N O T H
A C D A A K T R K C W T P V F S K A A X I Q A P
N T E N O R L D E U T E A P Y I E B O N K U M E
I A G G A H I B A K K U R H I S B R E V O R P D
A R Z A G G L A F R W V Z C O A S E G D U J A Y
H U S W E R B E H A I M E H E N N O I T G R A M
J X E P S U S L C H R O N I C L E S H D E S M E
```

Acts, Amos, Chronicles, Colossians, Corinthians, Daniel, Deuteronomy, Ecclesiastes, Ephesians, Esther, Exodus, Ezekiel, Ezra, Galatians, Genesis, Habakkuk, Haggai, Hebrews, Hosea, Isaiah, James, Jeremiah, Job, Joel, John, Jonah, Joshua, Jude, Judges, Kings, Lamentations, Leviticus, Luke, Malachi, Mark, Matthew, Micah, Nahum, Nehemiah, Numbers, Obadiah, Peter, Philemon, Philippians, Proverbs, Psalms, Revelation, Romans, Ruth, Samuel, Song of Solomon, Thessalonians, Timothy, Titus, Zechariah, Zephaniah

(Answer is on page 335)

Browsing God's Library

Summary: Generations to Joseph. Fascinating stories of people from Adam and Eve in Eden to Joseph in Egypt.

People: Adam, Eve, Abel, Seth, Noah, Ham, Shem, Japheth. Abraham, Sarah, Isaac, Jacob, Joseph, Judah

Places: Eden, Ararat, Babel, Ur of Chaldea, Haran of Mesopotamia, Canaan, Egypt

Unusual: The answer to which came first: the chicken or the egg (1:26)
The oldest man who ever lived (5:27)
A woman who became a salt statue (19:26)
A boy whose hand was older than his older brother (38:27-30)

Summary: Exit from Egypt. Millions of Hebrew slaves are rescued from Egypt to meet God at Mt. Sinai.

People: Pharaoh, Moses, Aaron

Places: Egypt, Red Sea, Mt. Sinai

Unusual: A bush that burned without burning up (3:2)
Walking sticks that became snakes (7:10-11)
Frogs everywhere—in beds, ovens, even in bread dough (8:3)
Sunlight for God's people when the rest of the country was dark (10:22-23)
The best-dressed man (28:2-4)

Summary: Levites and Sacrifices. Selecting priests and sacrifices for sin.

People: Moses, Levites

Places: Mt. Sinai

Unusual: Four-footed fowls (11:20)
Disease diagnosis based on hair color (13:3)
A totally linen wardrobe (16:3-4)
Families living outdoors in makeshift shelters (23:39-43)

For each book in God's Bible library, the big idea is captured in three words and its story is summarized in one sentence. Major people and places are listed in the order they occur. All places mentioned can be located on the map on page 54. And because truth can be stranger than fiction, there are some very unusual things to look for.

TESTAMENT

NUMBERS

Summary: Numbering the Hebrews.
A 40-year wilderness trek between two censuses.
People: Moses, Joshua, Caleb
Places: Mt. Sinai, Kadesh, Wilderness, Moab, Trans-Jordan
Unusual: A woman cured of leprosy as fast as she got it—instantly (12:9-13)
An animal that saw an angel (22:23)
Food delivered from Heaven that people didn't like (11:4-9)
A prophet who had a conversation with his donkey (22:28-30)

DEUTERONOMY

Summary: Duplicate of Law. The desert kids learn about God and His ways.
People: Moses
Places: Northern Moab, Mt. Pisgah
Unusual: A truly king-sized bed—13 feet long (3:11)
How to live longer (5:16)
Shoes that didn't wear out during 40 years of desert walking (29:5)
A man who died at the age of 120 in perfectly good health and a sound mind (34:7)

JOSHUA

Summary: Judgment on Canaan.
Joshua conquers and divides the Hebrews' "promised land."
People: Joshua, Caleb
Places: Canaan
Unusual: City walls that collapsed after people shouted (6:20)
Con artists who fooled a spiritual leader (9:4-16)
A battle won with large hailstones (10:6-13)
Two kings who fled from hornets (24:12)
The sun standing still a whole day for a general to finish a battle (10:13)

JUDGES

Summary: Jewish Sin Cycles. Seven times the Hebrews sin and are conquered but delivered by a "judge."

People: Deborah, Barak, Gideon, Jephthah, Samson

Places: Canaan, Moab, Philistia

Unusual: A man who gave soup to an angel (6:11-19)
Camels that wore necklaces (8:21-26)
42,000 men killed for mispronouncing one word (12:5-6)
A Bible hero who killed a lion with his bare hands (14:5-6)
300 foxes with their tails on fire (15:4-5)

RUTH

Summary: Romance of Redemption. A classic love story of a girl saved from poverty by Prince Charming.

People: Elimelech, Naomi, Ruth, Boaz, Obed

Places: Moab, Bethlehem of Judah

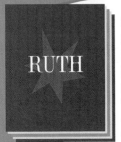

Unusual: A family that moved to another country to avoid starving (1:1)
A man who took off his shoe to seal a deal (4:7-9)
A daughter-in-law better than 7 sons (4:15)

1 SAMUEL

Summary: Samuel and Saul. The adventures of the last judge and first Hebrew king.

People: Eli, Hannah, Samuel, Saul, David

Places: Canaan (Ramah, Mizpah, Gibeah, Philistia)

Unusual: A priest who fell off his seat and broke his neck (4:15, 18)
A young man who killed a lion and a bear with only a club and his hands (17:34-36)
A king who hunted for a flea (26:20)
A man who ate veal cooked by a witch (28:11, 24-25)

2 SAMUEL

Summary: King David's rise and fall.

People: David, Joab, Abner, Bathsheba, Amnon, Absalom

Places: Canaan (Hebron, Jerusalem)

Unusual: A once-a-year haircut (14:26)
A rider whose hair caught in a tree and his donkey kept going (18:9)
A giant with 12 fingers and 12 toes (21:20-21)
A valiant warrior who chased a lion in the snow and killed it (23:20)

1 KINGS

Summary: Kingdom Is Divided.
The son of the world's wisest and richest man blows it.
People: Solomon, Rehoboam, Jeroboam, Ahab, Elijah, Asa, Jehoshaphat
Places: Canaan (Jerusalem in Judah, Samaria in Israel, Dan, Bethel)
Unusual: Fire that burned up stones (18:38)
A man who walked 40 days without eating (19:8)
A new suit of clothes that fell from the sky (19:19)
A man wearing iron horns (the first Viking?) (22:11)

2 KINGS

Summary: Kingdoms Taken Captive. Lots of good and bad kings lead to the Hebrews' final defeat.
People: Elisha, Joash, Amaziah, Uzziah, Jotham, Hezeklah, Josiah
Places: Canaan (Jerusalem in Judah, Samaria in Israel), Assyria, Babylonia
Unusual: A child who came back to life and sneezed 7 times (4:32-36)
Poison stew neutralized by adding flour (4:40-41)
An iron axe head that floated (6:5-7)
Kings who were 7 and 8 years old (11:21; 22:1)
Rotation of the earth temporarily reversed (20:11)

1 CHRONICLES

Summary: Commentary on David.
God's views on King David's life.
People: David, Joab, Abner, Amnon, Absalom
Places: Same as in 1 and 2 Samuel
Unusual: No mention of David's sin with Bathsheba
(God forgave him and "forgot" it)
A king who was killed for asking advice from a witch (10:13-14)
Music school with 288 students (25:7)

2 CHRONICLES

Summary: Commentary on Kings.
God's views on the rest of the Hebrew kings.
People: Same as in 1 and 2 Kings
Places: Same as in 1 and 2 Kings
Unusual: 88 children who all had the same father (11:21)
An 8-year-old boy who was king of the Jews for 100 days (36:9)
The reason Jews had to stay in Babylon 70 years (36:21)

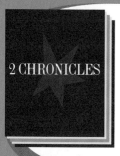

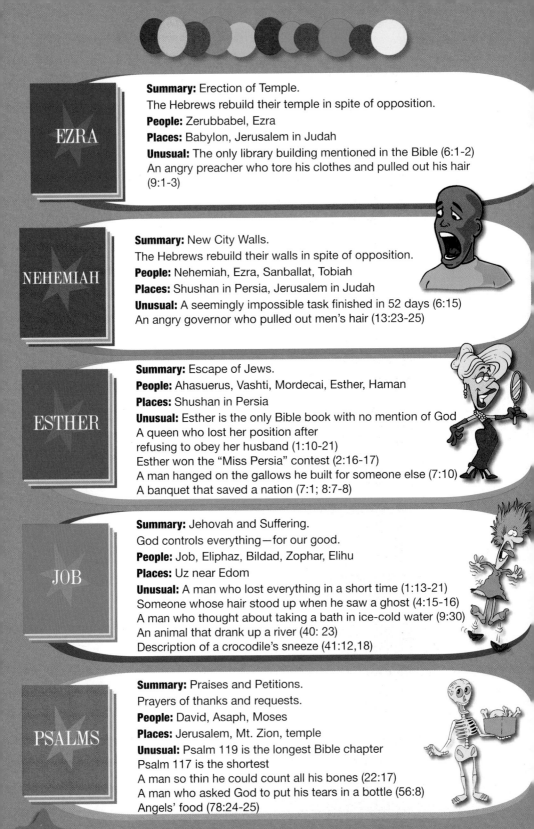

EZRA

Summary: Erection of Temple.
The Hebrews rebuild their temple in spite of opposition.
People: Zerubbabel, Ezra
Places: Babylon, Jerusalem in Judah
Unusual: The only library building mentioned in the Bible (6:1-2)
An angry preacher who tore his clothes and pulled out his hair (9:1-3)

NEHEMIAH

Summary: New City Walls.
The Hebrews rebuild their walls in spite of opposition.
People: Nehemiah, Ezra, Sanballat, Tobiah
Places: Shushan in Persia, Jerusalem in Judah
Unusual: A seemingly impossible task finished in 52 days (6:15)
An angry governor who pulled out men's hair (13:23-25)

ESTHER

Summary: Escape of Jews.
People: Ahasuerus, Vashti, Mordecai, Esther, Haman
Places: Shushan in Persia
Unusual: Esther is the only Bible book with no mention of God
A queen who lost her position after
refusing to obey her husband (1:10-21)
Esther won the "Miss Persia" contest (2:16-17)
A man hanged on the gallows he built for someone else (7:10)
A banquet that saved a nation (7:1; 8:7-8)

JOB

Summary: Jehovah and Suffering.
God controls everything—for our good.
People: Job, Eliphaz, Bildad, Zophar, Elihu
Places: Uz near Edom
Unusual: A man who lost everything in a short time (1:13-21)
Someone whose hair stood up when he saw a ghost (4:15-16)
A man who thought about taking a bath in ice-cold water (9:30)
An animal that drank up a river (40: 23)
Description of a crocodile's sneeze (41:12,18)

PSALMS

Summary: Praises and Petitions.
Prayers of thanks and requests.
People: David, Asaph, Moses
Places: Jerusalem, Mt. Zion, temple
Unusual: Psalm 119 is the longest Bible chapter
Psalm 117 is the shortest
A man so thin he could count all his bones (22:17)
A man who asked God to put his tears in a bottle (56:8)
Angels' food (78:24-25)

PROVERBS

Summary: Prudence in Life. How to skillfully live life as God intended.

People: Solomon, his son Rehoboam

Places: Jerusalem in Judah

Unusual: How to have a good, long life (3:1-2)
Garbage in—garbage out (4:23)
Most industrious insects (6:6-8)
Proof a dad loves his kid(s) (13:24)
Something better than gold or silver (16:16)

ECCLESIASTES

Summary: Emptiness in Life. Only God can satisfy people.

People: the Preacher (Solomon)

Places: Jerusalem in Judah

Unusual: A time for everything (3:1-8)
Why two are better than one (4:9-12)
A child who is better off than a king (4:13)
What it's like to grow old (12:1-7)
Our whole duty in life (12:13)

SONG OF SOLOMON

Summary: Sex in Marriage.
Marriage and family are God's beautiful ideas.

People: Shulamite maiden, Solomon

Places: Shunem

Unusual: Jewish boys couldn't read this book until age 30
A lily among thorns (2:2)
60 queens (6:8)

ISAIAH

Summary: Israel's Suffering, Glory. Israel's hard history will be outshined by their Savior's future kingdom.

People: Isaiah, Uzziah, Hezekiah

Places: Jerusalem in Judah

Unusual: Car parts?: hoods, rings, mufflers, chains and round tires like the moon (3:18-23 KJV)
A bed too narrow with a quilt too short (28:20)
The moon as bright as the sun (30:26)

JEREMIAH

Summary: Judah's exile, Return. Prediction the Jews would come back home after 70 years away (and they did).

People: Jeremiah, Josiah, Zedekiah

Places: Jerusalem in Judah

Unusual: A king who cut up and burned God's Word as it was read to him (36:23)
An author who ordered his book tied to a stone and thrown in a river (51:59-64)

LAMENTATIONS

Summary: Lament over Jerusalem.
An eye-witness account of Jerusalem's conquest.
People: Jeremiah
Places: Jerusalem in Judah
Unusual: Jeremiah is known as the weeping prophet.
Lamentations is laid out as an acrostic in its original Hebrew language
This book is recited today by Jews at Jerusalem's "Wailing Wall"

EZEKIEL

Summary: Expectations for Temple. Plans for a future grand temple in Jerusalem.
People: Ezekiel
Places: Judah (Jerusalem), Babylon
Unusual: A prophet who liked the sweet taste of a book (2:9; 3:3)
A sermon illustrated by a boiling pot of bones (24:3-6)
Two sticks that became one in a valley full of human bones (37:1-17)

DANIEL

Summary: Days of Gentiles. History of the non-Jewish nations foretold.
People: Daniel, Nebuchadnezzar, Shadrach, Meshach, Abednego, Gabriel
Places: Babylon
Unusual: A contest between vegetarians and meat eaters (1:11-16)
Four students with test scores 10 times anyone else's (1:19-20)
A phantom hand that wrote on a plaster wall (5:5-6)
A beast with iron feet and brass toe nails (7:7, 19)

HOSEA

Summary: Heart of Holiness.
God is love but He also has high standards.
People: Hosea, Gomer
Places: Israel (Samaria)
Unusual: A prophet who bought his wife back (3:1-2)
People as worthless as a half-baked cake (7:8)

JOEL

Summary: Judah's Judgment Day.
Insects punish a disobedient nation, but there's hope for individuals.
People: Joel
Places: Judah
Unusual: Locusts that ate up a country's vegetation (1:6-12)

BOOKS OF THE BIBLE

AMOS

Summary: Attitudes toward Law. Hard hearts need to be softened (and can be).
People: Amos
Places: Israel (Samaria)
Unusual: Proud socialites called cows (4:1)

OBADIAH

Summary: Obliteration of Edom. Edom will be wiped out for refusing to help their relatives.
People: Obadiah
Places: Edom (Petra)
Unusual: Accurate prediction the rock city Petra would remain desolate.

JONAH

Summary: Judgment Spared Nineveh. Israel's worst enemy gets converted and spared.
People: Jonah, sailors, Ninevites
Places: Tarshish, Mediterranean Sea, Nineveh
Unusual: A fish that caught a man (1:17)
A prophet who prayed inside a fish (2:1)
A prophet with seaweed wrapped around his head (2:5)
A preacher who got angry when a whole city converted after his message (3:1-5; 4:1)

MICAH

Summary: Morality in Society. God's laws apply to all aspects of life—for our good.
People: Micah
Places: Judah (Jerusalem), Bethlehem
Unusual: Volcanoes, earthquakes and floods together (1:4)
Prediction Jesus would be born in Bethlehem (hundreds of years before He was) (5:2)
Three things the Lord requires of people (6:8)

NAHUM

Summary: Nineveh's Soon Judgment. A century after Jonah Assyria's empire needed judgment again.
People: Nahum
Places: Nineveh in Assyria
Unusual: Accurate prediction a big city would be destroyed by a flood (and it was) (1:8)

83

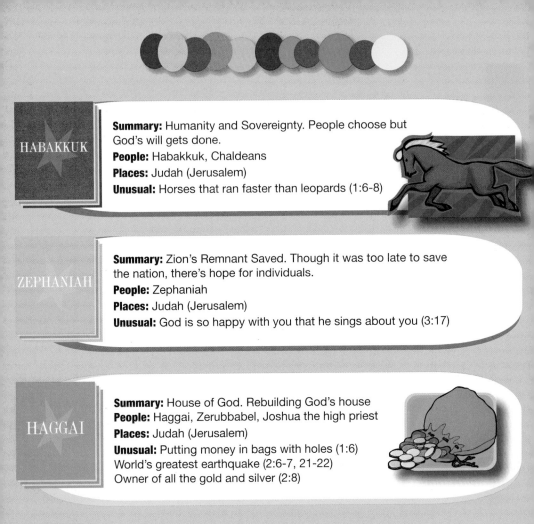

HABAKKUK

Summary: Humanity and Sovereignty. People choose but God's will gets done.
People: Habakkuk, Chaldeans
Places: Judah (Jerusalem)
Unusual: Horses that ran faster than leopards (1:6-8)

ZEPHANIAH

Summary: Zion's Remnant Saved. Though it was too late to save the nation, there's hope for individuals.
People: Zephaniah
Places: Judah (Jerusalem)
Unusual: God is so happy with you that he sings about you (3:17)

HAGGAI

Summary: House of God. Rebuilding God's house
People: Haggai, Zerubbabel, Joshua the high priest
Places: Judah (Jerusalem)
Unusual: Putting money in bags with holes (1:6)
World's greatest earthquake (2:6-7, 21-22)
Owner of all the gold and silver (2:8)

ZECHARIAH

Summary: Zion's Remnant Saved. The Jews rebuilding the temple on Mt. Zion in Jerusalem receive encouragement.
People: Zechariah, Zerubbabel, Joshua (high priest)
Places: Judah (Jerusalem)
Unusual: A writing scroll that flew on its own (5:1-2)
A woman carried through the air in a bushel basket (5:5-11)
A boy named Hen (6:14)

MALACHI

Summary: Messenger before Messiah. John the Baptist is predicted to come before Jesus.
People: Malachi, Elijah
Places: Judah (Jerusalem)
Unusual: Was Malachi the Italian prophet (mah-lot'-chee)?

Browsing God's Library

THE NEW TESTAMENT

MATTHEW

Summary: Messiah for Jews. The Jewish Savior fulfills Old Testament predictions.

People: Joseph, Mary, Jesus, John the Baptist, 12 disciples, Caiaphas, Herod, Pilate, Barabbas

Places: Bethany, Bethlehem, Capernaum, Decapolis, Jericho, Jerusalem, Jordan River, Judea, Nazareth, Sea of Galilee

Unusual: A man who ate insects and wore camel's-hair clothes (3:4)
Over 5,000 people who ate from a kid's lunch (14:15-21)
The devil quoting Bible verses (4:5-6)
Two men who walked on top of a sea (14:25, 29)

MARK

Summary: Messiah Is Servant. Christ came to serve and lay down His life for us.

People: John the Baptist, Jesus, 12 disciples, Jairus, Bartimaeus, Mary Magdalene, Pilate

Places: Same as Matthew except Bethlehem

Unusual: Two disciples nicknamed "Sons of Thunder" by Jesus (3:17)
A man who lived in a cemetery (5:2-3)
Jesus singing (14:26)
When a rooster's crow made a grown man cry (14:72)

LUKE

Summary: Likeness of Man. Human side of Jesus recorded by a doctor.

People: Mary and Joseph, Gabriel, Zacharias and Elizabeth, John the Baptist, Jesus, 12 disciples, Jairus, Lazarus, Mary, Martha, Zacchaeus

Places: Same as Matthew plus Samaria

Unusual: A disciple who was a "con artist" (22:21, 23)
A kingdom in which servants are the greatest (22:26, 29)
A man melted by a look and a rooster's crow (22:61, 62)
A man who could appear and disappear suddenly (24:15, 31, 36)

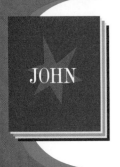

Summary: Jesus Is God. The divine side of Jesus is presented and proven.

People: John the Baptist, Lazarus, Mary, Martha, Nicodemus, 12 disciples, Herod, Pilate

Places: Same as Matthew

Unusual: Seven signs (miracles) and seven "I am..." statements by Jesus
200 gallons of water that became wine (2:1-11)
An ear cut off by a sword that was successfully reattached (18:10)
Chef Jesus cooking a fish breakfast on the beach (21:9-15)
A catch of 153 fish (21:11)

Summary: Apostles of Church. Jesus' disciples spread the Gospel and start new churches.

People: 11 disciples, Matthias, Ananias, Sapphira, Stephen, Paul, Barnabas, Cornelius, Dorcas, Mark, Silas, Timothy, Eutychus

Places: Jerusalem, Judea, Samaria, Gaza, Antioch, Tarsus, Cyprus, Asia Minor, Ephesus, Galatia, Thessalonica, Corinth, Athens, Macedonia, Achaia, Greece, Crete, Malta, Rome in Italy

Unusual: People who instantly learned a foreign language (2:1-4)
3000 people converted after one sermon (2:41)
An iron gate that opened by itself (12:10)

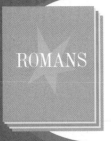

Summary: Righteousness of God. Everyone has sinned but God can give us the gift of being right with Him.

People: Paul, Caesar, Christians in Rome

Places: Rome in Italy

Unusual: God is color-blind (2:11)
Sin's wages (6:23)
A gift from God (6:23)
The most powerful love in the universe (8:38-39)
All leaders in government are ministers (13:1-4)

Summary: Church Problems Solved. Practical solutions to many church issues.

People: Paul, Christians in Corinth

Places: Corinth in Greece

Unusual: Adults who are still babies (3:1)
People are God's temple (3:16)
Something greater than faith or hope (13:13)
The last enemy God will destroy (15:26)
Greatest power on earth (15:57)

2 CORINTHIANS

Summary: Clearing Paul's Reputation. Paul defends himself and describes his ministry.

People: Paul, Christians in Corinth

Places: Corinth in Greece

Unusual: A house not made by human hands (5:1)
A rich person who became poor to make us rich (8:9)
Someone who survived three shipwrecks (11:25)
A preacher lowered from a city wall in a basket (11:32-33)
A man caught up into the third heaven (12:2)

GALATIANS

Summary: Gospel of Liberty. Christ came to set us free from old Jewish laws to be guided by His Spirit.

People: Paul, Christians in Galatia

Places: Galatia in Asia Minor

Unusual: A message received straight from Jesus (1:11-12)
The common bond that breaks down all human barriers (3:28)
A war within (5:17)
Fruit grown in us by the Holy Spirit (5:22-23)

EPHESIANS

Summary: Exaltation in Christ. How to be Christ's body on earth.

People: Paul, Christians in Ephesus

Places: Ephesus in Asia Minor

Unusual: People who are dead but also alive (2:1)
Seats in heavenly places (2:6)
How kids can live longer and better lives (6:1-3)
Christian's suit of armor (6:11-17)

PHILIPPIANS

Summary: Priority of Unity. Joy comes from being in fellowship with God and His people.

People: Paul, Christians in Philippi

Places: Philippi in Macedonia

Unusual: All the world will someday admit Jesus is God (2:10-11)
A missionary who almost died from overwork (2:25-30)
Source of real and lasting peace (4:7)
Power for living (4:13)

COLOSSIANS

Summary: Church's Ascended Head. Christ went back to Heaven so He could be head over His worldwide Church.

People: Paul, Christians in Colossae

Places: Colossae in Asia Minor

Unusual: Translating people (1:12-13)
An exact visible image of the invisible God (1:13, 15)
Hidden mysteries revealed (1:26-27)
What to put off and on (3:8-10)
How kids can please the Lord (3:20)

1 THESSALONIANS

Summary: Triumph before Return. Believers who have died are with Christ and will come back with Him.

People: Paul, Silas, Timothy, Christians in Thessalonica

Places: Thessalonica in Greece

Unusual: Someone raised from the dead
to deliver people from coming judgment (1:10)
Freedom from peer pressure (2:4)
A shout from Heaven to awaken the dead (4:16)
Living people snatched off the earth to meet others
in the air (4:16-17)

2 THESSALONIANS

Summary: Tribulation before Return. There will be a lot of trouble in the world before Jesus returns.

People: Paul, Silas, Timothy, Christians in Thessalonica, antichrist

Places: Thessalonica in Greece

Unusual: Jesus and His angels visible from Heaven (1:7)
A man who sets himself up as god (2:3-4)
The ultimate deceiver (2:8-12)
A missionary who didn't collect money for himself (3:7-9)
Welfare solution (3:10)

1 TIMOTHY

Summary: Trust in Timothy. Paul has confidence in his son in the faith who is now a pastor.

People: Paul, Timothy

Places: Ephesus in Asia Minor

Unusual: Eternal, invisible king (1:17)
Two men delivered to Satan (1:20)
Most attractive fashion style for girls (2:9-10)
Ministries made at home (3:4-5)
How to be well thought of even though you are young (4:12)

2 TIMOTHY

Summary: Teach the Church. A pastor's main job is to teach the truths of God's Word.

People: Paul, Timothy, Onesiphorus

Places: Ephesus in Asia Minor

Unusual: Three generations of faith (1:5)
Remedy for fear (1:7)
Spiritual multiplication (2:2)
Learning without learning (3:7)

TITUS

Summary: Truthless Teachers Denounced. Those who teach error must be opposed.

People: Paul, Titus

Places: Crete

Unusual: How to recognize true believers (1:15-16)
How to live in the present world (2:11-12)
Someone to look for daily (2:13)
How Christianity differs from other religions (3:4-7)

PHILEMON

Summary: Pardon of Onesimus. Paul asks forgiveness for a runaway slave who became a Christian.

People: Paul, Philemon, Onesimus, Apphia, Archippus

Places: Rome

Unusual: Letter from a prisoner (1)
Runaway slave who got converted to Christ (10)

HEBREWS

Summary: Hasten to Maturity. We must grow into a strong faith in Christ, who is better than any religious system.

People: Melchizedek

Places: unknown

Unusual: A real person who didn't have a father or mother, wasn't born and didn't die (7:1-3)
Three items hidden inside the ark of the covenant (9:4)
God's Hall of Faith Heroes (chapter 11)

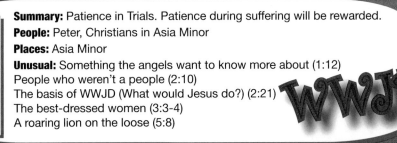

JAMES

Summary: Belief Behaves. Real faith in Jesus shows itself in good deeds.

People: James, scattered Christians

Places: Asia Minor

Unusual: People who look in a mirror but forget about what they see (1:23-24)
Pure religion tests (1:27)
How to recognize dead faith (2:17)
Fire in the mouth (3:5-6)

1 PETER

Summary: Patience in Trials. Patience during suffering will be rewarded.

People: Peter, Christians in Asia Minor

Places: Asia Minor

Unusual: Something the angels want to know more about (1:12)
People who weren't a people (2:10)
The basis of WWJD (What would Jesus do?) (2:21)
The best-dressed women (3:3-4)
A roaring lion on the loose (5:8)

2 PETER

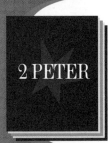

Summary: Purge False Teachers. Don't allow people to teach wrong things in the church.

People: Peter, Christians in Asia Minor

Places: Asia Minor

Unusual: Near-sighted Christians (1:9)
Source of the Bible (1:20-21)
Angels thrown into hell (2:4)
Teachers who don't know what they're talking about (2:12)
Where 1,000 years is 1 day (3:8)

1 JOHN

Summary: Joy in Fellowship. Sharing in God's light, life and love bring us true joy.

People: John

Places: unknown

Unusual: An eye-witness reporter of Christ on earth (1:1-3)
How there was light before the sun (1:5)
How to test spirits (4:1-3)
How to spot a liar (4:20)
How to know you have eternal life (5:13)

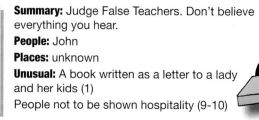

2 JOHN

Summary: Judge False Teachers. Don't believe everything you hear.
People: John
Places: unknown
Unusual: A book written as a letter to a lady and her kids (1)
People not to be shown hospitality (9-10)

3 JOHN

Summary: Joy of Hospitality. How to help ministers and missionaries.
People: John, Gaius, Diotrephes, Demetrius
Places: unknown
Unusual: Self-appointed big shot in the church (9)
Who's of God (11)

JUDE

Summary: Judgment on Apostates. Strong words against people who have turned their backs on God.
People: Jude
Places: unknown
Unusual: An argument between the devil and an archangel over Moses' body (9)
Men who are like clouds without water (12)
People pulled from a fire (23)

REVELATION

Summary: Revelation of Future. The bad news: the world will get worse. The good news: Jesus is coming back to make everything right.
People: John, Jesus, Christians, Jews, archangel Michael, Satan, antichrist, false prophet
Places: Asia Minor
Unusual: Seven groups of sevens (1:4, 12, 16, 20; 4:5; 5:1,6—7:12; 8:2; 10:3; 11:13; 12:3; 15:1; 16:1; 17:9, 10)
Insects with faces like men, teeth like lions and stinging tails (9:7-10)
A man who got a stomachache after eating a little book (10:10)
Hailstones that weighed 80 pounds apiece (16:21)
A whole city dropped into place from heaven (21:2)

BOOKS OF THE BIBLE

91

Buildings
Seven Wonders

Two thousand years ago, Ancient Greek and Roman tourists visited the world's great landmarks just as we do today. Ancient "travel agents" compiled lists of amazing things that travelers should see. These "wonders" were outstanding examples of human artistic or engineering achievement.

The seven most commonly listed monuments to human endeavor are called the Seven Wonders of the Ancient World. They all had qualities that made them stand out from the rest. Some were the most beautiful statues, others the largest structures of the day. Of the seven wonders, only one, the Great Pyramids, can still be seen today. The Hanging Gardens, the Temple of Artemis, the Statue of Zeus, the Mausoleum, the Colossus, and the Lighthouse at Pharos have all vanished or are in ruins.

Hanging Gardens

In 605 B.C. Nebuchadnezzar II, King of Babylon, built the Hanging Gardens in his kingdom. He planted many exotic plants on a brick terrace 75 feet above the ground. Machines worked by slaves watered the plants.

Colossus

The bronze statue of the sun god Helios towered 120 feet over the harbor entrance on the island of Rhodes in the Aegean Sea. Built in 292 B.C., it was about the same size as the Statue of Liberty.

Lighthouse

The Greek architect Sostratos designed the world's first lighthouse. It was built around 304 B.C. on the island of Pharos, Alexandria, Egypt. It stood about 440 feet high. A fire burned at the top to mark the harbor entrance.

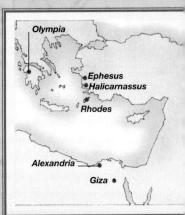

Olympia
Ephesus
Halicarnassus
Rhodes
Alexandria
Giza

of the Ancient World

Mausoleum

The Mausoleum at Halicarnassus (in modern Turkey) was a huge marble tomb built for Mausolus, a rich governor. It stood 135 feet high, with a base supporting 36 columns, under a stepped pyramid. An earthquake destroyed most of the mausoleum.

Temple of Artemis

This, the largest temple of its day, was dedicated to Artemis, goddess of the moon and hunting. Built almost entirely of marble by the Greeks at Ephesus (in modern Turkey), it burned down in 356 B.C., leaving only a few broken statues.

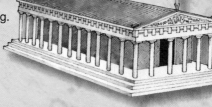

Pyramids

Three pyramids were built at Giza, Egypt, in about 2600 B.C. as tombs for three Egyptian kings. The largest, made from more than two million huge blocks of limestone, stands 482 feet high.

Zeus

The great Statue of Zeus, king of the Greek gods, stood 40 feet high at Olympia, Greece. Phidias, a famous Greek sculptor, created the statue in about 435 B.C. The god's robes and ornaments were made of gold, and the skin was of ivory.

Where the Wonders Were

The map shows the location of the Seven Wonders of the Ancient World. Travelers visited many of them by ship. Most of the wonders were destroyed by earthquakes or fire, but some remains can still be seen in the British Museum in London, England.

Babylon •

Noah's E-mail

Imagine Noah building his ark today:

TO:	Noah
FROM:	God
SUBJECT:	Ark Project

MESSAGE: Big rain coming — whole earth will be covered with water. Evil people will be destroyed. Want to save a few good people, and 2 of every animal. Build an Ark. You've got 6 months.

TO:	The Lord
FROM:	Noah
SUBJECT:	Ark Project Confirmation

MESSAGE: OK

TO:	The Lord
FROM:	Noah
SUBJECT:	Request for Extension

MESSAGE: Have run into some problems. I had to get a building permit, and Your plans didn't meet city code. I had to hire an engineer to redraw the plans. He insisted on adding a fire sprinkler system. My neighbors objected to the building of the Ark in my front yard. I had to get a variance from the city zoning board.

I had a big problem getting wood due to a tree-cutting ban to save the Spotted Owl. I had to convince U.S. Fish & Wildlife that I needed the wood to save the owls. However, they won't let me catch any owls.

The Carpenters' Union went out on strike. I had to settle with the National Labor Relations Board before anyone would pick up a saw or a hammer.

When I started gathering the animals, I was sued by an animal rights group. The Environmental Protection Agency stopped the project until I filed an environmental impact statement on Your proposed Flood. The Army Corps of Engineers wanted a map of the proposed new flood plain. I sent them a globe.

I'm still in a dispute with the Equal Employment Opportunity Commission over how many Croatians I have to hire. The IRS has seized all my assets, claiming I'm trying to avoid taxes by leaving the country. I just got a notice from the state about owing some kind of use tax.

Because of all these problems, I can't finish the Ark for at least 5 more years. Please grant an extension.

TO:	Noah
FROM:	The Lord
SUBJECT:	Ark Project Request for Extension

MESSAGE: Unfortunately, Project Ark lies in the critical path of Project Deluge.

REQUEST DENIED.

LEGOLAND USA

WHAT COULD YOU BUILD IF YOU HAD
MILLIONS OF LEGOS?
HOW ABOUT A WHOLE PARK?
LEGOLAND PARK IS MADE OF MORE
THAN 30 MILLION LEGO BLOCKS..

A favorite place in the park is Miniland USA, which has reproductions of famous American landmarks such as the White House and the Golden Gate Bridge. You can press a button and make things happen in the scenes, even though you can't touch the buildings. The park has life-sized giraffes, zebras and lions all built from Legos, and a Lego factory tour. But there's more than just Legos at Legoland.

The park also has rides and a "clubhouse" where kids get tips from Lego Master Model Builders. Mindstorm robotic sessions, where kids build and program their robots in conjunction with MIT's Media Laboratory are very popular with kids, too.

Most of the rides require kids to do something — drive, push, pull, pedal, steer, fly, pump, stomp, build, climb and, of course, laugh. More than 5,000 models made from Legos inspire and challenge young builders to create something new themselves in the construction areas around the park.

But Legoland doesn't rest on its bricks. New attractions are constantly being added like the Lego Racers 4-D Movie which, has animated actors and heart-pounding music while the audience dodges smoke, wind, snow, water, strobe lights and other special effects as the race roars across on a 36-foot big screen.

Did You Know?

Since Legoland opened in March 1999, 4.2 million kids of all ages have visited the theme park to discover fun and creativity. Guests are the ones who make everything happen. www.lego.com

Legoland is located on 128 acres in Carlsbad, California. There are also Legolands in Billund, Denmark, Windsor, England, and Gunzburg, Germany.

Calendars

Does Anyone Know the Date?

The Gregorian Calendar is used by the Christian church. It begins counting forward from the birth of Jesus Christ, the founder of Christianity. Pope Gregory XIII introduced this widely used system for keeping track of months and days in 582. This calendar is solar, based on the time it takes the earth to go around the sun. The yearly cycle is divided into 12 months.

The Jewish calendar begins at creation. The Jewish year is divided into 12 months which overlap the Gregorian months. The first Jewish month, Tishri, begins in mid-September and concludes in mid-October, and so on.

The Islamic Calendar begins with Muhammad's journey to Medina in A.D. 622 (known as the Hijrah, or migration). In the Islamic calendar, it is currently the 15th century. That is, the years 2000—2001 are equivalent to 1421 in the Islamic calendar. The calendar is based on a lunar year of 12 months.

Months of the Year

Gregorian	Hebrew	Hindu	Muslim
January	Shebat	Magha	Muharram
February	Adar	Phalguna	Safar
March	Nisan	Caitra	Rabi I
April	Iyar	Vaisakha	Rabi II
May	Sivan	Jyaistha	Jumada I
June	Tammuz	Asadha	Jumada II
July	Av	Sravana	Rajab
August	Elul	Bhadra	Shaban
September	Tishri	Asvina	Ramadan
October	Heshvan	Karitka	Shawwal
November	Kislev	Agrahayana	Dhu'l-Qa'dah
December	Tebet	Pausa	Dhu'l-hijjah

The Missing Day

Several years ago two scientists, Prof. Charles A. Totten of Yale University and Sir Edwin Ball, British astronomer, discovered that a day had been lost out of solar time. On July 8, 1970, Harold E. Hill, Curtis Engine consultant to the U.S. space program, reported that computer scientists at Green Belt, Maryland, found a day missing in space in total elapsed time.

Hmmmm, wonder if that has anything to do with the time in the fifteenth century B.C. when the sun "stood still," making the day long enough for Hebrew General Joshua to finish a battle (Joshua 10:13). Seven centuries later the sundial's shadow retreated 10 degrees (equal to 40 minutes) for Judean King Hezekiah (2 Kings 20:11).

Could these two events account for the missing day?

Happy Birthday!

Aren't birthday parties awesome? Well, thank the Egyptians of 3000 B.C. that you get to celebrate with a party. In olden times, people hardly ever celebrated birthdays. And kids' birthdays were never celebrated!

In 3000 B.C., the Egyptians came up with the idea of birthday parties...but only for royalty. These were fancy feasts and the guests all got presents instead of the birthday person.

The Greeks continued this custom and added a birthday cake which was served to the guests. They put lighted candles on the cake to honor Artemis, the Greek goddess of the moon.

Here's an interesting fact — early Christians didn't celebrate birthdays. They celebrated death days! Because when a person died — and went to heaven — was the important event. Christians did not even celebrate Christ's birth until the fourth century when the Catholic Church decided to have a "Christmas" (a mass or religious service) to honor Christ's birth.

About the same time that Christmas came into being, so did the birthday party as we know it. The custom began in Germany and was called a Kinderfeste, which means "children's party."

Kinderfeste started just before dawn. The birthday child was awakened by his family with a cake that had lighted candles on it. The candles kept lit until after dinner, when the cake was eaten for dessert. Then, the child blew out the candles after making a wish.

Did You Know?

Slaves, servants and "commoners" were all invited to Egyptian birthday feasts. Prisoners were often released from jail for the occasion.

The last Kinderfeste celebrated by a child was his 12th. At 13, the child was considered an adult.

"Happy Birthday to You" was originally titled "Good Morning to All." The song was written by two Kentucky sisters in 1893 and was first published in the book, *Song Stories for Children*. The words, "Happy Birthday to You," were added later.

Discover what happened on your birthday at This Day in History, published by the History Channel. Many of the stories have photos and video clips. www. historychannel.com/today

How You'll Spend Your Life

The average American now lives 75.37 years.
Here's how the average person spends those years.

20 years sleeping
14 years working
8 years in amusement (TV, internet, etc.)
7 years for bathroom and grooming
6 years eating
4 years waiting
4 years in transportation
4 years in conversation (including phone)
4 years in education
1 year reading
1 year searching for lost items
1 year in worship
8 months opening junk mail & viewing spam

What God Says About Your Life

"Don't let the excitement of youth cause you to forget your Creator. Honor him in your youth before you grow old and no longer enjoy living. Yes, remember your Creator now while you are young. Fear God and obey his commands, for this is the duty of every person" (Ecclesiastes 12:1, 6, 13 NLT)

"Seventy years are given to us! Some may even reach eighty...soon they disappear, and we are gone. Teach us to make the most of our time, so that we may grow in wisdom" (Psalm 90:10, 12 NLT).

"Those who are wise will find a time and a way to do what is right. Yes, there is a time and a way for everything" (Ecclesiastes 8:5, 6 NLT).

"So be careful how you live, not as fools but as those who are wise. Make the most of every opportunity for doing good in these evil days. Don't act thoughtlessly, but try to understand what the Lord wants you to do" (Ephesians 5:15-17).

Did You Know?

Countries where people live longer:

Japan	80.7
Singapore	80.1
Australia	79.8
Sweden	79.6
Canada	79.4
United Kingdom	77.7

Five southern African nations — Botswana, Zimbabwe, Swaziland, Malawi and Zambia — have the shortest life spans in the world — under 40 years — mainly due to AIDS.

A Day for Everything

Mark your calendar, and plan fun ways to celebrate these special days.

January
3 Sleep Day
4 Trivia Day
13 Make Your Dream Come True Day
14 Dress Up Your Pet Day
19 National Popcorn Day
29 National Puzzle Day

February
2 Groundhog Day
4 Thank a Mailman Day
6 Compliments Day
17 Random Acts of Kindness Day
22 Be Humble Day
24 Once Upon a Time Day

March
1 Peanut Butter Lover's Day
4 Hug a GI Day
12 Plant a Flower Day
17 St. Patrick's Day
19 Absolutely Incredible Kid Day
26 Make Up Your Own Holiday Day

April
1 April Fool's Day
2 International Children's Book Day
7 No Housework Day
11 YMCA Healthy Kids Day
20 Look Alike Day
30 Spank Out Day USA

May
1 May Day
3 National Day of Prayer
10 Clean up Your Room Day
11 Mother's Day (2nd Sunday)
20 Good Neighbor Day
25 National Missing Children's Day

June
3 Repeat Day
6 National Families Day
10 National Yo-Yo Day
14 Flag Day
16 National Hollerin' Contest Day
29 Camera Day

July
1 Creative Ice Cream Flavors Day
2 International Joke Day
8 Video Games Day
11 Cheer up the Lonely Day
15 Cow Appreciation Day
26 Aunt and Uncle Day

August
2 Friendship Day
8 Senior Citizens' Day
10 Lazy Day
16 National Tell a Joke Day
19 Aviation Day
28 Race your Mouse Day

September
6 Read a Book Day
9 Grandparents Day
12 Video Games Day
19 National Kids Day
21 World Gratitude Day
25 National Comic Book Day

October
5 Children's Day
8 American Tag Day
9 National School Celebration
12 Columbus Day
28 Plush Animal Lovers' Day
31 Halloween

November
1 All Saints' Day
11 Veterans' Day
14 Children's Goal-Setting Day
15 America Recycles Day
17 World Peace Day
20 Universal Children's Day

December
6 St. Nicholas Day
7 Pearl Harbor Day
16 National Chocolate Covered Anything Day
20 Games Day
25 Christmas Day
26 Boxing Day

Did You Know?

Find more special days at www.holidayinsights.com.

To send e-cards for special days go to www.annieshomepage.com.

CHRISTMAS

What's Wrong with This Picture?

Can you find at least 20 items that probably were not present when Jesus was born?
(The true story of Jesus' birth can be found in Matthew 2:1-12 and Luke 2:1-20.)

See page 335 for answers.

Did You Know?

The manger where Mary laid the baby Jesus was a stall or crib from which animals were fed (Luke 2:7). We don't know what animals, if any, were present.

It rarely snows in Bethlehem, and there is no evidence of it when Jesus was born.

The star stopped over a house, not the manger, which tradition says was in a cave (Matthew 2:9-11). The magi didn't visit the baby Jesus in the manger.

The "wise men" or magi probably weren't kings. We're not told how many wise men came to see Jesus, only that they brought three kinds of gifts: gold, frankincense and myrrh. Gold was the best currency at the time, and the other gifts are spices.

THE FIRST CHRISTMAS

orld history is divided by the birth of Jesus into B.C. (before Christ) and A.D. (anno Domini — Latin, meaning "in the year of the Lord"). It's been 2004 years since Jesus was born.

Many think Jesus was actually born in the year 6 B.C. because Cyrenius ordered a census in 7-6 B.C. (Luke 2:1, 2). And King Herod, who ordered children under age 2 to be killed, died in 4 B.C.

Jesus' birth was absolutely unique.
• His Father was God (John 3:16).
• His mother was a virgin (Matthew 1:23).
• He was conceived by the Holy Spirit (Luke 1:35).
• He came from heaven (John 6:38).
• Angels announced His birth (Luke 2:9-10).
• He received worship (Matthew 2:11).
• He hid His glory (Philippians 2:5-8).
• He inherited no sin (2 Corinthians 5:21).
• He was born to be the Savior of mankind (Matthew 1:21).

Hundreds of years before Jesus was born, His "birth certificate" was accurately completed. (You'll find the details in Isaiah 7:14; 9:6; 40:10-11; 42:6; 53:6, 12; Psalm 2:7; 16:10; Genesis 49:10; Micah 5:2.)

There is a sound of joy in every language's words for "Merry Christmas:" Boas Festas (Brazil), Buon Natale (Italy), Feliz Navidad (Mexico), Frohliche Weinachten (Germany), Glad Yul (Sweden), Joyeux Noel (France), Kala Christougena (Greece) and Meri Kurisumasu (Japan).

Christmas was first celebrated in North America at Jamestown, Virginia, in the year 1607.

Did You Know?

The first life-sized representation of a manger scene at Christmastime was built by St. Francis in 1223 in Greccio, Italy, using real people and live animals outdoors.

St. Francis may be the father of Christmas caroling. He set new religious words to popular tunes to be sung at his manger scene.

The first Christmas was planned over 4,000 years before it happened. God planned for the birth of His Son in Bethlehem before creating the earth (Ephesians 1:4).

Early Christians hid presents for the children to find on Christmas and pretended that they were from the Christ Child.

Christmas Islands are in the Indian and South Pacific Oceans.

Isaac Newton, Clara Barton, Conrad Hilton, Humphrey Bogart and Anwar Sadat were all born on Christmas Day.

Christmas has been commemorated by U. S. postage stamps annually since 1962.

Some of my Favorite Christmas Memories Are...

1.

2.

3.

4.

5.

The Best Present I Ever Gave Was...

The Best Present I Ever Got Was...

What Christmas symbol is described by these clues?

- About 10 octillion of these exist.
- They praise the God who made and named each one.
- God strictly forbids worship of them.
- One of these led the wise men to Jesus.

In Poland, the *Star* of Bethlehem is the most popular Christmas image. After dinner the Star Man arrives with the Star Boys, each dressed as a wise man, animal or other manger scene figure. The Star Man tests the children's knowledge of the catechism and rewards them with small presents. The Star Boys sing carols in exchange for refreshments.

Indian children in Alaska carry a star-shaped wooden frame covered with bright paper when they sing Christmas carols door to door in exchange for treats.

Can you guess what this common item might be?

- Two of them were on the first U. S. Christmas stamp in 1902.
- Sweden's Lucia wore a crown of these.
- They were used to decorate the earliest Christmas trees.

From earliest times Christians have used *candles* (meaning "to shine") to symbolize Jesus as the Light of the world. Austrian families make three special candles to light before dinner on Christmas Eve, Christmas Day and New Year's Day. As the family sings a hymn, each member stands on a stool, holds the lighted candle, and says three times, "Praise be to the Lord; Christ is born."

Who is this Christmas figure?

- Swiss, Austrian, German and Pennsylvania Dutch children think he brings gifts on Christmas Eve.
- He is pictured as a radiant angel with a crown, white robe and golden wings.
- Costa Rican children set out empty shoes for him to fill with gifts.

Early Christians placed presents for children to find on Christmas from the Christ Child. The Christ Child is a prominent part of Christmas in many lands.

Indians from Ecuadorian highlands arrive in colorful procession to place gifts of fruit and produce before the Christkind (German for "Christ Child"). Each child brings his specially-made or selected gifts to the Christkind in the community manger scene and asks a blessing for his family and animals. A great fiesta follows, featuring roast lamb and the exchange of gifts between the Indians and the ranchers.

Polish families keep empty places for absent members and the Christ Child at their Christmas Eve dinner.

What is this Christmas symbol?

- It began with Martin Luther.
- It was first mentioned by its modern name in 1561 in Germany.
- Mark Carr, a farmer from the Catskill Mountains of New York sold the first one in New York City in 1851.
- Franklin Pierce decorated the first one at the White House in 1856.

The earliest *Christmas trees* were decorated with lighted candles and natural ornaments — real fruits and flowers. Branches drooping from their heaviness prompted German glassblowers to produce lighter glass ornaments.

Czechoslovakian families paint eggshells for tree ornaments, while Swedes weave straw figures of animals. Using paper, Danes cut bells and hearts, and Japanese paint delicate butterflies and fans.

Some people make a "Christmas tree" for the birds by hanging seed balls on branches or railings outside.

Trees or wood are associated with Jesus' days on earth — the manger in which He was laid, boats in which He rode and the cross to which He was nailed.

From Saint to Santa Claus

St. Nicholas wouldn't recognize himself as the American Santa Claus, yet he is the original Santa. Nicholas was the church bishop in Myra (now Demre in Turkey). He was known for his humble generosity. He inherited great wealth and used it for others.

Writer Washington Irving made him elf-sized, flying about in a horse-drawn wagon to bring children presents. Poet Clement Moore created eight reindeer to pull his sleigh. Cartoonist Thomas Nast changed his name to Santa Claus and moved him to the North Pole. Coca-Cola ads in the 1920s gave Santa Claus his colors and set his appearance as we know it.

In Europe he is still St. Nicholas, a thin man in a bishop's robe riding a white horse. St. Nicholas' Day, December 6th, is the main day for gift giving in Europe. In Germany and Poland, boys dressed as bishops beg gifts for the poor. In the Netherlands and Belgium, St. Nicholas arrives on a steamship from Spain to ride a white horse on his gift-giving rounds. The Dutch share candies, chocolate initial letters, small gifts and riddles. Dutch children leave carrots and hay in their shoes for the horse, hoping St. Nicholas will exchange them for small gifts.

Gifts and Givers

1. What gift did Joseph of Arimathea give to Jesus? (Matthew 27:57-60)

2. What gift did Jesus give to Lazarus? (John 11:43-44)

3. Abraham offered this gift to King Ahimelech because he feared for his life. (Genesis 20:1-2, 11)

4. What special gift was given to Joseph by his father Jacob? (Genesis 37:3)

5. As Jesus stood watching in the temple, whose gift did he say was greater than that of the rich? (Luke 21:1-4)

6. What woman brought expensive gifts to King Solomon? (2 Chronicles 9:1, 9)

7. "For God so loved the world that he gave _____." (John 3:16)

8. From where does every good and perfect gift come? (James 1:17)

9. What expensive gift did a woman give Jesus? (Matthew 26:7)

10. Who sent gifts to his brother whom he had wronged twenty years earlier? (Genesis 32:9, 16-18)

(Answers are on page 336)

Operation Christmas Child

Every child should be able to enjoy Christmas.

Every child should have at least one gift to open. The Bible tells us that if we have enough money to meet our needs we should help those who don't. That's part of the reason Operation Christmas Child exists. Kids, families, grandparents – all kinds of people pack a shoe box full of gifts for children around the world. The shoe boxes might end up in Europe or Asia. Some are carried on camels to children in Afghanistan or on donkeys to South America.

Each and every Operation Christmas Child shoe box gift is joyously welcomed by the child who receives it. These gifts help North Korean orphans, children living in garbage dumps in Mexico and Macedonia, schoolchildren in Afghanistan, AIDS orphans in Thailand and kids in war-torn Sudan know that they are not forgotten.

Last Christmas 7 million children in more than 100 countries on 6 continents received personal, gift-filled shoe boxes through Operation Christmas Child. For many, the shoe box gift was the first present they ever received.

You can be a part of this children's Christmas project by filling a shoe box with personal gifts, school supplies, candy, necessity items, family photos and notes of encouragement. Boxes can be dropped off at 1,300 sites in all 50 states. To find the nearest location, call (800) 353-5949, or visit www.samaritanspurse.org (http://www.samaritanspurse.org).

For more photos and news visit http://www.demossnewspond.com/occ/photos/index.htm.

Did You Know?

The 24 million shoe boxes collected since Operation Christmas Child began in 1993 would make a stack 250 times higher than Mount Everest.

It takes 384,000 rolls of wrapping paper to wrap one year's worth of shoe boxes. That's enough to cover 255 football fields!

If all the children who have received shoe boxes to date held hands, they would form a line that reached more than halfway around the world.

Church Promiseland

Think of a place where:

Children have so much fun learning about how awesome God is that they don't want to miss a single week.

The music is so engaging that kids leave humming the tunes and singing the words that help them remember biblical truths all week.

Video and drama are effectively used to teach this media-driven generation about how to live the Christian life at home, at school and in their neighborhoods.

Children are part of a small group where they are known and loved.

Adult volunteers serve with joy and passion, knowing they are influencing the next generation of Christ's followers.

There is such a place! Promiseland is the children's ministry of Willow Creek Community Church in South Barrington, — of the fastest growing churches in the world. And one of the most copied.

"Promiseland wasn't always so promising," says director Sue Miller. "In 1989, we gave ourselves a C-." Promiseland has been rebuilt on 5 core values:

Child-Targeted. "Just as missionaries adapt to the culture of the people they are trying to reach, we plan activities that are fun for children."

Relevant. Every lesson focuses on three questions:
    Know what?   **So what?**   **Now what?**

Creative Bible Teaching. Realistic dramas, video clips, creative storytelling, contemporary music, surprises, games and fun activities, which vary each week, keep kids coming back for more.

Shepherded. Volunteers commit to stay with a group of children to care for them, know them and help them become more like Christ.

Fun! The goal is to make Promiseland the best hour of a child's week.

 Did You Know?

View "A Day in the Life of Promiseland" at www.willowcreek.org/promiseland.asp.

Only the First Baptist Church of Hammond, Indiana, has a larger Sunday school in America, with over 20,000 students. www.baptist-city.com/first_baptist.htm

RAGAMUFFIN ROUNDUP

People in England used to dread Sunday. It was the only day off work for the rowdy children who worked in the factories all week.

No public schools existed in 1780, and only the rich could afford private education. Robert Raikes, owner of the Gloucester Journal, started Sunday schools to teach children to read. Soon he had 100 children enrolled.

When children objected to coming in their ragged clothes, Raikes assured them all they needed was a clean face and combed hair. Reading lessons were from ten to two before lunch. Catechism lessons followed until five-thirty. Small rewards were given for mastering lessons or improving behavior.

Many of the youngsters were transformed by their Sunday school attendance. Swearing, rudeness and unruliness were replaced by a sense of duty and a desire to improve their minds. The crime rate dropped sharply. Factory owners and city officials publicly praised Raikes and his Sunday schools.

In the first 50 years Sunday schools grew to attract more than 1.3 million pupils in Britain and the United States.

In America, the founding of public schools made Sunday schools into places that only taught religion. The Sunday school moved west in the 1800s with the help of missionaries, who rode from town to town organizing schools and selling books. The most famous missionary, Stephen Paxton, once set up 47 Sunday schools in 40 days. His horse's name was Robert Raikes!

Did You Know?

Trying for a good Sunday school attendance record? Here's a target to shoot for. Roland E. Daab of Columbia, Illinois, attended classes for 3,351 consecutive Sundays. He didn't miss — even once — for more than 64 years!

There is a statue of Robert Raikes in Toronto, Canada. Sunday school is now in its third century — 223 years young.

Getting More Out of Church

What was the sermon about last Sunday? Can you remember the title or any of the pastor's main points? A regular attendee at church and Sunday school hears about 100 sermons and lessons a year. That's a lot of listening. But how much do we get out of it?

There are many things we can do to prepare ourselves to get more from the messages or lessons:
- Get plenty of rest the night before.
- Get up early and have an unhurried breakfast.
- Be in harmony with your family and other believers.
- Pray for the service and people's responses.
- Plan to worship God and encourage others.
- Look up Bible references as they are given.
- Jot down any questions that come to mind.

Taking notes on what we hear has a lot of benefits:
- Makes us more active listeners
- Keeps our minds from wandering
- Enables us to recognize the sermon's organization
- Aids retention

Notes may be short and simple. Jotting down just the highlights will double your intake. Begin with a blank sheet of paper and a firm writing surface like a notebook or clipboard. Record the title of the message, Scripture text, speaker's name, the date, all the main points, summary ideas, and any related Bible passages. Then note some personal application. Ask yourself: "What can I do about what I've heard?"

Compare notes with your family or a friend. Try to summarize the speaker's "big idea" in one sentence. Briefly talk through the message or lesson from your notes.

Review your notes later in the week, marking whether each point is **A, P, I** or **E.**
Everything in a message is either:

Application to our lives

Point the pastor or teacher wanted to emphasize

Illustrations (stories or examples used)

Explanation of the Bible text or topic

KIDS LETTERS TO PASTORS

DEAR PASTOR,
I know God loves everybody but He never met my sister. Yours sincerely, Arnold. Age 8, Nashville.

DEAR PASTOR,
Please say in your sermon that Peter Peterson has been a good boy all week. I am Peter Peterson. Sincerely, Pete. Age 9, Phoenix

DEAR PASTOR,
I'm sorry I can't leave more money in the offering, but my father didn't give me a raise in my allowance. Could you have a sermon about a raise in my allowance?
Love, Patty. Age 10, New Haven

DEAR PASTOR,
My mother is very religious. She goes to play bingo at church every week even if she has a cold. Yours truly, Annette. Age 9, Albany

DEAR PASTOR,
I would like to go to Heaven someday because I know my brother won't be there. Stephen. Age 8, Chicago

DEAR PASTOR,
I think a lot more people would come to your church if you moved it to Disneyland. Loreen. Age 9. Tacoma

DEAR PASTOR,
I liked your sermon where you said that good health is more important than money but I still want a raise in my allowance. Sincerely, Eleanor. Age 12, Sarasota

DEAR PASTOR,
Please pray for all the airline pilots. I am flying to California tomorrow. Laurie. Age 10, New York City

DEAR PASTOR,
Please say a prayer for our Little League team. We need God's help or a new pitcher. Thank you. Alexander. Age 10, Raleigh

DEAR PASTOR,
My father says I should learn the Ten Commandments. But I don't think I want to because we have enough rules already in my house. Joshua. Age 10, South Pasadena

DEAR PASTOR,
Who does God pray to? Is there a God for God? Sincerely, Christopher. Age 9, Titusville

DEAR PASTOR,
Are there any devils on earth? I think there may be one in my class. Carla. Age 10, Salina

DEAR PASTOR,
I liked your sermon on Sunday. Especially when it was finished. Ralph, Age 11, Akron

DEAR PASTOR,
How does God know the good people from the bad people? Do you tell Him or does He read about it in the newspapers? Sincerely, Marie. Age 9, Lewiston

Bulletin Bloopers

These are things that actually were printed in church newsletters and programs: Someone must have been embarrassed when they read these mistakes!

The eighth graders will be presenting Shakespeare's "Hamlet" in the church basement on Friday at 7 p.m. The congregation is invited to attend this tragedy.

Our youth basketball team is back in action on Wednesday at 8:00 p.m. in the recreation hall. Come out and watch us kill Christ the King.

Scouts are saving aluminum cans, bottles and other items to be recycled. Proceeds will be used to cripple children.

This afternoon, there will be a meeting in the south and north ends of the church. Children will be baptized at both ends.

For those of you who have children and don't know it, we have a nursery downstairs.

The music today was all composed by George Frederic Handel in honor of his 300th birthday.

Please place your donation in the envelope along with the deceased person(s) you want remembered.

Today is the fifth Sunday of Lint.

If you are blind or unable to understand English, please ask for assistance.

The men's group will hear a car talk at noon.

Great news! Doctors have performed a CAT scan on Pastor Wilson's head and report that they have found nothing.

The Scripture reading today is from the Gospel according to Luck.

Did You Know?

Teen Spiritual Activity

Of teens surveyed:

Nearly 9 out of 10 (89%) pray weekly.
Over half (56%) attend church on a given Sunday.
38% donate some of their own money to a church in a given week.
35% attend Sunday school in a given week.
35% read the Bible on their own each week.
More than 7 out of 10 are involved in some church-related activity in a typical week.
29% attend a small group each week that meets regularly for Bible study, prayer or Christian fellowship, not including Sunday school or a 12-step group.

Seven out of 10 American adults (71%) had a period of time during their childhood when they regularly attended church. A majority of those who attended church as a child still attend today (61%), while most who were not church goers as children are still absent from church today (78%)

The safest place to be is in church.

20% of all fatal accidents occur in automobiles.
17% of all accidents occur in the home.
14% of all accidents occur to pedestrians.
16% of all accidents involve air, rail or water transportation
Only .001% of all deaths occur in worship services in church, and these are usually related to previous physical disorders.

Zip Code 37234

LifeWay in Nashville, Tennessee, is one of the world's largest religious publishers. They send so much mail that they have their own zip code!

Who's Passing the Baton?

Nine out of 10 parents with kids under 13 feel it's their job to teach their children spiritual things. But most of them do not spend any time discussing religious matters or studying religious materials with their children. However, two out of three parents with children 12 or younger attend religious services at least once a month and usually take their children with them.

Boxcar Bunks

Have you ever wondered what it would be like to sleep in a railroad boxcar? Find out at Camp Willow Run in Littleton, North Carolina. Their dormitories are old railroad boxcars, part of the camp's unique railroad theme. The camp has 22 boxcars, a caboose, a 1911 Baldwin locomotive and two baggage cars. The dining hall is a replica 1890 depot!

Camp Willow Run is for kids in grades 3-12. The camp seeks to win kids to Christ, help mature those who are already Christians and demonstrate that Christians can have fun. Don't worry about being uncomfortable — the boxcars are paneled, air-conditioned and have bathrooms. All aboard! **www.campwillowrun.org**

10 Camp Questions

One of the best ways to choose which camp to attend is to talk to someone who has been to one. Here are 10 questions to ask:

1 What did you like best about the camp?

2 Will you go back again?

3 What were the counselors like?

4 Were there lots of activities? Did they include things like swimming, horseback riding and arts and crafts?

5 Where did you sleep? Cabin? Dorm? Tent?

6 What are the bathrooms and showers like?

7 How was the food?

8 Was the camp well-organized? (A good camp runs smoothly, even if the activities are zany and loud.)

9 Did the schedule include quiet or serious time?

10 Did these times help you learn more about God and the kind of person He wants you to be?

Did You Know?

Last year over 8 million people were involved in the 1067 camps and conferences that belong to Christian Camping International. 861 of these camps are for kids. To find one suitable for you, use the locator at www.cciusa.org.

The longest camping trip lasted 40 years and included millions of campers. See page 245.

Awana Know

What's a fun way to learn about the Bible, have fun with friends, make crafts and play games? Awana!

Awana stands for: "Approved Workmen Are Not Ashamed," referring to 2 Timothy 2:15 NIV: "Do your best to present yourself to God as one approved, a workman who does not need to be ashamed and who correctly handles the word of truth."

More than a million kids attend Awana's 9,841 clubs in 120 countries each week. The program for third through sixth graders is called T&T. That doesn't stand for Tacos and Tangerines. Nope, it stands for Truth & Training. Truth for the truth of God's Word, the Bible. Training for learning how to serve God with our lives.

T&T's web site is called "UA" because they want every kid to know about the Ultimate Adventure—not a video game or a movie or some sports thing. The Ultimate Adventure is knowing Jesus Christ. He loved you enough to die in your place and is the only Way to know God. To learn how to begin the Ultimate Adventure, a personal relationship with Jesus Christ, go to www.awana.org/ua/goodnews.html or see page 57 or 148.

Fun games, cool downloads, interesting Bible facts, a touch of humor — the Ultimate Adventure web site has it all. Go to www.awana.org/ua.

Did You Know?

If you don't already know about Awana, check it out! Make sure it's OK with a parent, then go there to find a church where you can join the fun: www.awana.org/ClubFinder.asp.

Awana has different programs for different ages. There's a special program, Cross-trainers, for inner-city preteens. Teens choose from Jr. Varsity (grades 7 and 8) or Varsity (grades 9 through 12). www.awana.org

Last year 9,056 kids earned one or more weeks of free summer camp through Bible memorization in Awana.

Awana teen mission trips offer life-changing, hands-on experience as a Missionary-In-Training.

It's fun to belong to a group where friendships can grow and you can learn helpful things at the same time. For almost a century, the Boy Scouts and Girl Scouts have helped boys and girls develop the values and knowledge they will need to become leaders in their communities. Scouting is a values-based program, with a strong code of conduct. The Scout Promise and Law help instill the values of good conduct, respect for others and honesty. Scouts learn skills that will last a lifetime, including basic outdoor skills, first aid, citizenship, leadership, technical skills, and how to get along with others.

On My

Scout

Boy Scout Promise
On my honor I will do my best
to do my duty to God and my
country, and to obey the Scout Law;
to help other people at all times;
to keep myself physically strong,
mentally awake, and morally straight.

Scout

Boy Scout Law
A Scout is:

Trustworthy	Obedient
Loyal	Cheerful
Helpful	Thrifty
Friendly	Brave
Courteous	Clean
Kind	Reverent

Scouting

Boys
Tiger Cubs (age 7; gr. 1)
Cub Scouts (ages 8-10; gr. 2-5)
Webelos Scouts (age 10; gr. 4-5)
Boy Scouts (ages 11-17; gr. 6 & up)
Varsity Scouts (ages 14-17)
Venturing (ages 14-20)

Honor

Promises

Girl Scout Promise
On my honor, I will try:
To serve God and my country,
to help people at all times,
and to live by the Girl Scout Law.

Laws

Girl Scout Law
I will do my best to be:
Honest and fair, Friendly and helpful,
considerate and caring,
courageous and strong,
and responsible for what I say and do,
and to respect myself and others,
respect authority, use resources wisely,
make the world a better place, and
be a sister to every Girl Scout.

Options

Girls
Daisey Girl Scouts (ages 5-6; gr. K-1)
Brownie Girls Scouts (ages 6-8; gr. 1-3)
Junior Girl Scouts (ages 8-11; gr. 3-6)
Cadette Girl Scouts (ages 11-14; gr. 6-9)
Senior Girl Scouts (ages 14-17; gr. 9-12)

Did You Know?

All scouts have the same motto: "Be prepared." Girl Scouts all around the world share special signs, a handshake, and the friendship squeeze that crosses over the barriers of language.

www.scouting.org and www.girlscouts.org are your links to explore scouting, their interesting magazines, the National Scouting Museum, how to locate scouting near you and more.

Computers
Who's On Line?

Percentage of kids aged 8 to 13 who say they use the computer:

Used computer yesterday	48%
Used computer out of school	40
Used computer at school	25

Average daily computer use
Per minute use of computer, aged 8 to 13 of those reporting any computer usage the day before:

	Boys	Girls
Games	38	20
School work	17	20
Web sites	16	11
Chat rooms	10	11
E-mail	7	9
Job related	6	3
Other	16	17

Why the Internet is used:

Chat	33%
E-mail	28
Games	42
Information	35
Schoolwork	36

Types of web sites visited
Share of kids aged 8 to 13 visiting each type of site the previous day (among those visiting any site):

Entertainment	46%
Gaming	31
Sports	18
Research/information	13
Shopping	10
Relationship/lifestyle	8
Search Engines	8
Family/Children	7
News	7

Where the Internet is accessed:

Home	72%
School	47
Friend's Home	24
Library	11

What Moves Your Mouse?

COMPUTERS

Web sites visited frequently by 9 to 12 year olds
Percent who visited selected site among those who visited any site

	Boys	Girls
AOL Kids Only	30%	50%
Nick Online	40	40
Disney Online	30	33
Nintendo	37	18
Yahooligans	18	30
Warner Brothers	37	5
Discovery.com	22	10
PBS, PBS Kids	7	10
Mattel	8	12

Things I do while on the computer

	Usually	Sometimes	Total
Watch TV	22%	32%	54%
Listen to radio	12	36	48*
Talk on phone	7	28	35
Read magazine	2	10	12

*increases to 58 percent for tween girls

Internet impact on other activities

	Increased	Same	Decreased
Listening to music	32%	62%	6%
Reading books	30	56	14
Time w/friends & families	16	78	6
Watching TV/videos	5	58	37
Reading newspapers & magazines	22	65	10
Using the phone	32	53	13
Making arts & crafts	31	58	6
Playing outside	14	74	11

(Parent's opinion as to change in child's activities since using Internet from home)

Notable Computer Software

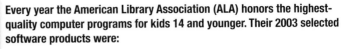

Every year the American Library Association (ALA) honors the highest-quality computer programs for kids 14 and younger. Their 2003 selected software products were:

Encarta Reference Library 2003 (Microsoft)

For ages 8 up. Pretty much everything you ever wanted to know — right at your fingertips. Use a basic version free at www.encarta.msn.com. (Full version free to MSN subscribers)

Inspiration 7 (Inspiration Software)

For ages 10 up. Create a graphic organizer that integrates multimedia files. Or choose from 50 school-related templates. Free trial at www.inspiration.com.

Math Arena Advanced (Sunburst Technology)

For ages 12 up. Practice advanced math skills or enter a competition to prove your knowledge. Online demos at www.sunburst.com/matharena.

Moop and Dreadly in the Treasure on Bing Bong Island

(Plaid Banana Entertainment)
For ages 5 to 10. Solve basic logic problems to collect items needed for the big quest. www.plaidbananagames.com

Nancy Drew: Ghost Dogs of Moon Lake (Her Interactive)

For ages 10 and up. Locate the clues to discover whether ghost dogs are really haunting a cabin. There are two levels of play. www.herinteractive.com/prod/dog

The Powerpuff Girls: Mojo Jojo's Clone Zone
(Learning Company/Riverdeep)
For ages 6 to 10. Use math, logic, language arts and geography skills to save Townsville. Five levels of difficulty. www.tlckids.com

PrintMaster Platinum 15 (Broderbund)
For ages 9 and up. Create a project from scratch or customize one of thousands provided to get professional-looking results. www.broderbund.com

Ultimate Ride Coaster Deluxe (Disney Interactive)
For ages 9 and up. Create and ride a roller coaster using one of five track types and a variety of environments. www.disney.go.com

Zoombinis Island Odyssey (Learning Company/Riverdeep)
For ages 8 and up. Math and logic and science problems. www.tlckids.com

For more information about Notable Computer Software for Children, visit www.ala.org/alsc/awards.html.

The Best of the

How many ways can you find on these 2 pages to have fun exploring and learning?

1. www.clubhousemagazine.com
2. www.cool2read.com
3. www.gp4k.com
4. www.pbskids.org
5. www.timeforkids.com
6. www.factmonster.com
7. www.guinnessworldrecords.com

Web for Kids

123

NET LINGO

A smiley is a sequence of characters on your computer keyboard. Tilt your head to the left to view them. [: = eyes, - = nose,) = mouth.] These little faces are also called emoticons because they are used to show emotion! :-) How many of the following can you match to their meaning?

:-)))	angel
:-\	bawling
:-)	big hug
:---)	blabbermouth
X-(	cat
:")	chin up
:3-]	confused
=8-0	crying
:-(0)	disappointed
'-)	dog
:-&	embarrassed
*<l:-)	foot in mouth
:-#	mad
:-S	Mickey Mouse
}:-X	my lips are sealed
:~-(	Pinnochio
0:-)	pouting
(((H)))	propeller head
;-(	real unhappy
:-e	Santa Claus
:-"	smile
:-V	shouting
X:-)	tongue-tied
:`-(	undecided
(:-D	very happy
8(:-)	whistling
:-!	winking
:-t	yelling
:-C	yikes!

SHORTHAND

To save time and keystrokes when typing quick messages, sometimes people use abbreviations. Once you learn the lingo, make up some shorthand of your own.

4	for
b	be
brb	be right back
g2g	got to go
h/o	hold on
im	instant message
j/k	just kidding
j/p	just playing
lol	laugh out loud
n/p	no problem
n2m	not too much
n2mjch	not to much, just chilling here
peeps	people
s/n	screen name
ttyl	talk to you later
u	you
w/	with
waz?	what's up?

(Answers on page 336)

Select-a-Site!

Check out these super-cool web sites to help with just about anything you're doing!

Look It Up:
www.itools.com
www.yahooligans.com
www.factmonster.com
www.infoplease.com
www.worldalmanacforkids.com
www.eduplace.com/kids
www.cia.gov/cia/publications/factbook
www.britannica.com
www.m-w.com
www.encarta.msn.com
www.catalog.loc.gov
www.refdesk.com
http://www2.nypl.org/home/branch/kids

Help with Homework:
www.school.discovery.com/homeworkhelp/
bjpinchbeck
www.ipl.org/div/kidspace
www.familyeducation.com
www.hhmi.org/coolscience
www.education.com/kidspace
www.ask.elibrary.com
www.askanexpert.com
www.schoolwork.org

Play Games:
www.christianitytoday.com/kids
www.bigidea.com
www.bigideafun.com

Have Fun:
www.Lego.com
www.looneytunes.com
www.mamamedia.com
www.pbskids.org
www.nick.com
www.toomunchfun.com
www.cyberkids.com/fg/ga/ad/sn
www.candystand.com/home.htm

Reading:
www.Cool2Read.com
www.leftbehind.com/channelkids.asp
www.abbyadventures.com
www.elizabethgail.com
www.forbiddendoors.com
www.marsdiaries.com
www.winniethehorsegentler.com
www.tolkien.cro.net
www.lordoftherings.net
www.noblenet.org/wakefield/tolkien.htm
www.thelordoftherings.com

Writing:
www.electricpenguin.com/
inkspot
www.kidpub.com/kidpub
www.thesaurus.com

Links:
www.beritsbest.com

Trivia:
www.uselessknowledge.com

MY 10 FAVORITE WEBSITES

1.

2.

3.

4.

5.

6.

7.

8.

9.

10.

Drama

ACTRESS BY ACCIDENT

Fifteen-year-old Mischa Barton never really meant to become an actress.

"My parents sent me to a summer camp when I was eight. I took a writing course there and wrote a monologue that I performed for the parents. No one knew that agents go to those things to look for kids who can act. I was very surprised when an agent called me. I was cast in my first play that same year!"

Since then, Mischa has performed in plays at the Lincoln Center and the Public Theater in New York City. She's acted in eight movies including *The Sixth Sense*, *Notting Hill* and *Lost and Delirious*. "I've played a deaf child and a British teenager," she says. "I always play something a little edgy or different."

She recently finished filming Disney's *A Ring of Endless Light*. "My favorite part of this film was going to Australia to work with the dolphins," Mischa says. "There was a trainer who taught me how to communicate with them by using simple hand movements. I could make them jump and do tricks."

Before Mischa's career required her to spend months at Australian beaches and other locations, she attended a regular school in New York. Now she works with a tutor on the movie set. "I definitely want to go to college," she says.

What advice would she give to kids who want to act? "Follow your heart and do what you want to do, but never put all your eggs in one basket. It's a difficult business. One minute you're popular and successful, and the next minute you're not. Get a good education so you have other options."

For now, Mischa is enjoying the success of her accidental acting career. She'll be filming another movie soon, and she'd like to do more theater. "Shopping and hanging out are also big priorities," she explains.

Who? Me? An Actor?

Have you thought much about drama? Does the thought of being in a play scare you or excite you? Here's some ways drama happens...

Readers Theater

You just have to be able to read — and speak for this. The actors have the scripts in front of them and read the parts. You still must rehearse, but you don't have to memorize!

Skits

These short dramas (3 or 4 minutes) with a single message, usually involve two or more actors. Often humorous, skits are a great way to make a point for a lesson, devotional or sermon.

Full-length plays

This involves a full cast — kind of like a movie in real time. There are longer (major) roles and smaller ones, too. A good play tells several stories that are woven together and usually involves several age groups. In churches, these are often done at holiday time.

Mime

For those who object, "I can't talk in front of people!" or "I can't memorize!" here's a good place to begin. Mime is just acting out the message — no words are spoken. Sometimes mime is done to music or while someone else reads a story.

Storytelling

Who doesn't enjoy a good story? Remember when your mom or dad read to you every night? Telling a story is a great way to get used to speaking in front of a crowd.

Top Ten Reasons to Do Drama

10. Get to wear really cool (weird) costumes.
9. Can be anything from a snooty socialite to a redneck, from a baby to a Bible character.
8. Get to try out funny accents.
7. Being part of a team (that's the cast, dude).
6. Build your confidence and maybe surprise yourself when you find out you can do it!
5. Experience the thrill of making people laugh (or cry)!
4. Get to "be someone else" for a while.
3. Hey, it's a great way to serve God.
2. It helps you get in touch with your "inner child" and start pretending again.
1. Rehearsal times make a good excuse for why your homework isn't finished.

The Play's the Thing

Stories are a great way to teach. Jesus used stories all the time. We call His stories parables, but they are stories, such as the Good Samaritan or the Prodigal Son. In fact, the Bible is full of really cool true stories — Daniel in the lions' den or David and Goliath, for example.

So what? How can drama be used in church? Lots of ways...

To start discussions for a youth group or Sunday school lesson
To illustrate the point of the sermon. Yeah, in BIG CHURCH!
Holiday programs

Hey, isn't drama just annnnnnnoooooottttttthhhhheeeeerrrrrrrrrr sermon? No Way! Humor or drama helps explain the message by showing how it fits into real life.

Games to "Loosen Up"

One of the first things little kids do is pretend! In fact, kids don't even have to learn to pretend — they just do it! However, as we grow up, some people get "stiff" or scared to let go and pretend in front of others. One way to loosen up is to play games like these:

The Freeze Game

Call a scene, such as playing catch. Two people silently act out that scene until the leader calls "Freeze." They freeze and a new person takes one of their places. He takes the same position, but must change the activity. You can't speak in this game!

The Stupid Game

Sitting in a circle, everyone thinks of a different "sound" to make. Each one demonstrates his sound for the group. Then, the first person makes his sound and someone else's sound. The person with that sound repeats his sound, then makes someone else's. Continue this, going faster and faster, until someone misses his sound and breaks the chain.

Story Add-on Game

One person starts a story. After 30 seconds, the leader calls "Stop"! Another person picks up where first storyteller stopped and adds his or her 30 seconds to the story. Continue switching storytellers until you have the weirdest, most discombobulated story ever!

Fairy Tale Retell

Tell your favorite fairy tale to the group, using three very different accents.

Clowning Around

Do you like to make people laugh?
Do you enjoy having fun?
Become a clown!

Clowns have been around for hundreds of years. They perform in churches, parades, malls, birthdays parties and, of course, on TV and in the circus.

There are four types of clowns, each with a unique personality.

The Whiteface clown is the elite of the clowns. His skills are more highly developed, and he appears to be smarter than the others. His costume is usually very elegant and colorful.

The Auguste clown is charming and naive. This clown is more "happy-go-lucky." But he is a little clumsy and seems to do everything wrong. Auguste is often in conflict with Whiteface. His costume is mixed-matched, bright and colorful.

The Hobo clown has a sad face and wears worn and tattered clothes. Hoboes have a knack for finding the good in a sad situation.

The Character clown wears very little makeup. His costume is an over-exaggeration of a person in everyday life. This clown may be a silly scientist, nurse or a super hero, for example.

Believe it or not, a great place to "clown around" is at church. Some churches have a clown ministry.

What can clowns do in church? They can go to hospitals and nursing homes to cheer up people. They can teach the Bible lesson in children's church or help the pastor illustrate his sermon.

Clowning can be hard work. There is a lot to learn about clowning, but don't forget to have fun. And you'll enjoy the response.

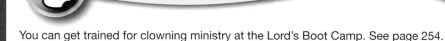

Did You Know?

You can get trained for clowning ministry at the Lord's Boot Camp. See page 254.

When you're in Milwaukee, Wisconsin, drop by the International Clown Hall of Fame. Or make a virtual visit at www.theclownmuseum.org.

Want to learn more about clowning? All the links you need are at www.clown-ministry.com.

Sandy Noe, who wrote this page, is a clown, comedian and storyteller. Meet Sandy at www.forhiskidz.com.

Puppets and Puppeteers

Churches around the world are learning that puppet ministry is a meaningful, effective ministry on both sides of the curtain. Children, of all ages, work the puppets. Audiences of all ages are taught Bible truths, entertained and spiritually challenged by what the puppets say and sing.

Each year, thousands of puppeteers are trained at puppet festivals, workshops and Christian education conferences. Dale VonSeggen, who founded One Way Street with his wife, Liz, answers your questions about puppet ministry.

Q. Is it hard to learn?
A. No, it's actually quite easy if the instructor/teacher knows the basics.

Q. Is it hard work?
A. It is at first, but the more you practice, the stronger your arm muscles become.

Q. What kind of puppets are used?
A. Most puppet ministries today use the moving-mouth "Muppet" style puppet. "People puppets" are the most common. There are also animal puppets and things like flowers, tools, books, stars, clouds.

Q. How is puppetry done?
A. The puppeteer's hand is put into the puppet's head: fingers in the upper part, and thumb in the lower jaw. The puppet's mouth is then opened on each syllable of the words spoken or sung.

The puppeteer usually kneels behind a curtain, with his/her arm straight up from the shoulder, tipping the hand forward so the puppet has proper eye contact with the audience. The puppet is moved so it appears to be alive; acting and reacting to the words and movements of the other puppets.

Q. What styles of performing are there?
A. The easiest style is for the puppet to "lip synch" to a prerecorded song or play. A more challenging style is "live voice" puppetry, where the puppeteer wears a microphone and speaks the words of the script as the puppet is manipulated.

Q. How popular are puppets?
A. Very popular! Puppets are used in television ads, movies, and in educational venues as well as in the church. In other parts of the world, various types of puppets have been used for centuries. The "Punch and Judy" puppets have been used by street entertainers in England for many centuries, and marionettes are very popular throughout Europe. In Asian countries, shadow puppets have been used for hundreds of years.

It's fun! It's cool! It's ministry!

Q. Where are puppets used in the church?
A. Children's Church, Sunday School classes, Vacation Bible School, seasonal programs, outreach ministries, banquets, and special programs. Normally a group of children or teens is directed and trained by adults, and encouraged to perform wherever the opportunity arises.

Q. What do you need to get started in puppet ministry?
A. First, you need a calling from God that leads you into this special ministry. Adult leadership is essential, plus several young puppeteers willing to be trained. You'll need several moving-mouth puppets, plus songs and scripts for the puppets to perform. A stage is necessary, but can be improvised at first. Then several sessions of training will be needed to learn the basic skills and strengthen the hand and arm muscles.

Q. What happens when you really get "good" at doing puppets?
A. First of all, your audience responses will be very positive and affirming. You'll want to attend regional or national puppetry competitions, and perhaps even take a ministry tour or mission trip. Individuals who become excellent puppeteers can even make puppetry a full-time career, working in television, performing nationally or teaching puppetry at conferences and seminars.

Q. Where can I get information to get started?
A. There are three better-known companies in the field of Christian puppetry. They are:

One Way Street, Inc. www.onewaystreet.com
Puppet Productions www.puppetproductions.com
SonShine Puppet Company www.sonshinepuppetco.com

Did You Know?

One Way Street, Inc. is the world's largest supplier of puppet ministry products. Their catalog has 250 different puppets, ranging from $3 finger puppets to $850 blacklight puppets that are six feet tall and operated by two puppeteers. (Web site above or PO Box 5077, Englewood, Colorado 80155. 1-303-790-1188)

Each year One Way Street sponsors 45 training conferences around the U.S. and an International Festival. Last year a total of over 20,000 attended.

You can get trained for puppet ministry at the Lord's Boot Camp. See page 254.

THE WORLD'S GREATEST STORYTELLER

Crowds followed Jesus and "listened to Him with great interest" (Mark 12:37 NLT). People like stories — especially about other people. Jesus is recognized as the world's all-time greatest storyteller.

Jesus often taught in parables — earthly stories with heavenly meaning. Forty of them are recorded in the first three books of the New Testament.

PARABLE	Matthew	Mark	Luke
Dishonest manager			16:1-13
Doorkeeper on watch		13:34-37	
Father, two sons	21:28-32		
Fishing net	13:47-50		
Friend at midnight			11:5-10
Fruitless fig tree			13:6-9
Good Samaritan			10:25-37
Growing seed		4:26-29	
Hidden treasure	13:44		
Houses on rock and sand	7:24-27		6:47-49
Leaven (yeast)	13:33		13:20-21
Leaves on a fig tree	24:32-33	13:28-29	21:29-31
Light under a bushel	5:15-16	4:21-22	8:16-17
Lost coin			15: 8-10
Lost sheep	18:12-14		15:3-7
Mustard seed	13:31-32	4:30-32	13:18-19
New cloth and old clothes	9:16	2:21	5:36
New wine and old containers	9:17	2:22	5:37, 38
Persistent widow			18:1-8
Pharisee and tax collector			18:9-14
Place of honor			14:7-14
Prodigal son			15:11-32
Ready servants			12:37-38
Reluctant guests			14:16-24
Rich fool			12:16-21
Rich man and Lazarus			16:19-31
Servant's duty			17:7-10
Sheep and goats	25:31-46		
Sower and soils	13:3-23;	4:2-20	8:4-15
Talents: three servants	25:14-30		19:11-27
Ten bridesmaids	25:1-13		
Two debtors			7:41-43
Unforgiving servant	18:23-35		
Valuable pearl	13:45-46		
Wedding feast	22:1-14		
Weeds	13:24-30		
Wicked tenants	21:33-44	12:1-12	20:9-19
Wise manager			12:42-48
Workers in the vineyard	20:1-16		

All of Jesus' parable stories are recorded in the first three Gospels. John has none.

It's interesting to compare the same story recorded by different writers.

Renee Spells Ballet

Would you be willing to move 2,000 miles from your family and friends to do something you are really good at and really love? Renee Crous did! Ballet is Renee's passion, so when she got the chance to study at The National Ballet School of Canada, she took it! She beat out 1,000 other 10-year-olds wanting to attend the classical ballet program.

When Renee was two, her parents took her to see "The Nutcracker." She danced around for months afterwards. Ballet had won her heart.

"I used to dance with the Jeunesse Classique Ballet Company," Renee says. "My favorite parts were dancing as the sugarplum fairy toy in 'The Nutcracker' and being a waltzer in 'Sleeping Beauty.' "

Renee's ballet troupe held an auction and performance to raise money for a children's hospital. One of the most special times God has answered Renee's prayers was when she asked famous Russian (now American) ballet dancer, Mikhail Baryshnikov, to send a pair of autographed slippers for the auction. They sold for $2,900! (Baryshnikov won't miss them: he has danced barefoot since 1990.)

Renee has also spent lots of time singing in the choir at Glenmore Christian Academy and studying devotionals with her mom. Now that she's living apart from her family, all of those good times help her get through lonely days.

"I pray a lot and try to read the Bible," Renee says. "But sometimes it's really hard to be a Christian. My favorite Bible verse is John 3:16. I like that verse, because it gives me comfort that Jesus loves me."

In Toronto, Renee has a host family, who takes her to Sunday school. "I'm really glad I have a church to go to," Renee says.

"I really like King David," Renee says. "He set lots of good examples for us, and he obeyed God. And I like his son Solomon, too. He was the wisest man ever."

Now Renee is learning to obey God and make wise decisions on her own. Being 11 and away from home isn't always easy, but she knows she's not alone.

Easter

Easter Fact and Fancy

Easter is amazing! For Christians, it is the most wonderful time of the year! We acknowledge and celebrate Easter because Jesus rose from the dead! Jesus spent 3 days in the grave. His followers were sad and confused. But, on Easter morning He was alive again and many of His followers saw Him and talked with Him. Their sadness quickly turned to joy!

SOME THINGS CHANGE

- Easter wasn't always celebrated on Sunday. It used to be on whatever day came after the Passover ended. But in 325 A.D., church leaders decided that Easter should always be on Sunday, the day Jesus' followers found His empty tomb.
- Years ago worshippers were required to stand up when they prayed on Easter and other Sundays to show that they were risen with Christ.
- A popular Easter hymn was almost lost. When he published the hymns of his brother Charles, John Wesley didn't include "Christ the Lord Is Risen Today." Fifty years later a hymn book editor discovered the lost hymn and added the "Alleluia!" Now millions of Christians sing it every Easter.

SEASONS AND STUFF

- North of the equator, Easter comes in the spring. But kids in the Southern Hemisphere celebrate Easter in the autumn.
- Easter is always the first Sunday following the first full moon in the spring. That's why the date changes from year to year. It can come as early as March 22 or as late as April 25. Do you know the date for Easter this year?
- Perhaps you've heard George Frederick Handel's "Hallelujah Chorus" at church on Easter. Don't be surprised if everyone stands up. When England's King George II first heard the Hallelujah Chorus celebrating Jesus' resurrection, he was so moved that he jumped to his feet. And people have done so ever since.

SOME EASTER FIRSTS

- The explorer Ponce de Leon sighted land on Easter Sunday 1513. He named it Florida from the Spanish name for Easter, Pascua Florida. (Pascua means Easter and florida means flowery.)
- An island off the coast of Chile was discovered on Easter Sunday, 1722. It's called Easter Island and is famous for ancient stone carvings.

Did You Know?

All over the Northern hemisphere, the customs of the Easter season are more or less alike. The Lenten penance and fasting; carnivals, egg exchanging, eating, decorating and egg hunts. Also there are Passion Plays and Easter parades.

The Hershey Easter Egg Hunt on April 14, 2001, set a new world record for the largest Easter egg hunt ever. Queen Victoria Park in Niagara Falls, Ontario, was filled with 8,200 children who collected 253,000 chocolate eggs. Thirteen hunters found gold-colored eggs, which were traded for scooters, bikes, a family weekend at a hotel, a year's supply of chocolate and more. One lucky child won a trip for four to Walt Disney World.

Symbols of Easter

Spring

Easter and spring belong together. It just seems perfect to celebrate Christ's new life and believers' new lives at the same time that nature is coming alive after winter. The green, yellow, pink and lavender colors of springtime are traditionally used at Easter.

New clothes

New clothes in pretty springtime colors are one of the fun things of Easter. These new outfits are a reminder of our new life in Christ.

Eggs

Eggs are a symbol of life. In Jewish tradition, they also symbolize a free will offering, the giving of more than is demanded. Jesus is God's free will offering. He is the gift of eternal life!

Did You Know?

What kids expect on Easter Sunday:
- -not much, really: 51%
- -an Easter basket packed with goodies: 30%
- -an Easter card: 5%
- -a box of chocolates: 4%
- -a few jelly beans, if I'm lucky: 4%
- -a stuffed animal: 3%

10 Best Easter

The White House Easter Egg Roll, Washington, D.C.

President Rutherford B. Hayes started this tradition on the White House grounds in 1878. It takes place on the morning after Easter. Call 202-456-7041 or check www.whitehouse.gov/history/tours/easter.html for info.

Easter Eggstravaganza

in Central Park, New York City

All kinds of fun activities and crafts are part of New York City's biggest egg hunt. This happens the day before Easter. Call 212-360-3456 or check www.newyorkled.com

Easter Eggstravaganza

at the University of Montana, Missoula, Montana.

Big Sky country's hunt in the school's tree-ringed Oval. This is the afternoon before Easter. Call 406-243-2488 for info.

Garden Egg Hunt

Santa Barbara, California

Egg hunters are first led on a nature walk through Santa Barbara's colorful Botanic Garden. This is the day before Easter. Call 805-682-4726 for details.

Garrison Farm Easter Egg Hunt

Homer, Georgia

This hunt is billed as the world's largest: 100,000 egg-shaped treats hidden in a 10-acre field, hunted by 5,000 to 15,000 kids. Join the fun on Easter Sunday afternoon. Call 706-677-3126 for details.

Egg Hunts

Zack Gordon Youth Center Easter Egg Hunt

Juneau, Alaska

This is egg hunting in nature. Ravens circling above have been known to swoop in and seize eggs at Adair-Kennedy field. This is the day before Easter. Call 907-586-2635.

United Methodist Church Easter Egg Hunt

Santa Claus, Indiana

In the town known to locals as Santa's summer home, children scramble for the candy-filled plastic eggs. This is the day before Easter. Call 812-937-2482.

Easter Egg Hunt in Costello Park

Manassas Park, Virginia

Kids ages 10-13 hunt with flashlights on Good Friday evening. Younger children search through the grass the next morning. Call 703-335-8872 for information.

Young's Jersey Dairy Easter Egg Hunt

Yellow Springs, Ohio

Over 4,000 boiled and colored eggs are hidden in the pasture for kids 10 and under. This happens on Easter Sunday. Call 937-325-0629 for information.

Easter Egg Hunt on the Slopes

Brian Head, Utah

At Brian Head Resort, children 12 and under can schuss down the trails, seeking out eggs. This is on Easter Sunday. Call 435-677-2035 for details.

For more interesting "10 Great" lists, visit www.10greats.usatoday.com.

139

Bee Contests

Spelling Bee

On May 29, 2003, Sai Gunturi won $12,000, a set of the *Encyclopedia Britannica* and *Great Books of the Western World*, a $1,000 U.S. Savings Bond and a reference library — all for correctly spelling **pococurante.**

The occasion: the 76th annual Scripps Howard National Spelling Bee in Washington, DC. Sai won against 251 other finalists ranging in age from 8 to 15 from every state and several territories and countries.

Sai, an eighth grader from Dallas, tied for 7th place in 2002, 16th place in 2001 and 32nd place in 2000. "Actually, I started studying in fourth grade and then I guess it's kind of like cumulative study all the way up to here," he said.

The Louisville, Kentucky *Courier-Journal* held the first National Spelling Bee in 1925 to stimulate interest in spelling with cash prizes and a trip to the U.S. capitol. The Scripps Howard News Service took over the Bee in 1941.

To find out how to enter, see pictures of all 251 finalists from last year and more, log onto www.spellingbee.com. For all the championship words from 1925 to 2003, see page 337.

Geography Bee

Each year over 5 million students in grades four through eight participate in the National Geographic Bee. The grand prize: a $25,000 college scholarship, a lifetime subscription to *National Geographic* magazine and a week at SeaWorld and Busch Gardens Adventure Camps. Second and third prizes are scholarships of $15,000 and $10,000. www.nationalgeographic.com/geographybee

James Williams, a homeschooled 14-year-old from Vancouver, Washington won the 15th annual National Geographic Bee in 2003. James captured the title by knowing that Goa in India was formerly a colony of Portugal.

Did You Know?

The word "bee" has long been used to describe a busy gathering of people who come together for a special purpose, such as quilting or building a barn. Maybe this is inspired by the busy insect of the same name.

SPELLBOUND is an award-winning film about the National Spelling Bee -- one of the highest rated specials on ESPN — a nail-biting face-off among kids who train as rigorously as any Olympic athlete. www.thinkfilmcompany.com/SpellboundMovie

JESUS HAD TO LEARN, TOO

Do you ever get tired of school? Tired of homework? Tired of studying? Well, just in case you think that kids in Jesus' day didn't have school — here's a little info on schools in those days: Jewish children were homeschooled as they studied the Torah – the Scriptures. Parents instructed their children formally and informally (Deuteronomy 6:6, 7). Of course, they only had the Old Testament to study. They learned the meaning of the Jewish feasts, they saw how God had always taken care of their people. Much of what they learned was done by repetition and memorization. The parents put great emphasis on proper attitudes and treating others with respect and kindness.

We know that Jesus studied the scriptures because He frequently quoted verses from the Old Testament. In the book of Luke alone, Jesus referred to passages from 16 Bible books.

The Bible doesn't mention that Jesus attended school, but He probably followed the custom of boys of His day. They usually went to a synagogue school beginning at age six. Priests led schools in every province and town in Judea at that time. We know that Jesus regularly attended the Sabbath services in the synagogue, the Jewish place of worship. He would have heard the Scriptures read in Hebrew there, and their meaning explained.

Along with other schoolchildren Jesus learned to read and write. We know this because He read from the book of Isaiah in a synagogue service (Luke 4:16—20). Also, He wrote on the ground (John 8:6, 8). He could read and converse in Hebrew, Aramaic and Greek.

Jesus also learned skills at home. His father, Joseph was a carpenter and Jesus learned carpentry from him. When Jesus began teaching in the synagogue in His hometown of Nazareth, people were surprised because they knew Him in His growing up years as "the carpenter" (Mark 6:3) and "the carpenter's son" (Matthew 13:55).

Jesus used things He had learned from His childhood and His work in carpentry in His teachings. He used things from everyday village and country life as examples in His teaching. He talked about a speck of sawdust in one's eye, building a house on a rock rather than on sand, the corroding effect of moths and rust, sewing patches to repair cloth, pouring of wine into wineskins, storerooms in a house, oil in lamps, value of coins, capstones, payment of taxes and flat roofs on houses.

Jesus was definitely God, but He was also a boy and had lessons to learn just like any other boy. There's no doubt that He was a good student!

School at Home

What do these people have in common?

Thomas Edison
Orville & Wilbur Wright
Benjamin Franklin
Anton Bruckner
Patrick Henry
Claude Monet
Douglas MacArthur
Albert Einstein
Joan of Arc
Thomas Jefferson
Mark Twain
Abraham Lincoln
C.S. Lewis
George Washington

Leonardo da Vinci
Irving Berlin
John Rutledge
Booker T. Washington
Felix Mendelssohn
George Washington Carver
Cyrus McCormick
Hans Christian Andersen
Charlie Chaplin
Charles Dickens
Andrew Carnegie
Dwight L. Moody
Florence Nightingale
Theodore Roosevelt

They were all homeschooled! That was more common 200 years ago than it is now. About 1.7 million kids in the U.S. were homeschooled during the 2001-2002 school year, mostly in Christian families.

Homeschooling brings some great results. By eighth grade, home schooled students perform four grade levels above the national average, according to a Fraser Institute study. Studies show that homeschooled children typically do better than their peers on standardized achievement tests and that they have generally excelled in college.

What are some reasons for homeschooling? Some parents homeschool because they want to be sure their kids get a good education that includes religious instruction. Others want to help their kids avoid peer pressure. It's working. Studies find homeschoolers more socially developed than their public or parochial school peers.

Some homeschooled kids use textbooks like those in public schools. Other kids learn from books such as biographies and missionary stories. They also do a lot of hands-on projects for subjects like science. Others do most of their schooling on the computer.

What It's Like to Be Homeschooled?

One homeschooled student says, "Every day is different. The main subjects I study are Science, Bible, Language, History and Math.

"There are days when we add different subjects. Sometimes we do Art. Other days we go on field trips for Social Studies like to a fish hatchery, a horse sanctuary or the electric company.

" I enjoy taking piano lessons, and I'm part of a children's choir. I also love to write and read. For fun, I've created newsletters for my family and neighbors. I have also written a book called *The 'Biggest' Dwarf*. And when I have extra time I love to email my family and friends."

Bill Gothard is founder and president of the Institute in Basic Life Principles, a nonprofit corporation dedicated to serving youth and families through their leaders (www.iblp.org).

After 15 years of working with inner-city gangs, church youth groups, high school clubs, youth camps and families in crisis, Bill wrote his master's thesis at Wheaton Graduate School on 7 Biblical, non-optional principles of life which, help in building good relationships in all areas of life.

For the past 36 years these principles have been taught in seminars around the world. Millions of people have been helped from this 32-hour seminar. Families continue to report life-changing transformations from the truths they learned at Basic Seminars.

The Institute has received invitations to come into public schools, juvenile court systems, prisons, and business and community leaders and has become an international service organization with training centers in several cities, representing several nations.

The work of the Institute involves:

* The Advanced Training Institute (ATI), a home-education program (www.ati.iblp.org)

* Oak Brook College, a law school (www.obcl.edu)

* Verity Education, a college (www.verity.iblp.org)

* The Air Land Emergency Response Team (ALERT) (www. alertacademy.com)

* Institute in Photographic Studies (IPS) (www.ips.iblp.org)

* Two orphanages

* Juvenile rehabilitation programs

* 60 other service programs

Bill is the third of six children born to William and Carmen Gothard. His father was the general manager of an engineering firm and later served various ministries, including Gideons International where he was its executive director.

Did You Know?

For more information about Bill, read his Life Chapters (www.billgothard.com/aboutme/chapters.php)

In the last 40 years over 2.5 million people have attended a basic IBLP seminar.

Character Qualities

Character is who you are—how you behave—when no one else is looking. God's desire is that His children become like His Son, Jesus. There are 49 different qualities to work on in developing a godly character:

Alertness — "Being aware of what is taking place around me so I can have the right responses."

Attentiveness — "Showing the worth of a person or task by giving my undivided concentration."

Availability — "Making my own schedule and priorities secondary to the wishes of those I serve."

Benevolence — "Giving to others' basic needs without having as my motive personal reward."

Boldness — "Confidence that what I have to say or do is true, right and just."

Cautiousness — "Knowing how important right timing is in accomplishing right actions."

Compassion — "Investing whatever is necessary to heal the hurts of others."

Contentment — "Realizing that true happiness does not depend on material conditions."

Creativity — "Approaching a need, a task, or an idea from a new perspective."

Decisiveness — "The ability to recognize key factors and finalize difficult decisions."

Deference — "Limiting my freedom so I do not offend the tastes of those around me."

Dependability — "Fulfilling what I consented to do, even if it means unexpected sacrifice."

Determination — "Purposing to accomplish right goals at the right time, regardless of the opposition."

Diligence — "Investing my time and energy to complete each task assigned to me."

Discernment — "Understanding the deeper reasons why things happen."

Discretion — "Recognizing and avoiding words, actions and attitudes that could bring undesirable consequences."

Endurance — "The inward strength to withstand stress and do my best."

Enthusiasm — "Expressing joy in each task as I give it my best effort."

Faith — "Confidence that actions rooted in good character will yield the best outcome, even when I cannot see how."

Flexibility — "Willingness to change plans or ideas according to the direction of my authorities."

Forgiveness — "Clearing the record of those who have wronged me and not holding a grudge."

Generosity — "Carefully managing my resources so I can freely give to those in need."

Gentleness — "Showing consideration and personal concern for others."

Gratefulness — "Letting others know by my words and actions how they have benefited me."

Honor — "Respecting those in leadership because of the higher authorities they represent."

Hospitality	"Cheerfully sharing food, shelter or conversation to benefit others."
Humility	"Acknowledging that achievement results from the investment of others in my life."
Initiative	"Recognizing and doing what needs to be done before I am asked to do it."
Joyfulness	"Maintaining a good attitude, even when faced with unpleasant conditions."
Justice	"Taking personal responsibility to uphold what is pure, right and true."
Loyalty	"Using difficult times to demonstrate my commitment to those I serve."
Meekness	"Yielding my personal rights and expectations, with a desire to serve."
Obedience	"Quickly and cheerfully carrying out the wise direction of those who are responsible for me."
Orderliness	"Arranging myself and my surroundings to achieve greater efficiency."
Patience	"Accepting a difficult situation without giving a deadline to remove it."
Persuasiveness	"Guiding vital truths around another's mental roadblocks."
Punctuality	"Showing esteem for others by doing the right thing at the right time."
Resourcefulness	"Finding practical uses for that which others would overlook or discard."
Responsibility	"Knowing and doing what is expected of me."
Security	"Structuring my life around that which cannot be taken away or destroyed."
Self-Control	"Rejecting wrong desires and doing what is right."
Sensitivity	"Perceiving the true attitudes and emotions of those around me."
Sincerity	"Eagerness to do what is right, with transparent motives."
Thoroughness	"Knowing what factors will diminish the effectiveness of my work or words, if neglected."
Thriftiness	"Allowing myself and others to spend only what is necessary."
Tolerance	"Realizing that everyone is at varying levels of character development."
Truthfulness	"Earning future trust by accurately reporting past facts."
Virtue	"The moral excellence evident in my life as I consistently do what is right."
Wisdom	"Making practical applications of truth in daily decisions."

Did You Know?

Specific action steps to practice each quality are at www.charactercincinnati.org. For example, how I can practice orderliness:

* Pick up after myself   * Keep my work and play areas clean and neat
* Put things back where they belong   * Use things only for their intended purpose
* Return lost things to their rightful owners

Good Teachers

The Bible is filled with individuals who modeled good or godly behavior. Here are just a few of them listed by one of the many good character qualities they illustrate.

COURAGE

David—fought a giant
Esther—saved the Jews
Gideon—fought thousands with only 300 men

FAITH

Elijah—called on God to send fire
Noah—built an ark on dry land
Woman—touched Jesus' robe to make herself well

FORGIVENESS

Esau—forgave Jacob for stealing his birthright
Jesus—forgave those who crucified Him
Joseph—forgave his brothers

FRIENDLINESS

Aquila and Priscilla—welcomed

believers into their home
Lydia—shared her home with early Christians
Rebekah—gave water to Abraham's servant and his camels

GENEROSITY

Barnabas—sold his land to help the needy
Naaman—sent gifts to Elijah
Ruth—worked in the fields to support Naomi

HUMILITY

Andrew—was happy for younger brother, Peter, to be "special"
John the Baptist—proclaimed Jesus the Messiah, not himself
Mary of Bethany—wiped Jesus' feet with her hair

LEADERSHIP

Deborah—led the Israelites to a great military victory
Joshua—led his people into the Promised Land after Moses' death
Paul—established the early Christian church

PATIENCE

Jacob—worked fourteen years for a wife
Job—was afflicted in every way, yet trusted God
Sarah—had her first son at age ninety

REPENTANCE

David—asked forgiveness for sending Uriah to war
Jonah—was sorry for not going to Nineveh
Paul—regretted persecuting Christians

REVERENCE

Mary Magdelene—followed Jesus
Samuel—heard God's voice and served Him
Solomon—built a great temple for worship

SELF-CONTROL

Balaam—refused to curse the Israelites
Daniel—spent the night in a den of lions

EXCUSES, EXCUSES

EXCUSES FROM PARENTS

Maybe some parents should have done more homework! Check out these actual excuses for absences turned in to Illinois schools (spelling unchanged)

Please eckuse John for been absent January 28, 29, 30, 32, and 33.

Chris has a acre on his side.

Mary could not come to school because she was bothered by very close veins.

John has been absent because he had two teeth taked out of his face.

My son is under the doctor's care and should not take PE. Please execute him.

Please excuse Joey Friday. He had loose vowels.

Please excuse from Blanche from Jum today. She is administrating.

Carlos was absent because he was playing football, he was hurt in the growing part.

Please excuse Jimmy for being. It was his father's fault.

EXCUSES FROM KIDS

Excuses actually heard by teachers as reasons for homework not being finished:

My dog ate it.
A bird took off with it.
Dad thought it was scrap paper.
It got caught in the garbage disposal.
I didn't hear you mention to do it.
I had friends sleep over all weekend!
What homework?
I forgot my book.
I left it at home on the bus.
I didn't have a pencil or pen.
We had to go shopping.
We had to go to my grandmother's house.
I had a game.
I didn't have time.
I was busy playing outside.
I lost it in my room.
My Dad forgot to put it in my bag.
My mother wasn't home last night.

Student: Do you believe someone should be punished for something they didn't do?
Teacher: No
Student: That's good, because I didn't do my homework.

Did You Know?

MOST KIDS BELIEVE THEY GET TOO MUCH HOMEWORK, BUT 73% REPORT SPENDING ONLY ONE HOUR OR LESS ON IT DAILY.

Evangelism

What Every Kid Should Know

If someone asked you, "How can I get to know God?" or "How can I become a Christian?" would you know how to answer?

Here is an easy ABC way of explaining God's plan for salvation.

A **Admit you are a sinner.**

"For all have sinned; all fall short of God's glorious standard" (Romans 3:23 NLT).

B **Believe Jesus can and will save you from your sins.**

"Believe on the Lord Jesus and you will be saved" (Acts 16:31 NLT).

C **Confess your sin to God.**

"If you confess with your mouth that Jesus is Lord and believe in your heart that God raised him from the dead, you will be saved" (Romans 10:9 NLT).

Talk to Him aloud. Tell Him that you believe He has died to forgive your sin. Let Him know that you want Him to be the most important thing in your life from now on.

These verses are especially good ones on the topic of salvation. Look them up and read them carefully in context.

John 3:3	John 14:21
John 3:16,17	Ephesians 2:8,9
John 14:6	1 Peter 2:24

The Story of Jesus for Children

The Story of Jesus for Children is a video/DVD that will give every kid on the planet a chance to see what makes Jesus so cool. It will answer your questions about God and explain why He sent Jesus, His Son, to earth.

Meet Lindsey

Lindsey Wholey plays Sarah. She was impressed with the peaceful, courteous and respectful atmosphere during the filming. "It was really neat. We prayed before each major scene, and that was really good." When asked what she liked the most about being a part of this film, she said, "I think the film is really good, because it tells kids about Jesus. It opens their eyes so they can see the Truth. It's good for kids and their parents to see this film."

The Story Behind the Story

The original *JESUS* film, based on the Gospel of Luke, was produced in 1979 and released in theaters by Warner Brothers Studios. It was filmed in the lands where Jesus actually lived. In 2000, new scenes were added to help children more easily understand the gospel message.

Six young actors eat the fish and loaves when Jesus feeds the multitude. They cry when He hangs on the cross—and celebrate when they hear He is alive.

All the scenes were filmed in a studio in Los Angeles, CA. This new footage was then spliced into the original to look like the kids are actually in the scenes from the 20-year-old film. See if you can tell any difference when you watch it!

Did You Know?

- You can learn the truth about God and Jesus.
- You can hear and see this historic event in 60 fast-action minutes.
- This account is told through the eyes of kids as it might have happened in A.D. 30.
- *The Story of Jesus for Children* has been translated into more than 40 languages.
- The original film is the most translated film of all time — 800 languages of the world.
- The *JESUS* film has been on television in 176 countries, and seen in every country.
- To learn more, go to www.jesusforchildren.org, or call 877-622-8747 or write to The JESUS Film Project; P.O. Box 72007; San Clemente, CA 92674-2007.

A Voice to the Multitudes

The house in Charlotte, North Carolina, where **Billy Graham** was born has been replaced by a giant IBM building. But, very thoughtfully, IBM has mounted a marker showing people the precise site of the birthplace of this world-famous evangelist.

Billy's home as a boy was a dairy farm, where he arose at 3 o'clock each morning to milk cows before going to school. Before he became a Christian at age sixteen, his ambition was to be a baseball player. He was pretty good, too. He played a few semipro games earning ten to fifteen dollars each.

After he turned his life over to Jesus, however, Billy suspected more and more that God might be calling him to be a preacher. He prepared for that service by studying at the Florida Bible Institute, and worked as a golf caddie and dishwasher to pay his way through. Then he moved to Wheaton, Illinois, and graduated from Wheaton College. A building on that campus bears his name today and the history of evangelism is shared through several displays and exhibitions.

Billy Graham preached his first crusade in 1949 in Los Angeles. Since that time his more than 60 years of ministry have given him the opportunity to preach the gospel to more than 210 million people in 185 countries. He has even shared the message of God's love to people in what used to be the Soviet Union. Mr. Graham is often included on lists of the most admired people in America – not because of what he has DONE – but because he has sought to be God's servant and share the message of God's love with as many people as possible.

The Wordless Book

EVANGELISM

It was an easy book to write – *or was it?* It's an easy book to read – *or is it?* It has no words at all. It has no pictures. It's only five pages long! It's called the Wordless Book and it has been used all over the world for more than 125 years to share the message of Christ's love for us. The different color on each page explains one part of the story of our sinfulness and Christ's death for us.

The gold page symbolizes Heaven, the perfect place that is God's home. He made all people and He loves every one of us. God wants us to be with Him in Heaven someday.

The black page stands for sin—the things we think, say or do that do not please God. No sin is allowed in Heaven – only sinless people can go there.

The red page explains Jesus' blood. He died on the cross as the sacrifice for our sins – even though He Himself did not sin at all. But in three days God raised Jesus from the dead.

The clean white page stands for forgiveness. When we understand that Jesus died for our sins and ask God to forgive us, we become His child. Jesus comes to live inside us. Now He is our Savior and we can enter God's Heaven someday.

The green page symbolizes new life from God. When Jesus becomes our Savior we have a new life. When we read God's Word and pray, we will become more like God. We will learn how He wants us to live.

Did You Know?

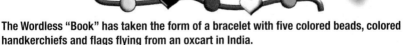

The Wordless "Book" has taken the form of a bracelet with five colored beads, colored handkerchiefs and flags flying from an oxcart in India.

In 1866, at the Metropolitan Tabernacle in London, Pastor Charles Spurgeon preached a sermon, "The Wordless Book," using three pages: black, red and white.

In 1875 in Liverpool, England, Evangelist Dwight Moody added the gold page and used the Wordless Book in a meeting with 12,000 children.

Child Evangelism Fellowship added the green page in 1939 and has printed the Wordless Book ever since. To learn more, go to http://www.gospelcom.net/cef/wordless/.

Families

CHORE CHART

BACK THEN...

Bible-time families could have many members living under one roof. There were husbands, wives, children, grandparents and sometimes servants. Later, married sons and their families often stayed in the home as well. Everyone had to pitch in and help.

A chart of chores for a Hebrew family in Bible times may have looked like this:

Earn a living by working a trade	men
Pay the bills	men
Collect the olives and dates	women
Grind the corn	women
Prepare the meals	women
Spin and weave the thread	women
Make the clothing	women
Take care of the animals	women
Fetch the water	women/children
Gather fuel	children
Teach sons a trade	men
Teach sons the laws and customs of Jewish religion	men
Teach daughters how to manage a household	women
Find suitable wives for sons	men
Care for cattle/tend flocks	older children

AND NOW...

Unfortunately, in today's society, chores are becoming just like the pioneer days—a thing of the past. Look at the facts:

The amount of time kids spent on chores declined 30 percent between 1981 and 1997.

Over the last 20 years, the average amount of time spent on chores by teens declined from more than five hours per week to just over three-and-half hours per week.

In 1976, 41 percent of high school seniors performed chores; in 1999, only 24 percent claimed daily chore duties.

One reason for the major shift, according to Dorothy Rich, president of the Home and School Institute of Washington, DC, is that most families choose to invest their children's free time in sports or academic brain-building projects. However, experts agree that chores are more than just kids doing work around the house. Says Rich, "Chores teach self-discipline, teamwork and help get kids ready for the work world."

8 Things Children Owe Parents

Respect

Honor your father and mother. This is the first of the Ten Commandments that ends with a promise. And this is the promise: If you honor your father and mother, you will live a long life, full of blessing (Ephesians 6:2, 3).

Obedience

Children, obey your parents because you belong to the Lord, for this is the right thing to do. (Ephesians 6:1)

Accept Discipline

As you endure this divine discipline, remember that God is treating you as his own children. Whoever heard of a child who was never disciplined? Since we respect our earthly fathers who disciplined us, should we not all the more cheerfully submit to the discipline of our heavenly Father and live forever? (Hebrews 12:7, 9)

Learn from Them

Listen, my child, to what your father teaches you. Don't neglect your mother's teaching. What you learn from them will crown you with grace and clothe you with honor. (Proverbs 1:8, 9)

Learn About Spiritual Things

Remember the days of long ago; think about the generations past. Ask your father and he will inform you. Inquire of your elders, and they will tell you (Deuteronomy 32:7)

Follow Their Lives

Follow God's example in everything you do, because you are his dear children. Live a life filled with love for others, following the example of Christ, who loved you and gave himself as a sacrifice to take away your sins. (Ephesians 5:1, 2)

Care for Them

If she has children or grandchildren, their first responsibility is to show godliness at home and repay their parents by taking care of them. This is something that pleases God very much. (1 Timothy 5:4)

Help Them

In Bible times children shared in the work of the family. Cain worked in the fields, and Abel looked after flocks (Genesis 4:2). Rachel tended sheep (Genesis 29:6), and Jethro's seven daughters also cared for his flocks (Exodus 2:16). David looked after sheep, too. (1 Samuel 16:11)

153

Birth Stories

The birth of a child is usually a joyous occasion (John 16:21). While girls were treasured in Bible times, every family hoped for at least one boy to receive the prized birthright. Children were considered a gift from God (Psalm 127), and a big family was a sign of God's special blessing.

At birth, salt was rubbed into the baby's skin to make it firm. And the child was wrapped in tight cloths to make the limbs grow straight. The name of the infant was carefully chosen to reflect something about the child's character. Babies were not weaned until they were two or three years old.

After giving birth, in order to be considered "clean" again, a mother had to sacrifice a pigeon and a lamb. In New Testament times, money was deposited in the offering boxes of the temple to "redeem" a firstborn son.

When a boy was eight days old, he was circumcised by his father or rabbi. The firstborn son was considered to belong to God in a special way and had to be bought back (redeemed) a month after circumcision by a payment to the priest (Exodus 13:13).

Every firstborn Jewish son received special privileges. These were part of his "birthright":
- Twice the amount of his father's inheritance (Deuteronomy 21:15-17).
- In early times, the privilege of priesthood (Exodus 13:1,2).
- Heir to his father's authority (2 Chronicles 21:3).

Esau, the firstborn son of Isaac, didn't care about his birthright when he was young. He sold it to his brother, Jacob, for a bowl of stew. Later, he realized the foolish mistake he had made (Genesis 25:29-34).

Reuben was the firstborn son of Jacob, but his disobedience kept him from keeping his birthright. Instead it was transferred to his younger brother, Joseph (1 Chronicles 5:1).

Bar means "son" in Aramaic. In New Testament times, it was used before names to mean "son of." Bar-Jonah, for example, means "son of Jonah."

Did You Know?

A famous prophet was killed during King Herod's birthday party (Matthew 14:6-12).

The day of the least births is May 22; the day of the most births is October 5.

President Grover Cleveland's daughter, Ruth, was the first child born in the White House in the 1920s. The Kandy Kake candy bar was renamed Baby Ruth in her honor.

What's Wrong with Grown-ups?

A group of kids was asked, "What's wrong with grown-ups?" Here's what they answered:

1. They don't keep their promises. Either they forget all about promises they make, or else they say it wasn't really a promise, just a maybe.

2. Grown-ups don't do the things they tell their kids to do—like pick up their things, or be neat or always tell the truth.

3. Grown-ups don't listen to their kids.

4. Grown-ups don't admit when they make mistakes. They pretend that they weren't mistakes or they blame someone else.

5. If a kid interrupts a grown-up, he gets in trouble. But, grown-ups interrupt kids all the time.

6. Grown-ups don't understand things their kids like. If it's something they don't like—even if the children have spent their own money for it—they say, "I can't imagine what you want with that old thing!"

7. Sometimes grown-ups punish children unfairly. It isn't right if you've done just some little thing wrong and grown-ups take away something that means an awful lot to you. Other times you can do something really bad and they say they're going to punish you, but they don't. You never know, and you ought to know.

8. Grown-ups are always talking about what they did and what they knew when they were 10 years old—but they never try to think what it's like to be 10 years old right now.

Make a Grandparent's Day

Nice things you can do for your grandparents (or anyone else for that matter).

1. Tape record a message and send it to them so they can listen to you anytime they want. Tell them how you're doing in school, your plans for the weekend or a funny joke you heard.

2. Write a story or draw a picture and send it to them.

3. When you visit them, show them books or toys that are special to you. Let them know what you're interested in.

4. Bake them a cake or some cookies and take it or send it to them.

5. Ask them to tell you stories about their childhood and younger adult life.

6. Send them a copy of your school picture. Or send a photo of you and your friends.

7. If they live close by, offer to help them with something around the house, like shoveling snow or raking leaves or cutting the grass.

8. Make a project of writing their life story. Interview them and ask lots of questions about where they were born, where they grew up, what jobs they had, and what interests they had. You can make and share the biography with other family members.

9. Offer to teach them something you know how to do, such as working on a computer.

10. Tell them you love them. No one ever gets tired of hearing those special words.

A Kid's Life in Bible Times

Family life in Bible times was quite different from our family life today. Then, the whole family— grandparents, parents, children, relatives and even servants—lived together. This group might be very large (as in the case of Abraham's family). The grandfather had complete authority over the family. When he died, his oldest son took over. Each family member had a clearly defined role in the home.

For Hebrew children, play, work and education were all closely tied to the home. Parents taught children their first lessons and prayers. The entire family attended worship on the Sabbath and festival days. Schooling for boys started when they were about six. Girls were not formally educated. The rabbi of the local synagogue gave moral and religious instruction based on the Torah, and the lessons were learned by repetition.

Work was an important part of childhood. Children had to help in the fields, workshop or kitchen as soon as they could manage the simplest task. Although the people in Bible times had to work hard, they did have times for social activities. God ordered one day in seven—the sabbath—to be set aside from ordinary work. It was a time to rest, relax and worship Him. Rich people had slaves and servants to do the hard work. The religious festivals were an opportunity to celebrate God. They also were welcomed as holidays and fun festivities for everyone.

Of course, there was opportunity to play as well. Children then played as children do today. Children in Bible times enjoyed toys and games. Rattles, dolls, and dollhouses have all been uncovered by archaeologists—even board and dice games, ball games and target games! Marbles were popular in Egypt.

At 13, during New Testament times, a boy became a man in a special ceremony called the Bar Mitzvah (meaning "son of the law"). After his coming of age, the boy was regarded as a responsible member of Israel in home, community and in the synagogue.

Marriage

Girls were usually engaged to be married between ages 13 and 17 in Bible times. Their suitors were generally young men around 17 or 18 years old.

Marriages were usually arranged by the parents. It was customary for a son's mother and father to choose his wife. If both families agreed with the arrangement, and if the son's family could pay the dowry (bride-price), a wedding took place.

The amount of the dowry depended upon what the bride was worth and how much the family could afford. Gold or silver was typical, but it could also be paid in jewelry, animals, goods or service (1 Samuel 18:22-25; Genesis 34:12). Fifty shekels was the usual price for a new bride. A widow or divorced woman was worth only half that amount.

There were several stages in a Middle Eastern wedding.

• **Betrothal**. One year before a man and woman wed, they promised themselves to one another. This promise was similar to today's engagement. It was a binding, legal arrangement with the terms in writing. Gifts were given to the bride-to-be and sometimes to her mother. The dowry could be paid at this time. Joseph and Mary were betrothed when they learned about Jesus' coming birth.

Did You Know?

Mary, the virgin mother of Jesus, was most likely a teenager.

Jacob worked 14 years for the right to wed Rachel and to pay off her dowry (Genesis 29:16-30).

Matters

- **Procession**. The bride waited for the groom to arrive. Her attendants lit clay oil lamps so the house stayed bright as evening approached. The bridegroom and his friends walked to the bride's home carrying torches. Together, they led a joyful procession through the village with musicians playing drums and tambourines, torchbearers, dancers, family and friends.

- **Wedding**. Both the bride and groom wore fine linen embroidered with gold thread. Her hair was often braided with jewels. The headdress was adorned with gemstones, gold ornaments, and later with gold and silver coins. Some wore a crown of flowers. Guests wore special clothes or wedding garments.

- **Feast**. An ongoing celebration was held at the bridegroom's house, and the new couple was blessed by their parents. Some feasts lasted between 7 to 14 days, depending upon the wealth of the families. Most weddings took place in the fall when the full harvest was in. Entire villages were often invited. It was considered very rude to turn down an invitation to a wedding.

While Jesus was attending a wedding feast, the bridegroom ran out of wine for his guests. To save the groom embarrassment and to glorify God, Jesus changed the water in six stone jars into delicious wine (John 2:1-11).

Fashion

From Fig Leaves to White Rob

The world's first couple were nudists, though many believe they were clothed with light. After they sinned, Adam and Eve wore fig leaves sewn together until God clothed them with animal skins. The last-mentioned clothes in the Bible are the white robes of the saints in Heaven.

What to Wear

Israelites wore clothing to express their relationship with God, or their feelings of joy or sadness. Clothing was usually white, purple, red, blue, yellow and black. At festivals, bright colors were worn. At funerals, black rough clothes were put on.

Ladies

1. Undergarment—long and tied with a bright sash.
2. Gown—long and fringed, sometimes with pointy sleeves.
3. Jacket—small, tight-fitting, beautifully embroidered.
4. Headdress—a plain shawl or a scarf set with pearls, silver, gold, or spangles.

Gents

1. Undergarment—sometimes short like an undershirt, sometimes long.
2. Tunic coat—worn sometimes to the ankle.
3. Girdle—a cloth or leather sash worn around the tunic.
4. Cloak—large and loose, worn for warmth.
5. Headdress—cap (worn by the poor), turban, or headscarf.

Clothing was cotton, wool, or silk depending upon the wealth of the wearer.

The folds of a cloth girdle acted like a pocket to carry small things. A leather girdle (worn by soldiers, desert dwellers, or herdsmen) was supported by a shoulder strap and held a sword, dagger, and small objects.

The most important piece of clothing for a man was his cloak. Sometimes it was called a mantle or robe. A cloak was used as a coat, a blanket and even a saddlecloth. God said if you take a neighbor's cloak as a pledge, be sure to return it by sunset. It is the only covering he has for his body.

A Bit About Shoes

Shoes were usually made of soft leather. Sandals were harder leather because they were made for rougher wear.

The soles of shoes were made of wood, cane, or palm-tree bark. They were attached to the leather with nails, and tied around the feet with "thongs."

Most travelers had at least two pairs of shoes.

A common way to confirm a business deal in ancient times was to pluck off your shoe and give it to the person you were making a deal with. Jonathan went a step further. After making a covenant with David, he took off his robe, tunic, sword, bow and belt and handed them over, too! (1 Samuel 18:4)

What They Wore in Bible Times

Adornment

Jewelry included earrings, nose rings or nose jewels, signet rings, toe rings, anklets, bracelets and necklaces.

Men also wore earrings and rings.

Expensive jewelry was crafted from gold, silver, ivory and precious jewels like red garnets and blue sapphires. Cheaper jewelry was made from bronze and glass.

Jewelry was taken as part of the war booty. It was also given in betrothal gifts. (Genesis 24:30)

High priests wore a breastpiece with precious stones. High officials wore gold chains.

Camels often wore jeweled crescents.

Makeup was used. Women painted their eyes, cheeks, and mouths. They also used a yellowish-orange paste on their fingernails and the palms of their hands.

Do's and Don'ts of Hair Care

Women:

Don't wear long hair loose in public.

Do braid it with flowers, ribbons, jewels.

Do use gold and ivory combs, gold hair pins and ribbons: gold hair nets, headbands, and jeweled tiaras, if you can afford it.

Men:

Do wear long hair and a beard if you are a Hebrew or Arab living in Old Testament times.

Do shave your beard if you are an Egyptian. (Genesis 41:14)

Do wear your hair short if you are a New Testament Jew.

Don't ever clip the edges of your beard. (Leviticus 19:27)

Did You Know?

Jesus' cousin, John the Baptist, wore a camelhair tunic with a leather belt. (Mark 1:6)

God says, "Don't be concerned about the outward beauty that depends on fancy hairstyles, expensive jewelry, or beautiful clothes. You should be known for the beauty that comes from within, the unfading beauty of a gentle and quiet spirit, which is so precious to God" (1 Peter 3:3-4 NLT).

Clothes Records

Most Valuable Pair of Jeans — A pair of jeans that sold 120 years ago for $1 were bought by jean maker Levi Strauss for $46,532 on May 25, 2001.

Most Valuable Dress — A Jean Louis gown worn by Marilyn Monroe when she sang Happy Birthday to President Kennedy in 1962 sold at Christie's, New York, on October 27, 1999, for $1,267,000.

Oldest Fashion Designer — British designer Sir Hardy Amies, born in 1909, is still actively involved in the fashion industry. His clothing designs were featured in Stanley Kubrick's 2001, A Space Odyssey.

Most Expensive Commissioned Shoes — For his self-coronation on December 4, 1977, Emperor Bokassa of the Central African Empire (now Republic) commissioned pearl-studded shoes from the House of Berluti, Paris, France, costing $85,000 USD.

Longest Saree — A silk saree created by Vikas Chajjer of Bangalore, India, measured 396 feet long and 45 inches wide. The saree was created in May, 1998, and featured hand-painted portraits of 127 women.

Longest Catwalk — A group of 11 models walked the entire length of a 3,645-foot catwalk, built in a parking lot in Bangkok, Thailand, between May 27–30, 1998.

Largest Necktie Collection — Tom Holmes of Walsall, England, collected 11,650 different ties over 70 years, including yearly birthday ties sent by the British Prime Minister.

Largest Swatch Watch Collection — Fiorenzo Barindelli, of Cesano Maderno, Italy, has a collection of 3,677 Swatch watches, including an example of every Swatch watch type produced since 1983.

Best-Selling Clothes Brand — Levi Strauss Co. is the world's biggest brand-named clothing manufacturer, and sells under the Levis, Dockers and Slates brands. The company's sales totaled $6 billion at the end of November, 1999.

Most Expensive Pop Star Clothing — An outfit worn by Geri Halliwell for the Spice Girls' 1997 Brit Awards performance was sold for a record $66,112 at Sotheby's, London, on September 16, 1998.

Did You Know?

The clothes and shoes of 600,000 Hebrews didn't wear out during a 40-year wilderness camping trip! (Deuteronomy 29:5; Numbers 11:21)

Abishag won the first beauty contest (1 Kings 1:3)

Biggest Fashion Chain

The Gap Inc. operates 3,676 stores in the United States, Canada, the United Kingdom, France, Germany and Japan (as of May 2001). The company's net sales for the year 2000 totaled more than $13.67 billion.

Real-estate developer Don Fisher and his wife, Doris, founded Gap in 1969. After exchanging a pair of jeans sent Don into a frenzy of frustration, he opened the first Gap store in San Francisco with a handful of employees. The name they chose for their store, Gap, referred to the generation gap. Gap sold classically styled, high-quality, casual clothes that everyone could afford.

The chain also includes GapKids, babyGap, GapBody, Old Navy and Banana Republic. In recent years they have raised the chic stakes by using stars in commercials. And they also have made shopping easier with their online stores.

Gap wants to help stop other gaps in the world! In 1977 the company established the Gap Foundation to fund international community programs like the building of a school for homeless children near New Delhi.

Biggest-Selling Designer Brand

The biggest-selling designer clothing brand in the world is **Ralph Lauren,** which had sales of $4.5 billion in 2000. The company has 240 Polo stores worldwide, and also sells its designs through 1,600 department stores and specialty shops.

Ralph Lauren was born Ralph Lipschitz in New York on October 14, 1939. He was brought up by his Jewish mother and shared a room with his two brothers. He created the famous Polo brand in 1967.

"I never went to fashion school," he says. "I was a young guy who had some style!" Starting off as a sales assistant, Ralph Lauren changed his name before opening his first store, which sold ties.

He is married with three children — Andrew, David, and Dylan. The Ralph Lauren name is about style — not fashion — and he named his specialty line after a sport that's all about elegance — polo.

For world records about everything, go to www.guinnessworldrecords.com.

Food

What Bible Kids Ate

Bible-time people usually ate two meals a day. Breakfast was bread, dried fruit and cheese. It was usually eaten on the way to the fields or workplace. The main meal was eaten with the family at the end of the workday.

Sack lunches were sometimes carried by workers or boys in the synagogue school. A typical lunch was two hollow loaves of bread filled with olives and cheese.

Supper Menu

FISH — salted or dried with a hint of mint or dill

CHICKEN — boiled or stewed with rice. Seasoned with a delicious blend of salt, onions, cumin and garlic

WILD FOWL (quail, dove) — boiled or stewed with rice in a rich gravy

LAMB — stuffed in coosa (squash) or wrapped in tender cabbage or grape leaves

SOUP — thick with peas, beans and lentils

PORRIDGE — made with fresh ground corn

FRUITS , NUTS, CHEESE — a tempting array of grapes, figs, olives, mulberries, pomegranates, apricots, plums, oranges, lemons, melons, dates, almonds, walnuts and cheese curds.

EXTRAS — boiled or roasted locusts, fried grasshoppers, roasted corn

DESSERT — dried figs boiled in grape molasses, honeycombs, honey donuts, locust biscuits, fig and cinnamon cakes

BEVERAGES — water, red wine, honey wine, goat's milk, grape juice

(All meals served with your choice of leavened, unleavened, sweetened or unsweetened bread)

Did You Know?

To make butter, fill a skin bag with goat's milk. Hang it between three sticks. Shake it and squeeze it lots until it turns into butter.

Red meat was mostly served on special occasions. Pork, rabbit and shellfish were not allowed to be eaten (Leviticus 11).

Egyptians ate their main meal at noon, rather than the end of the day (Genesis 43:16).

Drinking water was sold on the street in goatskins.

Fruits and vegetables were bought fresh from the market as often as was needed.

Jesus' cousin, John, lived on a diet of locusts and wild honey (Matthew 3:4).

TEN FOODS

10 Most Popular Fast Foods

What's your favorite junk food dinner? Where do you match up with the national average of top ten favorites?

1. Pizza
2. Chicken nuggets
3. Hot dogs
4. Cheeseburgers
5. Macaroni and cheese
6. Hamburgers
7. Spaghetti and meatballs
8. Fried chicken
9. Tacos
10. Grilled cheese sandwiches

10 Most Popular Ice Cream Flavors

Ice cream is a favorite snack around the world. What's your favorite flavor? These are the favorites from around the world.

1. Vanilla
2. Chocolate
3. Butter pecan
4. Strawberry
5. Neapolitan
6. Chocolate chip
7. French vanilla
8. Cookies and cream
9. Vanilla fudge ripple
10. Praline pecan

Test Food

These foods won't make you smarter than you are, but studies show that they can help you keep alert. Sometimes you need all the help you can get before taking a test, right? Try chowing down on some of these:

1. Apples
2. Broccoli
3. Fish (especially oysters)
4. Grapes
5. Lean beef
6. Low-fat yogurt
7. Nuts
8. Peaches
9. Peanuts
10. Pears

Did You Know?

Nearly $8 billion a year is spent on junk food.

40,000 kids die daily around the world from lack of food or clean water.

American kids consume an average of four pounds of candy every week.

A clever problem-solving teen invented the ice cream cone when he ran out of paper dishes at the 1904 World's Fair in St. Louis. He bought a stack of wafflelike confections and rolled them into cones to sell his ice cream.

Eleven-year-old Frank Epperson accidentally invented the popsicle. A jar of powered soda pop mixed with water was left on the porch and found frozen with the stir stick standing in it. He sold "Epsicles" for 5 cents in 1905, later calling them Popsicles after the main ingredient.

Strong man Samson in the Bible had a sweet tooth; he liked to eat honey.

STRANGE MEALS

Truth is stranger than fiction. Some parts of the Bible read like Ripley's Believe It or Not! Consider these unusual meals.

For 40 years in the wilderness the Hebrews ate manna that fell from the sky. Only what they collected on Friday kept overnight. Every other night the leftovers spoiled. (Exodus 16:35)

God sent quail to the Hebrews. But those who ate them died. (Numbers 11:18-35)

On his way to find a wife, Samson discovered a very unusual snack in a very unusual place. (Judges 14:1-9)

The prophet Elijah was fed by ravens. (1 Kings 17:6)

Elijah ate angel-baked bread. (1 Kings 19:5-8)

A dining hall meal at the prophets' school was mistakenly poisoned, but adding some flour to the pot made it safe to eat. (2 Kings 4:38-41)

Elisha the prophet fed 100 men with 20 loaves of bread and had lots left over. (2 Kings 4:42-44)

Jonah was a meal for a huge fish, but he gave it indigestion. (Jonah 1:17; 2:10)

Jesus and His disciples picked and ate grain on the Sabbath, causing a ruckus among the religious leaders. (Mark 2:23-28)

Jesus fed well over 4,000 people with 7 loaves and a few small fish and had 7 baskets of broken pieces left over. (Matthew 15:32-39)

Over 5,000 people attended an all-day seminar with Jesus and didn't bring any food. Jesus stretched a kid's sack lunch to feed them all. There was a basket of fish and chips left over for each of the servers. (Mark 6:35-44)

Much to everyone's surprise, Jesus went home to have dinner with a notable sinner named Zacchaeus. (Luke 19:1-10)

Jesus was severely criticized by the Pharisees for eating with a group of tax collectors at Matthew's house. (Matthew 9:9-13)

When Jesus ate with His disciples the night before His crucifixion, they all ate from one bowl. Jesus asked His followers to always remember Him when they shared bread and wine, and the Last Supper became the most famous meal ever. (Matthew 26:17-29)

Jesus cooked breakfast on the beach for a group of fishermen who had worked all night. (John 21:1-12)

Hunger Fight

Millions of people go to bed hungry every night. Thousands of children die of hunger every day. Beating world hunger is going to take cooperation and hard work – from everyone. Here are some things you can do:

1. Read newspapers and magazine articles about hunger around the world. Learn what countries struggle the most with this issue. Tell other people what you have learned.

2. Donate to organizations that supply food to other countries. One such organization is The Heifer Project. www.heiferproject.org

3. Adopt a foster child in another country. Check out organizations such as Compassion, International or International Children Aid Foundation.

4. See if there is a food pantry or homeless shelter in your town. Volunteer to help in any way you can.

5. Support World Food Day, October 16. www.worldfooddayusa.org

6. Skip a meal and feed the hungry! On the Thursday before Thanksgiving, many people skip a meal or fast for the whole day and donate the money they would have spent on food to Oxfam America. www.oxfamamerica.org

7. Check out UNICEF, an organization that helps lots of people around the world. www.unicef.org

8. Get moving and hold a CROP WALK. Ask people to donate money for each mile you walk. www.churchworldservice.org/CROP

9. Support the American Jewish World Service. This foundation organizes health and agricultural projects for people of all religions. www.ajws.org

10. Pray for others. Ask God to keep reminding you to pray for kids around the world who don't have enough to eat.

Pray for Hungry Children

You know how it feels to be hungry. Your stomach growls. You get weak. You have trouble concentrating. You might even get the shakes.

Millions of children in the world feel real hunger every day because they don't have enough food. Their bodies don't grow correctly, and they get sick easily. Many die young. The ones who live can't learn because their brains have been hurt by bad nutrition.

God cares about hungry people. They are so close to His heart that when we care for them it's like we are caring for Him (Matthew 25:34-40). God has pity on needy people (Psalm 72:13), and He gives food to the hungry (Psalm 146:7). If we ignore the needs of the poor on purpose, we insult God (Proverbs 14:31). In His eyes, we truly worship and walk with Him when we help people in need (Isaiah 58:6-7,10).

One way we can help hungry children is to pray. In fact, God tells us to! Lamentations 2:19 says, "Lift up your hands to him in prayer. Plead for your children as they faint with hunger in the streets."

Prayers That Make a Difference

Your prayers can make a difference for hungry people! Here are some things you can ask God to do:

1. "Father, draw hungry children to Jesus who is the Bread of Life. He promised that whoever comes to Him will never go hungry and whoever believes in Him will never be thirsty."

2. "Jesus, protect hungry children from diseases and protect their minds from harm. Shelter them during times of war, famine and disaster. Keep them safe and give them hope."

3. "Lord God, give Christians the desire to defend weak and fatherless people and the courage to speak up for those who cannot speak up for themselves."

4. "Heavenly Father, bless wealthy people with a heart to do good. Make them generous so hungry children can get the help they need."

5. "Show me, Lord, what I can do to help hungry children in a practical way. Make me a blessing to them."

For adventures with Jesus in prayer, go to www.navpress.com/Magazines/PrayKids!

169

LEFT BEHIND:

You Just Can't Stop Readn' 'Em

In one shocking moment, millions of people around the globe disappear. Those left behind face an uncertain future—especially the kids who now find themselves alone. As the world falls in around them, Judd, Vicki, Lionel and the others must band together to find faith and fight the evil forces that threaten their lives!

Read this gripping story in 40 installments, all best-sellers, all from Tyndale. More at www.leftbehind.com/channelkids.asp. The last 4 books in *Left Behind: The Kids* are due out this year. Reading any of these books is like eating good salty pretzels—you just can't stop!

#1 The Vanishings
#2 Second Chance
#3 Through the Flames
#4 Facing the Future
#5 Nicolae High
#6 The Underground
#7 Busted
#8 Death Strike
#9 The Search
#10 On the Run
#11 Into the Storm
#12 Earthquake
#13 The Showdown
#14 Judgment Day
#15 Battling the Commander
#16 Fire from Heaven
#28 The Mark of the Beast
#17 Terror in the Stadium
#18 Darkening Skies
#19 The Attack of Apollyon
#20 A Dangerous Plan
#21 Secrets of New Babylon
#22 Escape from New Babylon
#23 Horsemen of Terror
#24 Uplink from the Underground
#25 Death at the Gala
#26 The Beast Arises
#27 Wildfire!
#28 The Mark of the Beast
#29 Breakout!
#30 Murder in the Holy Place
#31 Escape to Masada
#32 War of the Dragon
#33 Attack on Petra
#34 Bounty Hunters

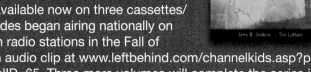

Look and Listen

Surrounded by state-of-the-art sound effects and a great soundtrack, you'll join the Young Trib Force as they courageously face an unraveling world in this unforgettable audio experience. The first 36 episodes *of Left Behind: The Kids Live Action Audio* are available now on three cassettes/CDs. These episodes began airing nationally on over 500 Christian radio stations in the Fall of 2000. Listen to an audio clip at www.leftbehind.com/channelkids.asp?pageid=262&channelID=65. Three more volumes will complete the series in 2004.

Enjoy the same action-packed adventures of the Left Behind series in comic book format. There are five "graphic novel" titles for each of the first two adult books in the series. There are some great previews at www.leftbehind.com/channelbooks.asp?channelID=53.

The first two dramatic videos in the series are already best-sellers: *Left Behind-The Movie* and *Left Behind II-Tribulation Force*. Link to previews, meet the cast, get the latest scoop on the coming TV series and more at www.cloudtenpictures.com.

You Said It

Preteens who wrote to authors Jerry Jenkins and Tim LaHaye say...

"All your books will leave you hanging."

"I like them a whole lot better than those 'Harry Potter' books. I started reading the first Harry Potter book (not knowing what I was getting into) and it wasn't exactly my type. When I started reading Left Behind I could not put the book down."

"This is one of the best books I have ever read. I cannot wait to read the other books."

"The situations that take place make my heart pump faster. The curiosity of wanting to know what happens next at the end of each chapter makes me want to keep on reading."

"After the first chapter I was hooked. Before Christmas I was an average seventh grader who only cared about his friends and himself. Your books have shown me that I should care about other people other than myself. Also, how to believe that God is real and will help me through tough times."

Did You Know?

Over 10 million copies of the *Left Behind: the Kids* books have been sold. End to end, they would stretch over 1,000 miles. The adult titles have sold over 40 million.

= 10 14 + 2 = 16 21 - 4 = 17 1+ 5 = 6 3 x 4 = 12 23 + 73 = 96 33 - 11
= 96 33 - 11 = 22 4 x 4 = 16 6 + 4 = 10 14 + 2 = 16 21 - 4 = 17 1+ 5 =
= 17 1+
16   6
23 + 7
6   21
2   4 x 4
3 x 4 =
14 + 2
33 - 1
1+ 5 =
6 + 4
+ 73 =
- 4 = 17
= 16
2   23
16   2
2   4 x 4
3 x 4 =
14 + 2
33 - 1
1+ 5 =
6 + 4
+ 73 =
6   33
7   1+ 5
6 + 4
+ 73 =
- 4 =
= 16
2   23
16   2
2   4 x 4
3 x 4 =
14 + 2

Calculating the Odds

The Old Testament contains 306 prophecies about Christ's first coming to earth. Each of them came true exactly as predicted. There are 540 prophecies awaiting fulfillment at Jesus' second coming. They will be literally fulfilled, too. The Bible prophesies about hundreds of other things, too.

What are the mathematical odds of all the Bible prophecies coming true? Professor Peter Stoner and others calculated the mathematical probabilities of just eight prophecies coming true and arrived at a conservative estimate of one chance out of a number with 26 zeroes (Science Speaks, Moody Press).

To visualize how big such a number is, imagine the state of Texas covered with silver dollars to a depth of three feet. Texas measures 710 miles by 760 miles and contains 262,134 square miles. Further imagine that one of those quintillions of silver dollars was painted red and a blindfolded person was asked to select one coin from anywhere within the state. What would be his "odds" of picking up the red one the first time? His chances of being correct the first time are the same as for only eight Bible prophecies coming true. But in reality, ALL the prophecies in the Bible came true!

Prophets in the News

FUTURE

Match each headline with the Bible prophet who fits it. For an extra challenge, answer choices are scrambled. When completed, the letters in the answer boxes will spell out a secret message.

1. Prophet Accuses King David of Murder!
2. Prophet Hires Baruch as Personal Secretary!
3. Prophet Seen Alive After Being Crucified!
4. Prophet Names Son Maher-Shalal-Hash-Baz!
5. Eyewitness Account of Jerusalem's Destruction! (prophet's book)
6. Prophet Commands Tithes Be Brought to Storehouse!
7. Prophet Writes Five Books Added to New Testament!
8. Prophet Swallowed by a Great Fish!
9. Prophet Predicts Savior to Be Born in Bethlehem!
10. Prophet Appears from Dead to King Saul!

Answer Choices (scrambled): (Answers are on page 338)

Chilama	Sujes	Hamic	Hantan	Najoh
Aheremij	Taslenmation	Honj	Lesuma	Haisai

1. _ _ [_] _ _ _ _
2. _ _ [_] _ _ _ _ _
3. _ _ _ [_] _
4. _ [_] _ _ _ _
5. _ _ _ _ _ _ _ _ [_] _ _ _
6. _ _ _ _ _ _ [_]
7. _ _ _ [_]
8. _ _ _ _ [_]
9. _ [_] _ _ _
10. _ _ [_] _ _ _

Did You Know?

True prophets must be 100% accurate or be killed. They were allowed no margin for error (Deuteronomy 13:1-5; 18:17-22).

Geography

World Records Set in Bible Lands

A lot of world records have been set in the lands we read about in the Bible.

Lowest

The Dead Sea's shore is the lowest exposed ground at 1,312 feet below sea level. The sea bed is 2,388 feet below sea level. It would be like climbing 3,000 stairs to walk from the bottom back to sea level.

Largest

The Sahara Desert, which stretches across North Africa into the Sinai Peninsula, covers 3,500,000 square miles, making it the world's largest desert.

Longest

The Nile River starts from Lake Victoria in Tanzania (Central Africa) and flows 4,145 miles through Uganda, Sudan and Egypt to reach the Mediterranean Sea. As the world's longest river, the Nile would stretch from Berlin, Germany, to New York City. The Suez Canal joins the Red Sea to the Mediterranean Sea, 108 miles to the north, making it the world's longest canal.

Oldest

The world's oldest canals were built in Iraq, which in ancient times was called Sumer, Mesopotamia and Babylonia. The oldest records of human civilization were also found in this region. (Should we be surprised? The Garden of Eden was located in this vicinity.)

Saltiest

Most oceans contain 3.5% salt. But the Dead Sea is six times saltier than Utah's Great Salt Lake. Even if you can't swim, you're guaranteed to float in the Dead Sea.

Firsts

Rome, Italy, was the first city in the world to have over one million people in 133 B.C. Alexandria, Egypt, was the second to reach this size in 30 B.C. (New York City wasn't this large until 1874.) Athens, Greece, hosted the first Olympic Games in 1896.

Worst

The world's worst earthquake happened in 1202 in the Middle East and North Africa, killing over one million people. In 79 A.D. Mount Vesuvius erupted, burying the Roman cities of Pompeii and Herculaneum and 20,000 citizens.

THE COUNTRIES OF THE WORLD

AFGHANISTAN
· ALBANIA · ALGERIA · ANDORRA ·
· ANGOLA · ANTIGUA AND BARBUDA ·
ARGENTINA · ARMENIA · AUSTRALIA · AUSTRIA ·
AZERBAIJAN · BAHAMAS, THE · BAHRAIN · BANGLADESH ·
BARBADOS · BELARUS · BELGIUM · BELIZE · BENIN · BERMUDA ·
BHUTAN · BOLIVIA · BOSNIA AND HERZEGOVINA · BOTSWANA · BRAZIL
· BRUNEI · BULGARIA · BURKINA FASO · BURUNDI · CAMBODIA · CAMEROON
· CANADA · CAPEVERDE · CENTRAL AFRICAN REPUBLIC · CHAD · CHILE · CHINA
· COLOMBIA · COMOROS · CONGO, DEM. REP. OF · CONGO, REP. OF · COSTA RICA ·
COTE D'IVOIRE · CROATIA · CUBA · CYPRUS · CZECH REPUBLIC · DENMARK · DJIBOUTI
· DOMINICA · DOMINICAN REPUBLIC · EAST TIMOR · ECUADOR · EGYPT · EL SALVADOR ·
EQUATORIAL GUINEA · ERITREA · ESTONIA · ETHIOPIA · FIJI · FINLAND · FRANCE · FRENCH
GUIANA · GABON · GAMBIA, THE · GEORGIA · GERMANY · GHANA · GREECE · GRENADA ·
GUATEMALA · GUINEA · GUINEA-BISSAU · GUYANA · HAITI · HONDURAS · HUNGARY · ICELAND
· INDIA · INDONESIA · IRAN · IRAQ · IRELAND · ISRAEL · ITALY · JAMAICA · JAPAN · JORDAN ·
KAZAKHSTAN · KENYA · KIRIBATI · KUWAIT · KYRGYZSTAN · LAOS · LATVIA · LEBANON · LESOTHO
· LIBERIA · LIBYA · LIECHTENSTEIN · LITHUANIA · LUXEMBOURG · MACEDONIA · MADAGASCAR
· MALAWI · MALAYSIA · MALDIVES · MALI · MALTA · MARSHALL · MAURITANIA · MAURITIUS ·
MEXICO · MICRONESIA · MOLDOVA · MONACO · MONGOLIA · MOROCCO · MOZAMBIQUE · MYANMAR
· NAMIBIA · NAURU · NEPAL · NETHERLANDS · NEW ZEALAND · NICARAGUA · NIGER · NIGERIA ·
· NORTH KOREA · NORWAY · OMAN · PAKISTAN · PALAU · PANAMA · PAPUA NEW GUINEA ·
PARAGUAY · PERU · PHILIPPINES · POLAND · PORTUGAL · QATAR · ROMANIA · RUSSIA ·
RWANDA · SAINT KITTS AND NEVIS · SAINT LUCIA · SAINT VINCENT AND THE GRENADINES ·
· SAMOA · SAN MARINO · SAO TOME AND PRINCIPE · SAUDI ARABIA · SENEGAL ·
SEYCHELLES · SIERRA LEONE · SINGAPORE · SLOVAKIA · SLOVENIA · SOLOMON
ISLANDS · SOMALIA · SOUTH AFRICA · SOUTH KOREA · SPAIN · SRI LANKA ·
SUDAN · SURINAME · SWAZILAND · SWEDEN · SWITZERLAND · SYRIA · TAIWAN
· TAJIKISTAN · TANZANIA · THAILAND · TOGO · TONGA · TRINIDAD AND
TOBAGO · TUNISIA · TURKEY · TURKMENISTAN · TUVALU · UGANDA ·
UKRAINE · UNITED ARAB EMIRATES · UNITED KINGDOM · UNITED
STATES · URUGUAY · UZBEKISTAN · VANUATU · VATICAN
CITY · VENEZUELA · VIETNAM · WESTERN SAHARA ·
· YEMEN · YUGOSLAVIA · ZAMBIA ·
ZIMBABWE

THERE ARE 196

COUNTRIES IN THE WORLD

Without looking at the names above, how many can you name?

Independent nation founded: 14 May 1948

Area:
> water: 440 sq km
> land: 20,330 sq km
> comparative: slightly smaller than New Jersey

Border countries: Egypt , Gaza Strip, Jordan, Lebanon, Syria, West Bank

Coastline: 273 km

Climate: temperate; hot and dry in southern and eastern desert areas

Terrain: Negev desert in the south; low coastal plain; central mountains; Jordan Rift Valley

Elevation extremes:
> lowest point: Dead Sea - 408 m
> highest point: Har Meron - 1,208 m

Natural resources: timber, potash, copper ore, natural gas, phosphate rock, magnesium bromide, clays, sand

Land use:
> arable land: 17.02%
> irrigated land: 1,990 sq km
> Sea of Galilee is an important freshwater source

Natural hazards: sandstorms may occur during spring and summer; droughts; periodic earthquakes

Population: 6,029,529

Age structure:
> 0-14 years: 27.1%
> 15-64 years: 63%
> 65 years and over: 9.9%

Life expectancy at birth:
> total population: 78.86 years
> female: 81.01 years
> male: 76.82 years

Ethnic groups:
> Jewish 80.1%
> non-Jewish 19.9% (mostly Arab)

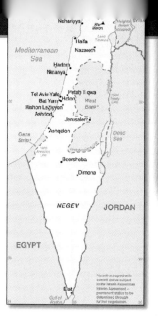

Religions:
>Jewish 80.1%
>Muslim 14.6% (mostly Sunni Muslim)
>Christian 2.1%
>other 3.2%

Languages:
>Hebrew (official)
>Arabic used officially for Arab minority
>English most commonly used foreign language

Literacy (age 15 and over can read and write): 95%

Government type: parliamentary democracy

Capital: Jerusalem

Holiday: Independence Day, 14 May (The Jewish calendar is lunar and the holiday may occur in April or May)

Inflation rate (consumer prices): 5.7% (2002 est.)

Industries: high-technology projects (including aviation, communications, computer-aided design and manufactures, medical electronics), wood and paper products, potash and phosphates, food, beverages, and tobacco, caustic soda, cement, diamond cutting

Currency: new Israeli shekel (ILS)

Exchange rates: new Israeli shekels per US dollar - 4.2757 (December 2001)

Internet country code: .il

Ports and harbors: Ashdod, Ashqelon, Elat (Eilat), Hadera, Haifa, Tel Aviv-Yafo

Disputes: West Bank and Gaza Strip are Israeli-occupied with permanent status to be determined; Golan Heights is Israeli-occupied (Lebanon claims the Shab'a Farms area of Golan Heights)

Did You Know?

You can read more about Israel and any of the world's 283 countries in The World Factbook produced by the CIA. www.cia.gov/cia/publications/factbook

A Bible Map for Non-Artists

Anyone can draw a map of the Bible lands. If you can draw a crooked line, you can do it!

A silly statement helps us remember the names of the rivers and seas which mark out the Bible lands: "E.T. purrs in the red tile med."

Going clockwise from the upper right of the map, note the Euphrates and Tigris Rivers, Persian Gulf, Red Sea, Nile (it rhymes with tile), and the *Medi*terranean Sea. The order of the "*E.T.*" rivers is easy because the *top* one starts with *T*. Just to the East of the Mediterranean Sea is the Sea of Galilee, out of which flows the Jordan River down to the Dead Sea.

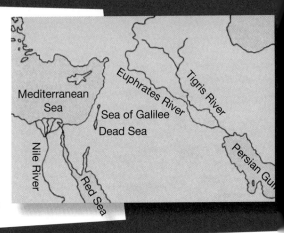

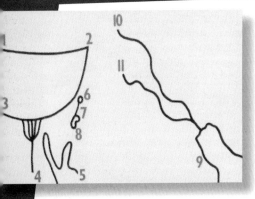

A silly story helps us draw this map: Imagine you are looking at the bow of a fishing boat (draw lines 1, 2 and 3). The fishing lines hanging from the boat got all tangled up (draw lines down to 4). A boy fell out of the boat and is standing on the bottom of the shallow lake. All we see of him are his two skinny fingers under the bow of the boat (draw lines to 5). Being well prepared, he sent a balloon toward the surface, with its string trailing (draw 6 and 7). So that it doesn't ascend too fast, he hung his mitten on the string (draw 8). Farther out ahead in the lake is the head of a water bug (draw 9). So that he can avoid all the action on his left, the bug puts out his two feelers to get safely past (draw 10 and 11).

Trace your finger or pencil over the map lines several times as you reread the above "fish story." Then turn away from the book and practice drawing the whole map. (You don't need to put in the numbers.) Name the water bodies from memory. See, you did it!

Here is how one kid, Henry Raficz (who *is* an artist), drew this freehand map. (The Mediterranean Sea is called the Great Sea in some Bibles.)

See the Bible story summarized on this map on page 54.

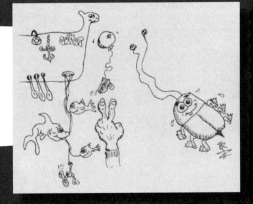

Take a Walk...Thru the Bible

Stories, games, puzzles, magic tricks and skits are all a part of a Kids in the Book Seminar.

It begins by turning the room into one gigantic map. All of a sudden you feel the waves of the Mediterranean Sea. (You may be one of the waves!) You know where the Sea of Galilee is. You walk with Jesus. Follow Paul on his missionary journeys. Sit atop Mount Sinai.

You're soaking in Bible history . . . places . . . characters. And you haven't taken a single note! Hand motions and catchy phrases work together to help you store vast amounts of Bible knowledge. All while you're having fun!

What's in it for You

When you attend either the Old or New Testament seminar you can expect to:

- Walk Thru the events of the Old Testament in 77 easy-to-remember steps—in less than three minutes! Or walk thru the events of Jesus' life and the Acts of the Apostles in 60 steps.

- Recall quickly the Bible books where you'll find the major people, places and events.

- Trace the major geographical movements in the Bible on one of the world's largest maps.

- Discover which 17 books contain the entire story of the Bible.

- Meet the Old Testament prophets up close through Walk Thru the Bible's unique "Prophets Shuffle'.

- Have a new desire to read and apply the Bible to your everyday life.

You'll learn a structure where you can plug in all of the Bible stories you know. You'll come away with a Bible overview that will stay with you for years to come.

Did You Know?

Hundreds of thousands have already attended a Walk Thru the Bible Seminar around the world.

Most kids who attend make a commitment to pray and read their Bibles every day.

Kids in the Book is two separate seminars, one for each of the Bible's testaments.

Get the scoop at **www.walkthru.org**.

God

God, Are You There?

Some people don't believe that God really exists and is a part of our world today. Here are five proofs that God does exist. Perhaps you can share these with your friends who aren't sure about God.

1

Movement. We know that the world is in motion. It turns on its axis, and it orbits around the sun. But nothing moves unless it is forced to move by something else. So who or what put the world into motion before any other force existed? **God.**

2

Nothing happens by itself. For example, a table doesn't just appear out of nowhere. It must be made with tools. Men make tools. And on it goes. But who or what caused the very first thing that ever happened? **God.**

3

Nothing comes from nothing. All physical things have a beginning and an end. So, before anything else existed, who or what created the very first thing ever made? **God.**

4

More or less. Objects and people in the world have different degrees of certain qualities, such as goodness. But we can only achieve our goal of more goodness by comparing our goodness to the maximum goodness. And who is maximum goodness? **God.**

5

The Director. Things in the world move toward specific goals. Day moves toward night, and winter moves toward spring, just as an arrow moves toward a target because the archer aimed it there. So, there must be an intelligent being who directs all things in the world to their proper goals. Who is that? **God.**

180

God in the Bible

Genesis 1:1 2 Kings 21-22 Romans 15:13	**God (god)** Creator of all and Lord over all; the only one who has always existed and always will; the one true God; the Trinity. The Bible is the story of God's deeds and efforts to restore a broken friendship with people. Did you know the Ten Commandments forbids the making or worshiping of false gods?
Genesis 31:19 Exodus 23:24 1 Corinthians 8:5-6	**god, gods (god, godz)** Deities of the Canaanites, Egyptians, Assyrians, and other ancient peoples; false, man-made substitutes for God; idols. The Israelites were supposed to destroy the Canaanites partly because of Canaanite idolatry. Instead, many Israelites themselves became worshipers of Asherah, Baal, Molech, and other such gods. The first of the Ten Commandments forbids the making or worshiping of false gods.
2 Timothy 3:16	**God-breathed (god-breethd)** A term used to describe Scripture. It means that God directed or guided the writers of Scripture to write what he wanted to say.
Ecclesiastes 8:12 Acts 13:26 Acts 17:17	**God-fearing (god-fihr-ing)** Another term for devout.
Colossians 2:9	**godhead, the (god-hed)** An older word for Deity.
Job 8:13 1 Timothy 47 2 Timothy 2:16 Isaiah 33:14 Proverbs 11:9	**godless (god-less)** •Adjective: Wicked; against or opposed to God; hostile to God. •Noun: People who are wicked, against God, or hostile to God.
1 Timothy 4:8 1 Timothy 6-3-6 2 Timothy 1:6-7	**godliness (god-lee-ness)** Respect for God; fear of the Lord; holiness; piety; sincere devotion to God.
2 Corinthians 7:10-11 2 Timothy 3:12 Psalm 43 Micah 7:2	**godly (god-lee)** •Adjective: Devoted to God; holy; pious; devout. •Noun: People who are devoted to God, holy, pious, devout.

GOD

WHAT'S GOD LIKE?

God has certain attributes or characteristics. They all work together in perfect harmony. For example, just because God is love doesn't mean He will ignore sin. He can't because He is also righteous. Here are some of God's other attributes:

God is eternal. That means He has no beginning or ending. He was never "born" and will never "die."

God is sovereign. He is the highest ruler. He is the Alpha and Omega (A to Z in the Greek alphabet). Nothing happens to us without His permission!

God is all-powerful. He is "omnipotent" (omni = all; potent = powerful). He has the power to keep all His promises to us!

God is omnipresent. That means He is present everywhere. We are never alone. God is always with us.

God knows everything. He is "omniscient" (scient = to see or know). God knows the end from the beginning.

God is holy. He is absolute perfection. God is the ultimate standard of purity. He will never compromise His standards.

God is righteous. Everyone is treated fairly and will get what he or she deserves. God doesn't play favorites—we're all His favorite!

God is truth. God is always consistent. His Word, the Bible, is our source of truth!

God is love. He has chosen to love us whether we are lovable or not!

God is changeless. His character will be the same forever. God will never stop displaying all these qualities.

EXPLAIN GOD

Before you read this, sit down with a piece of paper and a pencil and write down what you know about God. Afterward, see if you match what one boy wrote when he explained God like this:

One of God's main jobs is making people. He makes them to replace the ones that die. He doesn't make grown-ups, just babies. I think because they are smaller and easier to make. That way He doesn't have to teach them to talk and walk. He can just leave that to mothers and fathers.

God's second most important job is listening to prayers. An awful lot of this goes on, since some people, like preachers, pray at times beside bedtime. God doesn't have time to listen to the radio or TV because of this.

God sees everything and hears everything and is everywhere, which keeps Him pretty busy. So you shouldn't go wasting His time by going over your mom and dad's head asking for something they said you couldn't have.

Jesus is God's Son. He used to do all the hard work like walking on water and performing miracles. People finally got tired of Him preaching to them and they crucified Him. But He was good and kind, like His Father and He told his Father that they didn't know what they were doing and to forgive them and God said "OK"

God appreciated everything that Jesus did and all His hard work on earth so He told Him He could stay in heaven. Now He helps God out by listening to prayers and seeing things which are important for God to take care of and which ones He can take care of Himself without having to bother God. You can pray anytime you want and they are sure to help you because they got it worked out so one of them is on duty all the time.

You should always go to church on Sunday because it makes God happy, and if there's anybody you want to make happy, it's God. Don't skip church to do something you think will be more fun.

If you don't believe in God you will be very lonely, because your parents can't go everywhere with you, like to camp, but God can. It is good to know He's around when you're scared in the dark or when you can't swim.

But you shouldn't just always think of what God can do for you. I figure God put me here and He can take me back anytime He pleases. And that's why I believe in God.

God's Every-Where Spirit

Have you ever gone to a professional performance of a play, ice show, concert . . . anything of that type? How aware were you of the stage crew working behind the scenes to make everything happen? Hopefully, not at all. Your attention was directed to the stage, as it should have been.

The work of the Holy Spirit is similar to a stage crew—working silently and effectively to draw our attention to God. The Holy Spirit is God's invisible but powerful presence.

The following lines from the Celtic-style prayer "God's Every-where Spirit" help us understand more about the Holy Spirit.

"God's Spirit is always in front of me, leading the way."

The Holy Spirit helps us make daily decisions (Psalm 143:10).

"God's Spirit is always beside me, helping me and being my friend."

The Holy Spirit is always present everywhere and ready to help (Psalm 139:7-8).

"God's Spirit is always behind me, watching out for me."

The Holy Spirit can speak to you clearly and at any time — not audibly, but as an inward knowing (Ezekiel 36:26-27).

"God's Spirit is always underneath me, holding me up when I'm tired or sad."

The Holy Spirit is called "the Comforter" (John 16:7). He is God's powerful encourager in our lives (Acts 9:31).

"God's Spirit is always above me, praying for me in heaven."

The Spirit prays for us when we can't find words ourselves (Romans 8:26). He's the Someone who's always listening.

"God's Spirit is always inside me, talking to my heart about God's best for me today."

Jesus promised that the Holy Spirit would be our internal teacher (John 14:16-17, 26). He reminds us of Jesus' words and makes every day better.

God's Top Ten

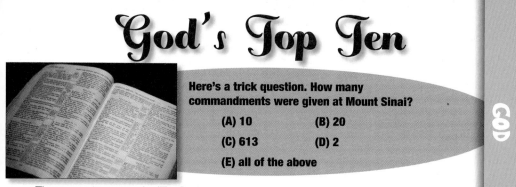

Here's a trick question. How many commandments were given at Mount Sinai?

(A) 10   (B) 20

(C) 613   (D) 2

(E) all of the above

The correct answer is (E). God gave Moses Ten Commandments written on rocks (Exodus 31:18). But (B) is also true because after Moses smashed the first set of rocks, God repeated them. After giving His "top ten" commandments, God continued to list 603 more. So (C) is also correct.

(D) is also right because Jesus summarized the whole Old Testament Law in two commands, "You must love the Lord your God with all your heart, all your soul, and all your mind," and "Love your neighbor as yourself" (Matthew 22:37-39 NLT).

Can you name the Ten Commandments in the order God gave them?

1. No other gods

2. No graven images

3. No vain (vane?) use of God's name

4. Keep the Sabbath day

5. Honor your parents

6. No killing

7. No adultery (a dull tree?)

8. No stealing

9. No bearing false witness

10. No coveting

Be among the first to check out the Kids' Ten Commandments Project at: http://www.k10c.com/. It's a big deal!

Did You Know?

All 613 commands that God gave at Mt. Sinai are recorded in Exodus 20:1 — Numbers 10:10.

Angels delivered God's words to Moses on Mt. Sinai 3500 years ago (Galatians 3:19).

The New Testament contains 1,051 commands from God — more than the Old Testament Law. Most of them are written in Romans through Jude. Some of these commands are for past or future times or specific people, but most are for us today!

Nine of the Ten Commandments are restated in the New Testament as commands for us. The only one that is omitted is the commandment to honor the Sabbath (Saturday), because the early church set aside the first day of the week (Sunday) to worship and remember Jesus' resurrection.

10 Things I'd Like to Ask God

1.

2.

3.

4.

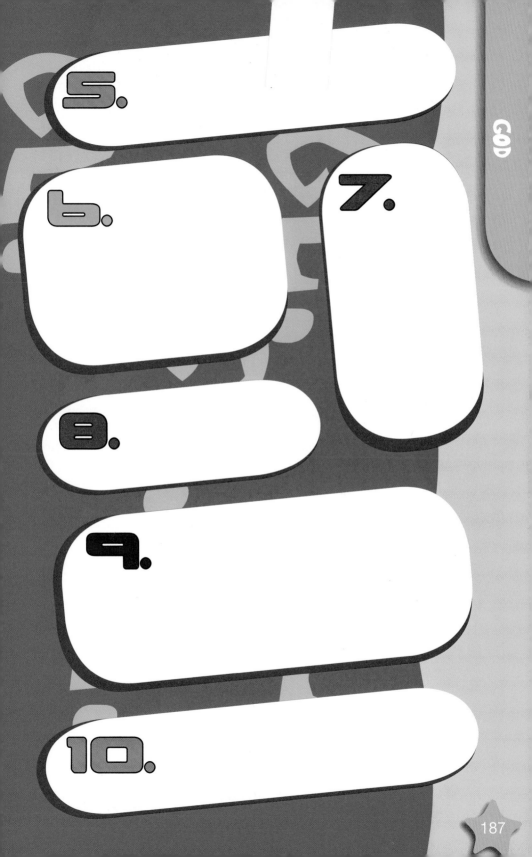

White House Surprises

The White House isn't just for grown-ups! Through the years, it has been home to many kids, too. Some of the things they did will surprise you!

1. 1860s: "Soldier" Tad Lincoln

Tad, youngest of Abraham Lincoln's sons, received a pretend military commission from the Secretary of War. Taking his "job" seriously, Tad wore a Union Army uniform and once bombarded the Cabinet Room door with a toy cannon.

2. 1880s: Fights in the East Room

Irvin and Abram Garfield were 11 and 9 when their father, James Garfield, became President. The boys had pillow fights in the East Room. They also raced around on the polished floors on large-wheeled tricycles called velocipedes.

3. 1890s: His Whiskers and Baby McKee

Benjamin Harrison's grandson, Benjamin "Baby" McKee, often rode around the grounds in a goat cart. Once the goat, called His Whiskers, raced out onto Pennsylvania Avenue dragging Baby McKee with it. The President himself chased after them!

4. 1900s: Snakes and Elevators

The lively family of Theodore Roosevelt turned the White House into a playhouse. The younger ones roller-skated through hallways and threw spitballs at presidential portraits. Quentin, the youngest, loved animals. Once he borrowed a selection of snakes from a pet shop. Racing home to show his father, he burst in on an important meeting and dropped the snakes on his father's desk! When Archie got the measles, Quentin decided a visit from the family pony would cure him. So he smuggled the animal onto the elevator and into Archie's upstairs bedroom.

5. 1960s: Fort Oval Office

When his family arrived at the White House, John Kennedy, Jr., was just two months old. Soon he discovered that the President's huge desk in the Oval Office made a perfect fort. John-John would crawl around his father's feet and hide behind a panel that opened and closed his fort.

6. 1970s: Homework Helper

Amy Carter was ten when her dad, Jimmy Carter, became President. One Friday Amy had a homework question about the industrial revolution. Her mother asked an aide to call the Department of Labor for help. On Sunday a truck delivered piles of computer printouts. A Labor Department computer team thought the question came from the President and worked all weekend on it.

Laughable Laws

There are many old (and strange) laws still on the books around the country. Most were passed a long time ago and must have made sense back then to somebody. Fortunately it appears they are not being enforced today.

It is illegal to:

Make faces at dogs in Oklahoma.

Walk a tightrope in Wheeler, Mississippi, if you're a young girl, but it's okay inside a church.

Slurp your soup in public on Sunday in Gilman, Connecticut.

Have an unusual haircut in Mesquite, Texas, if you're a youngster.

Read comics while riding in a car in Norman, Oklahoma.

Eat unshelled, roasted peanuts while attending church in Idanha, Oregon. Nor can churchgoers eat watermelon on Sunday.

For a girl to telephone a boy and ask for a date in Dyersburg, Tennessee.

Swing a yo-yo anywhere in public on Sunday, and especially in church or during Sunday school, in Studley, Virginia.

Stop a child from jumping over a puddle in Hanford, California.

Race turtles on Sunday in Slaughter, Louisiana, and not within 100 yards of a church at any time.

Roller-skate on the streets of Quincy, Massachusetts.

Be assisted by firemen during a Sunday fire in Leona, Kansas, unless you're fully dressed (if you're a woman of any age).

Eat everything in the refrigerator if you're baby-sitting in Altoona, Pennsylvania.

Carry a slingshot to church in Honey Creek, Iowa, unless you are a policeman.

Let sheep run wild in schoolyards in Vermont.

Shoot whales from an airplane on Sunday while church is in progress in Garysburg, North Carolina. (But it's legal to do so at other times.)

Play hopscotch on the sidewalk in Missouri.

Pretend your parents are rich in the state of Washington.

Throw snowballs at trees in Mount Pulaski, Illinois, if you're a boy.

Remove your shoes if your feet smell while you're in a theater in Winnetka, Illinois.

(Do you have a verifiable laughable law to submit? See page 350.)

Who Runs (in) the White House?

White House photo by Paul Morse

First Dog, **Spotty** is an English Springer Spaniel. He is named after Scott Fletcher, a former Texas Rangers baseball player. Spotty loves playing tennis with the President, who hits the ball and Spotty chases it. His favorite treats are bacon-flavored dog treats.

The White House may seem familiar to Spotty because he was born there on March 17, 1989. His mother, Millie, belonged to President George Bush, father of President George W. Bush. They gave Spotty to George and Laura Bush and he went to live in Texas with them.

Don't miss Spotty's very own White House tour at www.whitehouse.gov/kids/tour. It's a real treat!"

Spotty's Running Mates

Barney enjoys playing tennis with the President and Spotty. He's a 3-year-old Scottish Terrier. Milk-flavored dog treats are his favorite snacks. When Barney isn't napping in his bed, he is studying or videotaping. Read his White House ABCs at www.whitehouse.gov/kids/abc. Look at the White House through Barney's eyes while you're there.

White House photo by Paul Morse

India "Willie" is a 10-year-old black cat who enjoys hiding from her owners. She likes tuna-flavored kitty treats and naps under the bed. India has some interesting history quizzes, too. www.whitehouse.gov/kids/india

White House photo by Paul Morse

There Oughta Be a Law

The next time someone says it's the law, you could ask, "What kind?"

Blue Laws

Also known as Sabbath laws. They were passed to close certain businesses and restrict recreation on Sunday, which is the Christian day of rest.

Common Laws

Rules based on custom or long usage, which are usually not recorded as laws. They began in England.

God's Law

May refer to the whole Bible, its first five books, or the Ten Commandments.

Law of the Land

A phrase from the Magna Charta, the basic document of English law. Today the term refers to laws that are fundamental to democracy.

Martial Law

Temporary rule by the military imposed on citizens during a war, an emergency (like a natural disaster), or a political or economic crisis. Under martial law, military laws are followed instead of civil laws.

Moral Law

The law of one's conscience.

Moore's Law

The number of transistors on a microprocessor will double approximately every 18 months. (Intel cofounder Gordon Moore)

Murphy's Laws

1. Nothing is as easy as it looks.

2. Everything will take longer than you think.

3. If anything can go wrong, it will.

(No one is sure who Murphy was, but these laws are well-known.)

Parkinson's Law

"Work expands to fill the time allotted to it; or, conversely, the amount of work completed is in inverse proportion to the number of people employed." Simply said: If you have an hour to do a 5-minute job, it will take an hour to do it. A large number of people accomplish less work than a smaller number of people. (C. Northcote Parkinson, a British writer)

Did You Know?

Hammurabi, the king of Babylon in the 18th century B.C., is often mentioned as the first to record laws and their consequences. But God preceded him. The first law for humans was enacted by God for one person who lived in Eden at the time. It had severe consequences attached to breaking it. (Genesis 2:15-17)

Holidays

Secret Birthday Pal

Imagine it's your birthday, but no one's hanging balloons or baking a cake. No one's giving you presents, and not a single person even wishes you a happy birthday.

That happens to many kids at homeless shelters around the country. Parents are struggling to find work and a place to live. They don't have money to spend on birthday parties and gifts for their kids.

Here's an idea – throw a party for a kid who won't otherwise have one. Work with a shelter in your area to find out when the kids' birthdays are. Then plan birthday parties for them.

Find out what theme the birthday boy or girl might enjoy. Then buy decorations, make a cake and get a gift. If you really want to be a secret birthday pal, just plan the party, don't attend it. Let it seem like the kid's parents have thrown the party.

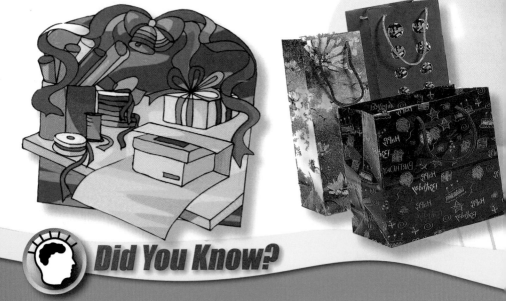

Did You Know?

Countless kids are making a difference in their world. Do you know a preteen who's making the world a better place? Please tell us about him or her. See page 350.

194

MY YEARLY SACRED PLANNER
If found, return to Bar-Iri of Bethlehem

MONTH		SPECIAL DAY	NOTES
NISAN (April)	14	Feast of Passover	Most important. Celebrates God's rescue of Jews from Egypt. Eat unleavened bread, wine, bitter herbs, lamb. Retell Passover story. (Leviticus 23:5)
	15	Feast of Unleavened	Celebrate with Passover Feast. All Jews, healthy and "clean" must attend above festivals. That means me! (Leviticus 23:6)
	21	Close of Passover	
SIVAN (June)	6	Feast of Pentecost	Close of wheat harvest. Sing, dance, give thanks to God for crops and for giving law on Mount Sinai. Attendance required, Bar-Iri! (Leviticus 23:15-22)
TISHRI (Oct.)	1-2	Feast of Trumpets	Hebrew New Year or Rosh Hashanah. Another day off! Blow horns and trumpets! Read God's law and feast. (Leviticus 23:23-25)
	10	Day of Atonement or Yom Kippur	Forgive my sins, God. Will fast. Must attend. (Leviticus 23:26-27)
	15-21	Feast of Tabernacles	Live in tents to remember how our forefathers lived in the wilderness. Offer sacrifices. A week of great joy! (Leviticus 23:33-34)
KISLEV (Dec.)	25	Feast of Lights or Hanukkah	Celebrates rededication of temple to the Lord. Light the menorah for 8 days!
ADAR (March)	14	Feast of Purim	Remembers victory of Queen Esther and Mordecai over Haman. Give food gifts to friends, needy. Read story of Esther.

Other Notes: During one-day festivals, there is no work!
During 7 or 8-day festivals, there is no work on the first and last day!

The Real St. Patrick

Imagine being kidnapped and sold into slavery! When you were finally able to escape, would you go back to the land where you had been a slave? One youth did just that. Thanks to his courage, Ireland heard the Gospel—and young Patricius of Roman Britain became Saint Patrick.

Patricius was only 16 when he was kidnapped by Irish raiders and sold into slavery. For six years he worked as a shepherd. He spent a lot of time in prayer while he walked around the pastures.

One day a voice in a dream told him, "Soon you will go to your own country. See, your ship is ready." Patricius escaped and walked over 200 miles to the coast—only to find no ship would take him, because he couldn't pay the fare! Determined, he asked God for help, and soon sailed for home.

His family welcomed him back, but it quickly became clear how much he had changed. The easygoing boy was now filled with Christian faith.

Patricius had another dream, in which the Irish people begged him to come back and bring them the Gospel. His family pleaded with him to stay home, but Patricius returned to Ireland.

Patricius was a good speaker and had a gift for explaining things. During one sermon about the Trinity he picked a shamrock, then showed how it had three leaves yet was one plant. The example helped many people understand and accept Christianity. To this day the shamrock remains a symbol of Ireland. By the time Patricius died on March 17, 461, Ireland had become a Christian nation.

Today we celebrate March 17 as Saint Patrick's Day. The humble Patricius would probably be embarrassed by all the parades we now hold in his honor. He would also be the first to say that he never drove out the snakes—there never were any snakes in Ireland, before or after St. Patrick! And he wouldn't even want to take credit for bringing Ireland to Christianity.

Did You Know?

To find out more about the history of St. Patrick's Day celebrations, click on www.historychannel.com/exhibits/stpatricksday

The Great Turkey Hunt

How many turkeys can you find (and keep) as you find your way out of the woods? Start in the center of the woods and hunt with your pencil. Each time you come to a turkey, "catch" him by correctly answering the Thanksgiving question. The goal: Get home with as many turkeys as possible. (Answers are on page 338.)

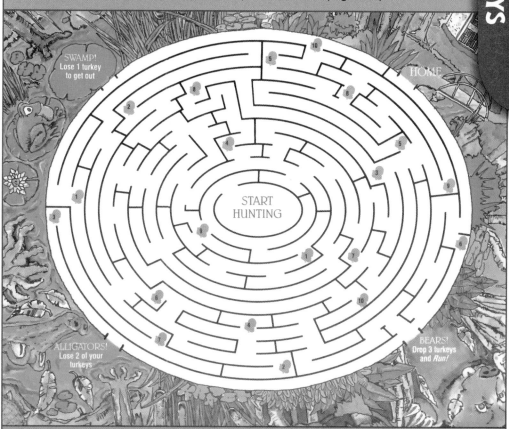

1. On the first Thanksgiving Day, the American colonists ate with their neighbors, the _____.
2. Out of 10 healed lepers, how many thanked Jesus?
3. Who gave thanks to God from inside a great fish?
4. In what state was the first American Thanksgiving observed?
5. About how long ago was the first American Thanksgiving Day observed? (Must be within 25 years of correct answer.)
6. Who was thrown to the lions because he publicly thanked God three times a day?
7. What is the famous rock called where the pilgrims landed?
8. What is the name of the American governor who proclaimed the first Thanksgiving Day?
9. What book of the Bible has the most mention of praise and thanksgiving?
10. "Give thanks to the Lord, for he is _____. His love endures forever."

Humor

Does God Have a Sense of Humor?

Laughter is a God-given gift for our benefit and enjoyment!

Bible Jokes

1. How long did Cain hate his brother?
2. Who was the shortest man in the Bible?
3. Who was the tiniest man in the Bible?
4. Who was the straightest man in the Bible?
5. When was tennis played by two Bible characters?
6. What time of day was Adam created?
7. What did Adam and Eve do after God expelled them from Eden?
8. When was a rooster's crow heard by every living creature on earth?
9. Who was the most successful doctor in the Bible?
10. Who was the first Irishman mentioned in Scripture?

Answers:

1. As long as he was Abel ("able;" Genesis 4:8)
2. "Knee-high-miah" (Nehemiah; Nehemiah 1:1)
   or Bildad the Shoe-height (Shuhite; Job 2:11)
3. Peter, the disciple who slept on his watch (Matthew 26:40)
4. Joseph, because Pharaoh made him into a ruler (Genesis 41:42-43)
5. When Joseph served in Pharaoh's court (implied in Genesis 41:38-46)
6. A little before Eve (Genesis 2:7, 21-22)
7. They raised Cain (Genesis 3:23; 4:1)
8. In Noah's ark (Genesis 7:13-23)
9. Job, because he had the most "patients" (patience; James 5:11)
10. Nick O'Demus (Nicodemus; John 3:1-5)

Seen in Church Bulletins

The men's group will hear a car talk at noon.
Today is the fifth Sunday of Lint.
For our Sunday evening gathering, Pastor Brown will show slides of his recent trip to the Roman ruins, including his wife and mother-in-law.
The pastor spoke briefly, much to the delight of the audience.

Seen on Church Bulletin Boards

Come to church Sunday. If you have no sins, bring someone who does.
Come in and pray today. Beat the Christmas rush.
The Lord loves a cheerful giver. He also accepts from a grouch.
All new sermons, no reruns.

Fun Reads

Find good jokes at www.clean-funnies.com. Most kids' web sites and magazines have a joke section. For example, tickle your funny bone at www.gp4k.com/lol, www.clubhousemagazine.com and www.cyberkids.com/fg/fb/jo.

Squeaky Clean Jokes for Kids by Bob Phillips and Steve Russo (Harvest House) is a fun goofy joke book.

A BIBLE RIDDLE

God made Adam out of dust, but thought it best to make me first;

So I was made before the man,

according to God's most holy plan.

My whole body God made complete, without arms or hands or feet.

My ways and acts did God control,

but in my body He placed no soul.

A living being I became, and Adam gave to me a name.

Then from his presence I withdrew, for this man Adam I never knew.

All my Maker's laws I do obey, and from these laws I never stray.

Thousands of me go in fear, but seldom on the earth appear.

Later, for a purpose God did see, He placed a living soul in me.

But that soul of mine God had to claim,

and from me He took it back again.

And when this soul from me had fled,

I was the same as when first made;

Without arms, legs, feet, or soul, I travel on from pole to pole.

My labors are from day to night, and to men I once furnished light.

Thousands of people both young and old,

did by death bright lights behold.

No right or wrong can I conceive;

the Bible and its teachings I can't believe.

The fear of death doesn't trouble me;

pure happiness I will never see.

And up in Heaven I can never go, nor in the grave or hell below.

So get your Bible and read with care;

you'll find my name recorded there.

(The answer is on page 339)

Bible Crossword
Creator's Character

Down

1. Old Glory
2. Company symbol
3. Spent
4. Girl's name
5. Wheel holders
6. Kind of sandwich
7. Sad song
8. What Jesus called Himself (2 words; Mark 14:14)
9. Horse food
10. Before
11. That's right
19. Claim Jesus made (4 words; John 10:7)
20. A boy
23. Folk tale
24. Bongo is one
25. Collar label
26. Belongs to a girl
27. How Jesus entered Jerusalem
28. Kind of school report
33. Strong denial (2 words)
34. Smallest Greek mark (Luke 16:17 KJV)
36. Fess up
37. One of David's writings
39. Very small amount
40. Salt Lake state
41. Ripped
42. Church song
43. Plane pusher
44. Just me
45. Eli Whitney's invention

Across

1. Reason to skip school
4. Created
8. Others
12. ___ Angeles
13. Figure skater's jump
14. Big bunny?
15. How old you are
16. Make angry
17. See-ers?
18. Our Creator's character (3 words; 1 John 1:5)
21. Goes with oohs
22. Gives way
26. Smell
29. Polynesian person
30. Cartoon character
31. After Santa in California
32. Potato state
34. School essay
35. Movie and singer
37. Pumpkin is one
38. Our Creator's character (3 words; John 3:33)
43. Caesar's clothes
46. Surrounds a castle
47. Disney's story
48. Army group
49. "___ be okay"
50. Hand holder?
51. Old singing cowboy
52. Now wild
53. Egg layer

200

Young Puzzlers

"I started out making crosswords for my school newspapers," says Mike Shenk, Crossword Puzzle Editor for the Wall Street Journal. "When I was 14 I decided to try to get a puzzle accepted by a national magazine and sent one to *Games Magazine*, and after some changes, it was accepted.

"Over the next few years I had a few more puzzles published, but a lot more rejected. You learn by trying things and making mistakes. Eventually I became a professional puzzlemaker and editor. Twenty years later that's still what I do for a living.

"I've had a lot of puzzles published in publications like 'Scholastic News' and 'Games Junior'.

In fact Mike has his own series of kids' crossword books. *Crosswords for Kids*, *Great Crosswords for Kids* and *Super Crosswords for Kids* and *Challenging Crosswords for Kids*.

16-year-old Tyler Hinman's first puzzle appeared in the New York Times in July 2000 after four tries. Hinman began working crosswords after a teacher gave him a Times puzzle in a study hall. Creating was the next logical step.

"After several months of solving, one day I thought, *Hey, I could make these things*," says Tyler, the youngest constructor used by Will Shortz, current crossword editor for the Times. Tyler has his own puzzle site at www.angelfire.com/games3/quandary27.

Mike Miller's first puzzle was published in the New York Times when he was 13. That set the record as the youngest puzzler. "I was just a kid who enjoyed playing around with words," he said.

So if records are made to be broken, here's one waiting for you.

Did You Know?

Newspaperman Arthur Wynne created the first crossword puzzle in 1913 for the New York World.

Professional crossword puzzle constructors are called cruciverbalists. It literally means "crossing words."

You can "eavesdrop" on the pros discussing puzzles, words and clues. They help "newbies," too — of any age. The Cruciverb-I newsletter and web site are free at www.cruciverb.com. You'll also find links to software and online puzzles (most are free).

Timothy Parker was named the "World's Most Syndicated Puzzle Compiler" by Guinness World Records. www.amuniversal.com/ups/features/univ_crossword/parker.htm

Picture Books

Identify the Bible books pictured phonetically below. Clues give extra help.

1.

2.

3.

4.

5.

6.

7.

8.

Clues
1. The author was a former tax collector
2. God's commentary on the Hebrew kings (2 books)
3. Predicted that Jesus would be born to a virgin (7:14)
4. Two censuses give this book its title
5. One of two pastors to whom Paul wrote
6. A record of the Holy Spirit working through Jesus' apostles
7. A book about patience by a disciple who wasn't
8. Second New Testament book

The answers are on page 339.

THE BIBLE ACCORDING TO KIDS

**These biblical "interpretations" are actual answers from students.
(Note: Spelling has not been "corrected.")**

Adam and Eve were created from an apple tree.

Noah's wife was called Joan of Ark.

Noah built an ark, which the animals came onto in pears.

Samson was a strongman who let himself be led astray by a Jezebel like Delilah.
Samson slayed the Philistines with the axe of the apostles.

Moses led the Hebrews to the Red Sea, where they made unleavened bread,
which is bread made without any ingredients. The Egyptians were all drowned
in the dessert. Afterwards, Moses went up on Mount Cyanide to get the Ten
Amendments.

The first Commandment was when Eve told Adam to eat the apple.

The Fifth Commandment is to humor thy father and mother.

Moses died before he ever reached Canada.

The greatest miracle in the Bible is when Joshua told his son to stand still and
he obeyed him.

David was a Hebrew king skilled at playing the liar. He fought with the
Finklestines, a race of people who lived in Biblical times.

Solomon, one of David's sons, had 300 wives and 700 porcupines.

When Mary heard that she was the mother of Jesus, she sang the Magna Carta.

When the three wise guys from the east side arrived, they found Jesus in
the manager.

St. John, the Blacksmith, dumped water on Jesus' head.

It was a miracle when Jesus rose from the dead and managed to get the
tombstone off the entrance.

The people who followed the Lord were called the 12 decibels.

The epistles were the wives of the apostles.

One of the opossums was St. Matthew who was by profession a taximan.

The Bible is against polygamy, because it says that no man can serve
two masters.

TAXI

The 10 Funniest Jokes I've Ever Heard Are...

1.

2.

3.

4.

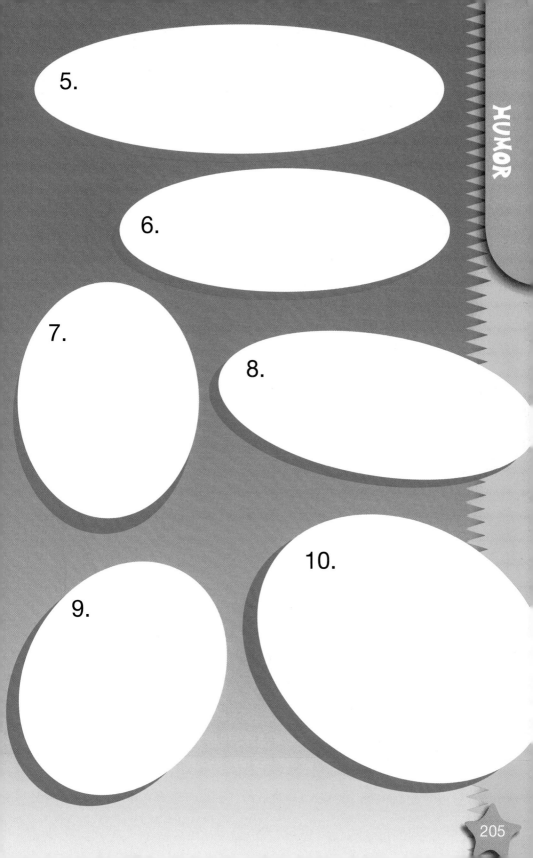

5.

6.

7.

8.

10.

9.

Inventions Bible Firsts

(Bible references are to Genesis unless otherwise noted.)

Author: Moses	(Exodus 24:4)
Bigamist: Lamech	(4:19)
Black-out: In Egypt	(Exodus 10:21-23)
Boat builder: Noah	(6:14—22)
Bottle: Hagar's water container	(21:14)
Circuit-riding judge: Samuel	(1 Samuel 7:15—17)
City-builder: Cain	(4:17)
Coffin: For Joseph	(50:26)
Command: By God, "Let there be light"	(1:3)
Command to write: To Moses	(Exodus 17:14)
Cremation: King Saul and his sons	(1 Samuel 31:12)
Drunk person: Noah	(9:20—21)
Embalming: Of Jacob	(50:2)
European converted to Christ: Lydia	(Acts 16:14—15)
Farmer: Cain	(4:2)
Female governor: Deborah	(Judges 4:4—5)
Gardener: Adam	(2:15)
Gold deposits: In Havilah	(2:11)
Governmental execution: Pharaoh's chief baker	(40:20—22)
Harpist and organist: Jubal	(4:21)
Hebrew: Abraham	(14:13)
Herdsman: Lamech	(4:20)
High priest: Aaron	(Exodus 29:1—9)
Hunter: Nimrod	(10:9)
I.Q. test: Queen of Sheba to Solomon	(1 Kings 10:1—3)
Made clothing of animal skins: God	(3:21)
Kiss: Jacob	(27:26—27)
Labor union: Silversmiths in Ephesus	(Acts 19:24—28)
Land purchase: Abraham	(23:3—20)
Left-handed person: Ehud	(Judges 3:15)
Letter: King David	(2 Samuel 11:14)
Liar: Serpent	(3:1-5)
Metal worker: Tubal-cain	(4:22)
Murderer: Cain	(4:8)
National food rationing: Joseph	(41:33—36)
Navy: King Solomon's	(1 Kings 9:26)
Priest: Melchizedek	(14:18)
Prisoner: Joseph	(39:20)
Prophecy: The serpent would be mankind's enemy	(3:15)
Prophetess: Miriam	(Exodus 15:20)
Pulpit: For Ezra	(Nehemiah 8:4)
Question: By the serpent	(3:1)
Rainbow: A sign from God	(9:13—14)
Riddle: By Samson	(Judges 14:12-18)
Ring wearer: Joseph	(41:42)
Saddle: Used by Abraham	(22:3)
Shaver: Joseph	(41:14)
Shepherd: Abel	(4:2)
Shepherdess: Rachel	(29:9)
Twins: Jacob and Esau	(25:21—28)

Kids' Creations

Louis Braille, a blind boy from France, was only 17 when he invented a "language" of raised dots that could be "read" by blind people.

Chester Greenwood loved ice skating but hated the fact that his ears got cold. So when he was 15 years old, he invented earmuffs.

Robert Patch is the youngest inventor ever. In 1962, when he was only 5, he designed a toy truck that could be taken apart and put back together.

Eric Van Paris, from Belgium, was 14 when he invented a "cooling fork" that blew air onto hot food so that kids could eat more easily.

Becky Schroeder received a patent at the age of 14 for creating a way of reading and writing in the dark. She used phosphorescent paint on paper underneath her writing paper. She was inducted into the Ohio Inventors Hall of Fame.

Eight-year-old Theresa Thompson and her 9-year-old sister, Mary, were the youngest sisters to ever receive a U.S. patent. They invented a device that they called a Wigwam—a tepee which was warmed by solar energy.

When Matt Balick and Justin Lewis were only 8 years old, they had an idea for turning the little plastic stands used in pizza boxes into little toys called Flip-Itz. They sold their idea to a toy company.

At age 9, Margaret Knight invented a safety device used in cotton mills that protected workers from injury. She went on to invent the machine that makes the square-bottom paper bags we still use for groceries today.

Chelsea Lannon at the age of 8 received a patent for her "pocket diaper" a diaper that has a pocket to hold a baby wipe and puff filled with powder.

When Suzanna Goodin was 6, she got tired of having to clean the cat food spoon. Her solution was an edible, spoon-shaped cracker. She won a grand prize for her invention in Weekly Reader's National Invention Contest.

AMERICA'S YOUNG INVENTORS

On May 3, 2003, five new inductees were welcomed into the National Gallery for America's Young Inventors.

Allan Chu, 18, Saratoga, California

"LZAC Lossless Data Compression: A Novel Approach to Minimum Redundancy Coding"

A new dictionary-based universal lossless data compression engine shrinks file sizes and improves the uploading of computer files. This process makes Internet speed three times faster, while requiring less memory.

After graduation, Allan plans to pursue a degree in physics, and work in nanotechnology.

Tessanie Marek, 11, Salado, Texas

"The Easy Crutches"

An adjustable leg support is added to one crutch. This allows the user to rest the injured leg directly on the crutch thereby avoiding strain or muscle cramps. The attached lever and pedal can be used to rest the leg in a forward position or to support the shin in a bent leg position.

Tessanie's goal after graduation is to study law at Texas A & M.

Mark Mazumder, 18, Little Rock, Arkansas

"Encased Stent for Rapid Endothelialization for Preventing Restenosis"

A metal stent is encased by a polymer sheath to provide biocompatibility and corrosion inhibition while remaining capable of expansion. Antithrombogenic drugs are embedded in the coating to promote the growth of new cell tissue while preventing re-blockage.

After graduation, Mark plans to attend college where he will pursue a degree in either writing or science.

Brandon Michael Palmen, 19, Rochester, Minnesota

"Efficient Re-Targeting of Virus Vectors for Gene Therapy"

A measles vaccine virus is genetically engineered to display on its surface an additional "ZZ" protein. A protein can be added to the surface of a measles vaccine virus particle so that it could be quickly and conveniently targeted to attack cancer cells.

Brandon is studying biochemistry at Harvard. After graduation, he plans to pursue a PhD in biochemistry, and possibly attend medical school.

Justin Riebeling, 12, Millstadt, Illinois

"Speed Grain Cart"

The Speed Grain Cart makes the feeding of cattle easier and faster. This modified wagon holds nearly 25 gallons of feed. A remotely controlled chute dispenses grain directly into the feeding trough while the cart is moving.

After high school, Justin plans to attend college where he will study farming.

Did You Know?

The Partnership for America's Future is looking for some creative students (K-12).
Enter any idea for a new way to demonstrate an educational concept, or an idea for a new product (or an improvement for an existing product or procedure). www.pafinc.com/gallery/index.htm

The best student idea in each division (K-8 and 9-12) each month wins $100. Winning entries may be eligible for induction into the National Gallery for America's Young Inventors. You may even get royalties for your idea as seen on CNN and featured in the FREY Scientific catalog (www.freyscientific.com).

Wander through worlds of innovative genius at the National Inventors Hall of Fame and Inventors Workshop in Akron, Ohio. www.invent.org (http://www.invent.org)

The Kids' Invention Book by Arlene Erlbach (Lerner Publications) profiles 11 kid inventors, describes the steps involved in inventing a new product, and discusses contests, patents, lawyers and clubs.

"To invent you need a good imagination and a pile of junk." — Thomas Alva Edison

Jesus

Jesus' Life from A to Z

Jesus' life on earth is recorded in the first four books of the New Testament, called the Gospels (Matthew, Mark, Luke, John). Gospel means "good news."

Here are the highlights of Jesus' life alphabetized in the order they happened.

A Angels appeared to Zechariah, Mary, Joseph and the shepherds regarding Jesus. (Nazareth, Jerusalem; Matthew 1:18-25; Luke 1:5-38)

B Birth. An incredible miracle: God became a man through the virgin Mary. (Bethlehem; Matthew 2:1-12; Luke 2:1-20)

C Carpenter. Jesus was an apprentice in Joseph and Sons Carpentry Shop. (Nazareth; Matthew 2:19-23; Luke 2:39-52)

D Dove. The form of the Holy Spirit coming on Jesus at His baptism. (Jordan River; Matthew 3:11-17; Luke 3:15-22)

E Enemy. Jesus overcame Satan's temptations using God's Word. (wilderness, northeast Judea; Matthew 4:1-11; Luke 4:1-13)

F Followers. Jesus chose 12 disciples to train for the next 3 1/2 years. (Galilee; John 1:19-51; Mark 3:14-19)

G Guest. Jesus did His first public miracle as a wedding guest. (Cana; John 2:1-11)

H Housecleaning. Jesus cleaned His Father's house of the moneychangers. (Jerusalem; John 2:13-22)

I Interview with Nicodemus, who needed a second birth. (Jerusalem; John 3:1-21)

J Jacob's Well, where many Samaritans believed in Jesus. (Sychar, Samaria; John 4:5-42)

K Kin. Jesus presented Himself as the Messiah to His extended family. (Nazareth; Luke 4:16-31)

L Location. Jesus moved His base of operations to Peter's home. (Capernaum; Matthew 4:13-22)

M Message, known as the Sermon on the Mount. (Capernaum area; Matthew 5—7)

N Nature. Jesus showed His miraculous power over nature, healing many people, raising the dead, stilling a storm at sea and feeding 5,000 with a kid's lunch. (Capernaum area, Galilee; Luke 7:1-35)

O Opposition peaks from the Jewish leaders who refuse to accept Him as their Messiah. (Capernaum; Matthew 12:22-50)

P Parables. Jesus only told one story-sermon before the Pharisees rejected Him; now dozens are recorded. (Capernaum area; Matthew 13:1-53; Mark 4:1-34)

Q Question. Peter had the right answer when Jesus asked, "Who do you think I am?" (Caesarea Philippi; Matthew 16:13-28; Luke 9:16-20)

R Revelation of Jesus' glory to 3 wide-eyed disciples. (A high mountain, probably Mt. Hermon; Matthew 17:1-13)

S Stoning. The Jews tried to kill Jesus for claiming to be God. (Jerusalem; John 10:22-39)

T Tomb. Jesus raises Lazarus to life from his tomb. (Bethany near Jerusalem; John 11:1-44)

U Upset. Jesus again upset the merchants' tables in the temple. (Jerusalem; Matthew 21:12-17)

V Vision of the end times given to His disciples. (Jerusalem, Mt. Olivet; Matthew 24—25)

W Washing the disciples' feet to teach servanthood. (Jerusalem, Upper Room; John 13:1-17)

X Xecution. Pardon the phonetic spelling for Jesus' crucifixion. (Jerusalem; Matthew 26:30—27:56)

Y Yes! Jesus is God, proven by His resurrection from the dead. (Jerusalem, Judea, Galilee; Matthew 28; Luke 24:1-49)

Z Zion, another name for Jerusalem, where Jesus ascended back to Heaven. (Jerusalem, Mt. Olivet; Luke 24:50-53; Acts 1:1-12)

Did You Know?

For complete references to Christ's life in chronological order, consult a "harmony" of the Gospels—all four books printed side-by-side in synchronized columns. Most reference Bibles contain such a chart.

God's Great News for Children by Rick Osborne and Marnie Wooding (Tyndale) is an easy-to-understand "biography" of Jesus' life. This collection of stories will help you get to know Jesus as a man who walked and talked and saved us from sin.

AKA: IMMANUEL (AND OTHER ALIASES)

A name tells a lot about a person. No ONE name can capture who Jesus is or all He does. These are just some of the names and titles given to Jesus in the Bible. ("aka" stands for "also known as.")

Almighty Revelation 1:8
Alpha and Omega Revelation 22:13
Amen Revelation 3:14
Ancient of Days Daniel 7:9
Beginning and the End Revelation 22:13
Blessed Hope Titus 2:13
Branch Zechariah 3:8
Bread of Life John 6:35
Bridegroom Mark 2:19
Christ Matthew 16:16,20
Cornerstone Isaiah 28:16
Counselor Isaiah 9:6
Creator Isaiah 40:28
Deliverer 2 Samuel 22:2
Emmanuel Matthew 1:23 (KJV)
Everlasting Isaiah 63:16
Everlasting Father Isaiah 9:6
Everlasting God Isaiah 40:28
Faithful and True Revelation 19:11
Faithful Witness Revelation 1:5; 3:14
Father of Lights James 1:17
First and the Last Revelation 2:8
First Begotten of the Dead Revelation 1:5
Fortress 2 Samuel 22:2
Foundation Isaiah 28:16
Fountain of Living Waters Jeremiah 2:13
God Matthew 1:23
Head of the Corner Matthew 21:42
Heir Mark 12:7
High Priest Hebrews 8:1
Holy One Luke 4:34
Immanuel Isaiah 7:14
Jehovah Isaiah 12:2
Jesus Matthew 1:21
Key of Knowledge Luke 11:52
King Matthew 25:34
King of Kings Revelation 17:14
Lamb Revelation 5:6
Landowner Matthew 20:1
Life John 14:6
Light of the World John 8:12
Lion Revelation 5:5

Lord Revelation 18:8
Maker Isaiah 17:7
Mighty One Isaiah 30:29
Morning Star Revelation 22:16
Peace Micah 5:5
Physician Luke 4:23
Prince of Peace Isaiah 9:6
Prophet Luke 4:24
Redeemer Isaiah 49:7
Refuge 2 Samuel 22:3
Resurrection and the Life John 11:25
Rock Matthew 7:24
Root and Offspring of David
Revelation 22:16
Savior Isaiah 19:20
Servant Isaiah 42:1
Shepherd Psalm 80:1
Shield 2 Samuel 22:3
Son of God John 3:16
Son of Man Matthew 8:20
Star Revelation 22:16
Stone Mark 12:10
Sun of Righteousness Malachi 4:2
Sword Isaiah 49:2
Tower 2 Samuel 22:3
Truth John 14:6
Vine John 15:5
Way John 14:6
Witness Revelation 3:14
Wonderful Isaiah 9:6
Word John 1:1,14
Word of God Revelation 19:13

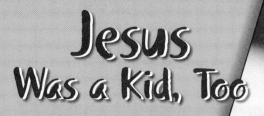

Jesus Was a Kid, Too

Dr. Luke, a physician, summarized Jesus' whole childhood for us.

"When Jesus parents had fulfilled all the requirements of the law of the Lord, they returned home to Nazareth in Galilee. There the child grew up healthy and strong. He was filled with wisdom beyond his years, and God placed his special favor upon him.

"Every year Jesus' parents went to Jerusalem for the Passover festival. When Jesus was twelve years old, they attended the festival as usual. After the celebration was over, they started home to Nazareth, but Jesus stayed behind in Jerusalem. His parents didn't miss him at first, because they assumed he was with friends among the other travelers. But when he didn't show up that evening, they started to look for him among their relatives and friends. When they couldn't find him, they went back to Jerusalem to search for him there. "Three days later they finally discovered him. He was in the Temple, sitting among the religious teachers, discussing deep questions with them. And all who heard him were amazed at his understanding and his answers.

"His parents didn't know what to think. 'Son!' his mother said to him. 'Why have you done this to us? Your father and I have been frantic, searching for you everywhere.' 'But why did you need to search?' he asked. 'You should have known that I would be in my Father's house.' But they didn't understand what he meant.

"Then he returned to Nazareth with them and was obedient to them; and his mother stored all these things in her heart. So Jesus grew both in height and in wisdom, and he was loved by God and by all who knew him." (Luke 2:39-52 NLT)

TOP 10 KiDS
WHO NEVER FAILED AT ANYTHING

10 Jesus
9
8
7
6
5
4
3
2
1

Did You Know?

Jesus had brothers and sisters. His four brothers are James, Joseph, Judas and Simon. His sisters aren't named (Mark 6:3).

Something to think about: How would you like to live with an absolutely perfect brother? He always obeyed his parents and never talked back. He never did anything wrong.

213

His Closest Friends

Jesus selected 12 men to be His closest companions (Matthew 10:1-4). They would be with Him constantly for the next three years. Later they would become the 12 Apostles ("sent ones"), who continued Jesus' work after He returned to Heaven.

Andrew: a fisherman, Peter's brother
Bartholomew: also called Nathaniel
James: a fisherman, son of Zebedee
James: son of Alphaeus
John: a fisherman, son of Zebedee
Judas Iscariot: Jesus' betrayer
Matthew: a tax collector
Philip: from Bethsaida
Simon: renamed **Peter** by Jesus, a fisherman
Simon: the Canaanite
Thaddeus: also called Jude
Thomas: also known as "doubting Thomas"

The Ultimate Proof

Ten of the original 12 Apostles became voluntary martyrs for Christ. Their only "crime" was believing and preaching that Jesus Christ was God come in a human body. If they had denied their faith, they could have been freed. If they had displayed Jesus' dead body, they'd have been spared. But they were convinced that Jesus was God and that He had risen from the dead and gone back to Heaven.

Andrew: ordered crucified on an X-shaped cross in Achaia, Greece by Governor Aepeas, enraged after his wife and brother became Christians.
Bartholomew Nathanael: flayed alive with sharp knives in India as a foreign missionary.
James, John's brother: beheaded by King Herod to please the Jews.
James, Alphaeus' son: crucified in Egypt and his body cut in pieces.
Thaddeus: killed with arrows at Ararat after a successful evangelistic ministry
Philip: hanged in Heiropolis and his body wrapped in papyrus and burned.
Simon the Zealot: crucified.
Thomas: killed with a spear near Madras, India

Each refused an "easy" escape of renouncing his allegiance to Christ as Savior and Lord.

What's He Doing Up There?

Before He left earth to return to Heaven, Jesus said He is going to prepare a place for us and someday come back and get us (John 14:1–3). From Heaven He is also providing many gifts to His children. Here are 26 things believers in Christ receive from their risen Lord.

Adoption as God's child (Ephesians 1:5)

Birth from above (1 Peter 1:23)

Completeness in Christ (Colossians 2:10)

Deliverance from darkness (Colossians 1:13)

Eternal life (John 3:16)

Forgiveness of sins (Ephesians 1:7)

Gifts for service (Romans 12:6—8)

Hope in heaven (1 John 3:2, 3)

Inheritance reserved (1 Peter 1:4)

Joy (Jude 24)

Kingship and priesthood (Revelation 1:6)

Life abundant (John 10:10)

Member of Christ's Body (1 Corinthians 12:13)

New creation (2 Corinthians 5:17)

Open access to God (Ephesians 2:18)

Power of God (Ephesians 1:19)

Quick return of Christ (Revelation 3:11)

Redemption (Ephesians 1:7)

Song in the heart (Ephesians 5:19)

Transformation (1 Corinthians 15:51)

Union with Christ (Romans 6:4—9)

Victory in Jesus (1 John 5:4, 5)

Workmanship of God (Ephesians 2:8—10)

e**X**altation in God (1 Peter 5:6, 7)

Years with Christ (Revelation 20:6)

Zion, the city of God (Hebrews 12:22—24)

(eXcuse the creative use of the letter X)

Jobs From Ambassador

There are 191 different occupations

ambassador	courier
apostle	craftsman
archer	creditor
armorbearer	cupbearer, butler
astrologer	dancer
athlete	deacon
baker	deaconess
banker	debtor
barber	disciple
beggar	diviner, soothsayer
bishop, overseer	doctor
blacksmith	drawer of water
bodyguard	dreamer, foreteller
bricklayer	drummer
builder	elder
butcher	embalmer
buyer, merchant	enchanter
captain, leader, official	evangelist
captive, prisoner	executioner
carpenter	exorcist
caulkers, shipwrights	expert, skilled craftsman
census taker	farmer, husbandman
centurion	fisherman
chariot driver	foreman
charmer, enchanter, medium	fortune-teller
chief priest	fowler
chief, ruler, minor king	fruit tender, fruit picker
concubine	fuller, bleacher, washerman
cook	gardener
coppersmith	gatekeeper
counselor	gem cutter

216

gleaner

governor

grape gatherer

grave digger

grinder, miller

guard, doorkeeper, watchman

guide, leader, commander

hairdresser

handmaid, maidservant

harpist

harvester, reaper

herald

hireling, hired laborer, day worker

horseman, cavalryman

hunter

innkeeper

interpreter

jailor

judge

king

laborer, worker

lawyer

leathermaker

lender

magician, soothsayer

magistrate, official

maidservant, female slave

manservant, male slave

mason, stonecutter, quarryman

masterbuilder

merchant

messenger

metal worker

midwife

minister

minstrel

money changer

mourner

music director, chief musician

musician

necromancer

officer, foreman

overseer, supervisor, captain

pastor

peacemaker

Pharisee

pharmacist, apothecary

philosopher

physician, doctor, healer

piper, flute player

plasterer

policeman, constable, officer

porter, doorkeeper

potter

preacher

priest

prime minister

prince

princess

proconsul

procurator, guardian

prophet

ABE'S POTTERY

HALF PRICE!

SPECIAL TODAY!

BEL'S OASIS

VACANCY

Turn the page for more Bible occupations

217

MORE BIBLE OCCUPATIONS

prophetess

prostitute, harlot

psalmist

quack, worthless physician

queen

rabbi

reader

reaper

recorder

refiner (of metals)

retailer, huckster, peddler

ringleader

robber

rower, oarsman

Sadducee

sailor

satrap

scholar

scribe, secretary, clerk

sculptor

seer, diviner

servant, helper

shepherd

silversmith

singer

slave, servant

slinger

sluggard, unemployed, lazy man

smith, artisan

snake charmer

soldier, military man

soothsayer, enchanter

sorcerer

sower

spy

standard bearer

steward, foreman

stonecutter

string player, musician

student

swimmer

tanner

taskmaster

tax collector

teacher

tent maker

tetrarch

tiller, plowman

traveler, wayfarer, caravaner

treasurer

tribal chief

trumpeter

vine dresser

wardrobe keeper

watchman

weaver, embroiderer

widow

wine (grape) treader

winemaker

winnower

wiseman

witch

wizard

woodcutter, woodsman

zealot

Kids' Kitchen

JOBS

Sagen Woolery was only in the second grade when she felt the urge to help others. "I had wondered what happens to the children during the summer when the free-lunch program ends at school—what did they eat?" says Sagen, now 12.

Sagen decided her community of Warner Robbins, Georgia, needed a summer feeding program for children and sought advice from elderly Sam Guimond, who oversaw a soup kitchen for many years. Guimond taught her how to organize a feeding kitchen and planted ideas about how to bring her vision to reality.

By the summer of 1998, Sagen had the support of 10 churches for the community's first "Kids' Kitchen." With Guimond in the background, Sagen supervised the ministry. Only child volunteers would do the work, she decided. For two highly successful summers, the team served 600 lunches on a typical Wednesday, and recipients could take leftovers home to share with their families at dinner.

Sagen has won many awards, including the 2000 Prudential Spirit of Community Award presented to her in the nation's capital. The award came with a promise of $25,000 in merchandise for her to distribute to children in need. The Lands' End clothing company named her one of three "Born Heroes" and donated $5,000 in her name to Christmas for Kids, a nonprofit organization serving the needs of low-income children throughout central Georgia.

Battling aggressive adolescent scoliosis, which results in a painful curvature of the spine, Sagen must wear a body brace for 20 hours each day for four years. Because she can't do any bending or stooping, Sagen has groomed her 9-year-old brother, Kamen, to take over for her.

"If you have a dream," Sagen says, "just pursue it, and if you want it bad enough you can change your world by helping someone else. I believe that if one person is fed and not hungry, it is a big accomplishment. I think we are all responsible for each other."

Did You Know?

Read about other youthful heroes and heroines at www.thekidshalloffame.com.

WHEN I GROW UP

I'D LIKE TO BE...

_____

_____

_____

_____

_____

_____

_____

_____

_____

SEE PAGES 216-218 FOR SOME IDEAS

OTHER JOBS I MAY CONSIDER

SEE PAGES 216-218 FOR SOME IDEAS

221

Kids

Top Kids' Interests

Girls 8-12

music
nature & animals
famous people
arts & crafts
fashion
dance

Boys 8-12

participation in sports
watching sports
nature & animals
music
science
famous people

Greatest Fears

Death of parents, self, family member	14%
violence (like kidnapping, someone trying to kill)	14
accidents (airplane or car crash or heights)	11
animals (snakes, dogs, spiders)	12
horror (like monsters, ghosts, scary movies)	6
dark/being alone	4

Worries and Concerns

Percent reporting they are	worried	at least somewhat concerned
parent's dying	61%	83%
guns in school	49	75
drugs	47	72
dying	43	74
kidnapping	42	72
war*	42	73
fighting in school	34	68
neighborhood crime	33	71
pollution	30	80
environment	30	74
AIDS	29	51
divorce of parents	25	42
alcohol	28	53
being poor	26	51
being left alone	22	53
homelessness	23	61
peer pressure	20	61

(*at time of USS Cole bombing)

Some teenagers were polled to see what they believe about

* A Southerner has always been President of the United States.

* South Africa's official policy of apartheid has not existed during their lifetime.

* Cars have always had eye-level rear stoplights, CD players and air bags.

* We have always been able to choose our long distance phone carriers.

* Weather reports have always been available 24-hours a day on television.

* "Big Brother" is merely a television show.

* Cyberspace has always existed.

* Barbie has always had a job.

* Telephone bills have always been totally incomprehensible.

* Prom dresses have always come in basic black.

* A "Hair Band" is some sort of fashion accessory.

* George Foreman has always been a barbecue grill salesman.

* Afghanistan has always been a front-page story.

* They have no recollection of Connie Chung or Geraldo Rivera as serious journalists.

* Peter Jennings, Dan Rather and Tom Brokaw have always anchored the evening news.

* The U.S. and the Soviets have always been partners in space.

* Mrs. Fields' cookies and Swatch watches have always been favorites.

Mind-sets

various things in our world. Do you agree with these points:

KIDS

* Nicholas Cage, Daryl Hannah, Eddie Murphy and John Malkovich made their first major film impressions the year they were born.

* The GM Saturn has always been on the road.

* Fox has always been a television network choice.

* Vanessa Williams and Madonna are aging singers.

* Perrier has always come in flavors.

* Cherry Coke has always come in cans.

* A "hotline" is a consumer service rather than a phone used to avoid accidental nuclear war.

* Genetic testing and DNA screening have always been available.

* Electronic filing of federal income taxes has always been an option.

* Magnetic Resonance Imaging (MRI) has always been available to doctors.

* Trivial Pursuit may have been played by their parents the night before they were born.

* Julian Lennon had his only hit the year they were born.

* Sylvan Learning Centers have always been an after-school option.

* Hip-hop and rap have always been popular musical forms.

* They grew up in minivans.

* Scientists have always recognized the impact of acid rain.

225

Make a Wish

"I wish to go... to Disney World for my birthday."

When volunteers from the Make-A-Wish Foundation met Erica, she had already given her wish much thought. She wanted to celebrate her ninth birthday at Disney World. Erica's wish was the Western Pennsylvania & Southern West Virginia chapter's 5,000th wish since its inception in 1983!

Erica was the guest of honor for Pittsburgh's Light Up Night. (This starts Pittsburgh's holiday season and fell on the night before Erica's trip.) She was picked up in a limousine and brought to the city. Hundreds of well-wishers were waiting for her. Everyone—including Santa Claus—sang "Happy Birthday" to her and chowed down on cookies. Erica even blew out candles on an early birthday cake.

The family departed the next morning for the Sunshine State. U.S. Airways upgraded them—Erica, dad Richard, mom Estella and brother Richard, Jr.—to first-class. In Florida, they stayed at Give Kids The World, a resort that provides accommodations, attraction tickets and meals for children with life-threatening illnesses and their families.

Erica's favorite part of her trip was meeting Mickey and Minnie Mouse on her birthday, and she loved all the fuss they made over her. Her favorite ride was the Amazing Adventures of Spider-Man 3-D thrill ride at Universal Orlando. All the while, the new 9-year-old wore a special birthday pin into all the parks.

Erica's parents claim she met every character in every park and got their autographs. Her mom called the trip "more than a dream come true." The family even had to purchase an extra duffel bag to hold all of the souvenirs.

Did You Know?

More stories like Erica's are at www.wish.org. Read how Make-A-Wish started on April 29, 1980, when 7-year-old Chris Greicius was picked up in a police helicopter and sworn in as the first and only honorary state trooper in Arizona history.

To date, more than 97,000 wishes have been granted to children with life-threatening illnesses.

The four most requested wishes are
* I wish to go...   * I wish to be...
* I wish to meet...   * I wish to have...

Bible Kids

Kids are important – there are lots of kids mentioned in the Bible and some of them did some pretty important things:

Cain — oldest son of Adam
Abel — son of Adam killed by Cain
Seth — third son of Adam
Ishmael — son of Abraham and Hagar
Isaac — the son Abraham almost sacrificed
Esau — hairy twin brother of Jacob
Jacob — Esau's twin who tricked his father Isaac
Miriam — sister of Moses
Moses — baby boy who became Israel's leader
Joseph — son of Jacob who was sold by his brothers
Benjamin — Joseph's youngest brother
Samuel — child who served with Eli in the temple
David — shepherd boy who became king of Israel
Manasseh — 12-year-old King of Judah
Joash — 7-year-old king of Judah
Josiah — 8-year-old king of Judah
Daniel — young prisoner of Babylon who gained the king's favor
Shadrach, Meshach and Abednego — Daniel's three Hebrew friends
John the Baptist — Jesus' cousin who later baptized Him
Jesus — God's Son
Rhoda — girl who left Peter standing at the gate (Acts 12:13)

(* listed in order of appearance)

Some children are talked about . . . but we are never told their names:

Child fought over by two mothers (1 Kings 3:22-28)
Son of the widow of Zarephath (1 Kings 17:9-15)
Children eaten by bears for laughing at Elisha (2 Kings 2:23,24)
Shunammite's son who was raised from the dead (2 Kings 4:18-37)
Boy with loaves and fishes (Mark 6:30-44)
Son of widow of Nain whom Jesus raised from the dead (Luke 7:11-16)
Jairus' daughter whom Jesus raised from the dead (Matthew 9:18-26)

KIDS

Aaron John Luke
Adam Saul

227

Organizations For

Check out any of these organizations that work in areas you're interested in.

ABA Center on Children and the Law www.abanet.org

Al-Anon/Alateen www.al-anon.alateen.org

Alpha Club www.optimist.org/jooi-faq.html

American Anorexic/Bulemia Association www.aabaine.org

American Federation of Riders www.afr1982.org

American Student Council Association www.naesp.org/students/asca.htm

Amnesty International Children's Human Rights www.amnestyusa.org/children/index.html

Boys and Girls Clubs of America www.bgca.org

Big Brothers/Big Sisters of America www.bbbsa.org

Boy Scouts of America www.scouting.org

Boys Town www.boystown.org

Camp Fire USA www.campfire.org

Cancer Kids www.cancerkids.org

Childhelp USA www.childhelpusa.org

Common Sense About Kids and Guns www.kidsandguns.org

Covenant House www.covenanthouse.org

and About Kids

4-H www.4h-usa.org/

Girl Scouts of the USA www.gsusa.org

Hearts and Minds www.heartsandminds.org

Hit Home Youth Development International www.1800hithome.com

Hug-A-Tree and Survive www.tbt.com/hugatree

International Assn. for the Child's Right to Play www.ipausa.org

Jack & Jill of America Foundation http://jackandjillfoundation.org

Kids at Hope www.kidsathope.org

Kids Eat Here www.kidseathere.org

National Beta Club www.betaclub.org

National Coalition Against Domestic Violence www.givedirect.org

National Council on Child Abuse and Family Violence http://nccafv.org

National Crime Prevention Council www.ncpc.org

National Information Center for Children and Youth with Disabilities www.kidsource.com/NICHCY

National Jewish Council for the Disabled www.ou.org/ncsy/njcd

National School Safety Center www.nsscl.org

Reading Is Fundamental www.rif.org

StandUp for Kids www.standupforkids.org

Toys for Tots www.toysfortots.org

Winners on Wheels www.wowusa.com

YMCA of the United States www.ymca.net

How do you spend your money? Check your spending against this average of how kids your age spent a couple of years ago:

How Much Kids Spend Weekly

	8-9's	10-12's
less than $5	80%	59%
more than $5	20%	41%

What Kids Buy for Themselves

candy	64%
games/toys	44
nail polish/perfume (girls)	42
clothing (10-12's)	29
soda pop	39
books	39
snack food	31
fast food	16
clothing (all tweens)	16

$pend Money

KIDS

Average Household Spending on Each Kid
(Ages 9-11)

total	$8,650
housing	2,820
food	1,790
transportation	1,250
clothing	530
health care	660
child care/education	580
misc	1,020

What Kids Are Saving for

60 percent of kids say they're saving for something special. Their top choices:

Top choices:

Boys:	**Girls:**
video games	gifts and presents
scooter	CDs

Languages

Signs and

Using things we can see to remind us of something we can't see is
The skies display of His marvelous craftsmanship" (Psalm 19:1). He set the
gave Noah the rainbow as a symbol that He would never again destroy the
symbols Christians have used.

Alpha & Omega — Jesus is the beginning and the end
(and everything in between)

Apple — Temptation; sin

Broken Bread — Jesus' body was broken for our sins

Butterfly — Easter; resurrection; new life

Candle — Light; Jesus, the light of the world

Circle — Eternity; wedding ring

Cross — Jesus died for our sins

Crown — Christ our King

Crown of Thorns — Christ is our suffering Savior

Dove — God the Holy Spirit

Empty tomb — Jesus is our risen Lord

Dove with olive branch — Peace, forgiveness

Fire, Flames — Presence of God as holy

Fish — Salvation; secret symbol of early Christians

Grapes or Goblet — Jesus' blood was shed for our sins

Heart — Love

Lamb — Christ, the Lamb of God; Old Testament sacrifices

Lily — Easter; Resurrection

Menorah — God's Law, especially the Old Testament

232

Symbols

God's ideas. "The heavens tell of the glory of God.
bright lights in the sky as signs (Genesis 1:14) and
world with a flood (Genesis 9:12). Here are some

Palm branches — Jesus triumphantly entering into Jerusalem on a donkey; victory

Rainbow — God is faithful; He won't destroy the earth again with water

Shepherd's Crook or Staff — Jesus is our good shepherd

Star (5 points) — Jesus' birth in Bethlehem

Star (6 points) — Star of David; Judaism; country of Israel

Sun — Jesus, the sun of righteousness

Sword — God's Word, the sword of the Spirit

Tablets — Ten Commandments; God's Law

Tree — Tree of Life; Jesus said, "I am the vine."

Trefoil (Shamrock)— The Trinity (God the Father, Son and Holy Spirit); God's love

Triangle — The Trinity (God the Father, Son and Holy Spirit)

Did You Know?

The Fish was a secret sign used by the early Christians to identify themselves to one another and mark their meeting places. The Greek word for "fish" is *Icthus*. Each letter stands for a Greek word, written in Latin letters. It was a simple statement: "Jesus Christ, God's Son, Savior."

Find more about Christian symbols at http://www.umcbelton.org/miscellaneous/symbolsicons.htm.

UNCLE CAM

Cameron Townsend went to Central America to sell Spanish Bibles when he was only 21 years old. He would eventually begin the world-renowned mission, Wycliffe Bible Translators.

Cam Townsend hiked the back trails of Guatemala, Honduras, El Salvador and Nicaragua or rode on a mule with his Bibles. He survived the jungle insects, and learned to eat such treats as bugs, worms and fried tadpoles.

One day Townsend plopped down to rest beside an old Cakchiquel Indian, pulled a Bible from his backpack and gave the man a cheery "Buenas tardes." The Indian returned only a grunt and finally blurted out in his own language, "If your God is so great, why can't He speak my language?" Townsend knew only a few Cakchiquel words, but it was enough for him to pick up the Indian's point.

Townsend set out to learn the Cakchiquel language. He was the first outsider to attempt it. He built a house of logs and cornstalks among the Indians and settled in to stay. After 12 hardworking years, he had learned the difficult language, reduced it to writing, and produced a Cakchiquel New Testament, which he presented to the president of Guatemala. In the meantime he built schools, a clinic, a printing press and an orphanage. Having the New Testament in their own tongue transformed the Indian tribe. Churches sprang up. Witchcraft decreased.

Townsend recruited and trained students to do what he was doing. He launched a "missionary air force" called JAARS (Jungle Aviation And Radio Service). One goal consumed "Uncle Cam," as people affectionately called him: To make it possible for every person alive to read the Bible.

Wycliffe currently has 5,318 missionaries working in 1,023 languages in 70 countries and on all continents except Antarctica. Computer technology has greatly accelerated the work of Bible translation. There are still over 3,000 languages—380 million people who speak a language that has no Scripture.

Learn more about this exciting work at www.wycliffe.org.
Click on "Kids" for a really cool site.

CAUTION: THIS QUIZ
IS FOR GENIUSES ONLY.

How Well Can You Read English?

How many of these "common" proverbs can you translate back into plain English? The first, for example, is "Like father, like son." (It's okay to use a dictionary or ask someone. Answers on page 339)

(Answers on page 339)

1. A beheld vessel never exceeds 100 degrees C.
2. Prodigality is produced by precipitancy.
3. It is not proper for mendicants to be indicative of preference.
4. It is fruitless to become lachrymose because of scattered lacteal fluid.
5. Articles which coruscate are not fashioned from aureate material, at least not necessarily.
6. Your immature galliformes must not be calculated prior to their being produced.
7. Lithodial fragments ought not to be hurled by tenants of vitreous material.
8. A feathered creature clasped in the manual members is the equivalent, value-wise, of a brace in the bosky growth.
9. Cleave gramineous matter for fodder during the period when the orb of the day is refulgent.
10. A perissodactyl ungulate mammal may be addressed toward aqueous.

Words That Don't Exist, But Should

Carperpetuation: The act, when vacuuming, of running over a string or piece of lint at least a dozen times, reaching over and picking it up, examining it, then putting it back down to give the vacuum one more chance.

Disconfect: To sterilize the piece of candy you dropped on the floor by blowing on it, assuming this will somehow remove all the germs.

Elbonics: The actions of two people maneuvering for one armrest in a movie theater.

Frust: The small line of debris that refuses to be swept onto the dust pan and keeps backing a person across the room until they finally decide to give up and sweep it under the rug.

Phonesia: The affliction of dialing a phone number and forgetting whom you were calling just as they answer.

Pupkus: The moist residue left on a window after a dog presses its nose to it.

Did You Know?

The 500 most commonly used English words have more than 14,000 different meanings.

Magazines

Christian Comics

Do you enjoy drawing cartoons? Many cartoonists are Christians who are finding great ways to use their cartooning talents for God. Whether your interest is comic books, book illustrations or newspaper comic strips, there is a place to use your skills.

Comic Books and Graphic Novels

You've probably seen comic books such as Spiderman, Superman, the X-Men and even non-superhero comics like Archie and Barbie. Did you know that there are comic books available with Christian themes?

Archangels (9 titles in a series set) has sold 685,000 copies. Check out Timestream's web site at www. cahabaproductions.com.

PowerMark Series One and Two. 15 titles (9 more coming). www. powermarkcomics.com

Left Behind: A Graphic Novel of the Earth's Last Days has five volumes based on the best-selling series Left Behind.

Kids books

Hundreds of kids' books are available with Christian messages. Many of these books are Bible stories, but they are written and illustrated just for kids. Some books are based on videos, such as the series from VeggieTales and Bibleman.

The popular Cow Adventure Series is written and drawn by Todd Aaron Smith. Follow the adventures of a barnyard cow and her friends as they learn about life and God. Read more about it at www.cowontheweb.com.

Comic strips

Several well-known cartoonists are also Christians who have been drawing the comics in the newspapers for many years. Sometimes their cartoons even have a good message about God that is printed in the newspaper!

Johnny Hart, who writes and draws the comic strip B.C. and Wizard Id, is the most widely read cartoonist on the planet. Johnny is a Sunday school teacher and is planning books of B.C. and Wizard of Id comic strips, including a collection of religious-themed cartoons. www.creators.com

Bill Keane, writes and draws The Family Circus, syndicated in 1,500 newspapers. Bil writes this comic strip based on his real-life family. Three TV specials and 60 books have been made with Keane's characters.

Charles Schulz created and drew the wildly popular Peanuts comic strip for 50 years. Meet the whole Peanuts gang, view 30 days of strips, send e-cards and play games with Snoopy and his friends at www.snoopy.com.

Did You Know?

You can have a fun outing at a Christian bookstore. Lose yourself among the myriad of books, games, videos, computer software and, yes, even Christian comics. A store locator is at www.cba.know-where.com/cba. Or search for any subject or title above at www.amazon.com.

The Cartoonist's Workbook by Robin Hall (Sterling) is a great book for beginners. Have a laugh on every page as you learn to draw.

Cartoon Animation by Preston Blair (Walter Foster) is the best to turn your drawing skills into animation.

10 Magazines
You Need to Know About

Clubhouse Magazine presents a fun mix of contemporary, classic and biblical tales, articles and games in an entertaining and appealing style. Each issue reinforces Christian values with hands-on activities, challenging puzzles and exciting stories. For kids 8-12. www.clubhousemagazine.org

Clubhouse Jr. Children ages 4 to 8 love to learn with the fun stories, games and puzzles in this activity-filled magazine. www.family.org

Contact Kids zeroes in on science, nature and the hottest technology. Every issue is filled with fascinating facts, questions with amazing answers and eye-opening discoveries—plus stories, puzzles, mazes, and contests. www.321contact.com

Explore is out to foster curiosity and challenge kids to think critically about how the world works. This is a cool magazine that kids will enjoy learning from. www.exploremagazine.com

Guideposts for Kids is for kids ages 7-12. Each issue is full of stories and activities that educate and inspire. Kids love Wally the turtle, the magazine's guide and mascot. www.gp4k.com

Highlights for Children has entertained and enlightened kids for more than 50 years. It improves reading skills and helps develop values like honesty, thoughtfulness and tolerance. All the children know is that they like it. www.highlights.com

Kid City explores the world through a kid's eyes—focusing on sports, science, animals, entertainment and more. It's loaded with puzzles, stories, jokes and activities that spark imagination, encourage creativity and enhance self-esteem. www.321contact.com

National Geographic Kids is packed with cool educational stuff that kids love to find out about. Have fun exploring the world and all that's in it. www.nationalgeographic.com/ngkids

Sports Illustrated for Kids features games, fantasy leagues, the latest sports news, trivia, polls and more. Stories and features on the web site are updated daily so kids can always find something new. www.sikids.com

Sports Spectrum gives you all the sports stuff you need with the values you want. In each edition, they cover a wide variety of sports. Each issue contains exclusive interviews with top Christian athletes. It is the No.1 Christian magazine for sports. www.sport.org

 **Did You Know?**

Most of these magazines accept reader submissions. Call on your creativity and get published (if nothing more than sending in your favorite jokes).

The Joppa Journal

Have fun with the Bible by playing the part of a newspaper editor during Bible days. What you "publish" looks somewhat like a modern-day newspaper, except everything in it is based on a part of the Bible. The items in The Joppa Journal example were all created by kids using stories and ideas found in the Book of Jonah.

Some possible features for a Bible newspaper:

- Masthead at top of first page
- Headline and lead news story
- Other news stories
- Editorials
- Want ads
- Advertisements
- "Photos" (drawings, stick figures, clip-art)
- Letters to the editor
- Cartoons
- Crossword puzzles
- Interviews
- Fashions, Domestics, Recipes
- Sports, Travel, Business
- Short "human-interest" items

THE JOPPA JOURNAL

BUSINESS NEWS: SHIPPING STOCK PLUMMETS WITH NEWS OF ENTIRE CARGO LOST AT SEA.

EXCLUSIVE: INTERVIEW WITH GREAT FISH

"What is it like to harbor a disobedient prophet?"

"How would you describe your creator?"

EDITORIAL

At first I felt Nineveh deserved to be destroyed. But God has shown me my mistake, and now I rejoice because of their repentance.

NINEVEH NOTES

Leaders begin worship services in palace ballroom.

BOAT FOR SALE CHEAP

ONLY BEEN IN 1 STORM

RIDE THE BIG FIZH

BUY NINEVEH BONDS

~OBITUARY~ AMITTAI, FATHER OF JONAH DIED TODAY.

INSTANT SHADE BUY THEM FOR ONLY 4.6 DRACHMAS AT ASSYRIAN HOUSE PLANTS. PLANT ONE AT NIGHT HAVE COOLING SHADE THE NEXT DAY.

Did You Know?

SCORPION ENSEMBLE

What does the future look like for soldiers? Scientists are constantly working to streamline uniforms and make them more sophisticated.

CNN.com reports that soldiers will someday wear uniforms that will monitor vital signs and plug them into a massive network of satellites, unmanned planes and robotic vehicles.

When dressing for battle in the so-called "Scorpion ensemble," soldiers will put on no more than 50 pounds, making them much more mobile than today's troops, who carry up to 120 pounds of gear.

The ensemble will plug the soldier into the military's planned Future Combat System of tanks, powerful computer networks and fleets of remote-controlled airplanes and robotic ground vehicles.

Soldiers will wear an undershirt netted with sensors that monitor heart rate, body temperature and respiration. Their uniform will have built-in tourniquets that can be tightened and loosened remotely.

The most high-tech component will be the helmet, with tiny, built-in cameras to spot enemies hiding in the dark or concealed by bushes. The cameras' images will appear on semitransparent screens attached to the helmets.

Soldiers will view maps, global-positioning coordinates and other data on their location. The same data could be used to call in air strikes. Images from drones, robotic vehicles or other members of the unit also may appear on screen.

The way the soldier will interact with the system is still under development. The goal is to give soldiers important information without overloading them.

Concepts on the drawing board include chameleon-like camouflage to make a soldier almost invisible. Other research involves uniforms that close pores between fibers to block out chemical weapons, or fibers that stiffen to form a cast or splint on a broken bone.

Another project under development at MIT envisions thin films that would monitor a soldier's breath for exposure to toxins, then signal the system to release the appropriate medicine.

Christian Armor

God provides armor Christians can put on to protect them from the Devil (Ephesians 6:10-17).

1. Buckle the BELT OF TRUTH around your waist.

Always tell the truth, and admire others who are honest. Remember that God never lies. (Psalm 119:142)

2. Strap the BREASTPLATE OF RIGHTEOUSNESS on your chest.

Be careful what kind of feelings are in your heart. Do not be mean to others. When others hurt you, forgive them, and then forget about it. (Isaiah 54:14)

3. Fit your feet with the GOSPEL OF PEACE.

God is happy when we live in peace with each other. (Matthew 5:9)

4. Take up the SHIELD OF FAITH.

Trust God to take care of you. Don't worry about what might happen. Remember that God promises to help us get through anything. (Psalm 56:11)

5. Wear the HELMET OF SALVATION on your head.

Believe that Jesus is God, that He came back to life after being crucified, and that when you die you will go to Heaven. (Romans 10:9)

6. Hold the SWORD OF THE SPIRIT in your hand.

The Bible is the Word of God and is a mighty weapon against evil. Read and memorize it and it will help you through anything. (Hebrews 4:1)

241

Military Masters

Some of God's followers were amazing soldiers and leaders. He called them to lead and protect His people. Other famous soldiers in the Bible fought against God's people.

1. **Joshua**—Led the Israelites into the Promised Land

2. **Gideon**—Led 300 men against the Midianites

3. **Deborah**—With Barak, led the Israelites against Sisera

4. **Samson**—Killed a thousand Philistines using the jawbone of a donkey

5. **Abner**—Was commander-in-chief of Saul's army

6. **Saul**—Fought the Phllistines all of his adult life

7. **David**—Killed Goliath, and as Israel's greatest king, led many battles

8. **Joab**—Won many victories as the commander of David's army

9. **Naaman**—Was a great Syrian army commander whom Elisha cured of leprosy

10. **Cornelius**—Was a Roman soldier with whom Peter shared the Gospel

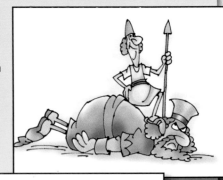

Biblical Battles

War is very much a part of the history of Israel. From early on, every man was expected to be a soldier to help defend God's "holy people" from the pagan tribes that often attacked them.

Even then, the everyday life of the Israelite family was ordinary and routine, jolted only here and there by war. Here is a quick look at war during Bible times:

- When Saul was appointed king, he chose 3,000 men as the first permanent army of Israel.

- King David was a military genius. Under him, the Israelites learned new methods of warfare. He was the first king to have a bodyguard of great warriors.

- The kings built fortresses to protect the land.

- Soldiers usually went to war in spring, when food was available.

- War was rarely declared; the element of surprise was important.

- The ram's horn, called a shofar, was blown to gather troops.

- Israelites often consulted prophets before facing battle.

- Before battle started, the priest offered a sacrifice to God.

- An attack on a city often took place just before dawn.

- From the city walls, defenders of a city hurled down burning arrows, boiling oil and stones in an attempt to keep the attackers at bay.

- After a city was taken, soldiers were usually free to take what they wanted. The walls were broken down and the city was burnt.

- Wars were sometimes settled by a single battle.

- The New Testament was not written against a background of war. The Mediterranean world was at peace under Roman government.

Miracles
A Whale of a Tale

One of the most famous Bible stories is that of Jonah and the whale. For many people it's a hard story to swallow.

In February 1891, the ship Star of the East was off the Falkland Islands when the crew spotted an 80-foot sperm whale. Two rowboats of crewmen were launched to capture the whale. Closing in, one harpooner threw his weapon and hit the whale, which lashed out, almost overturning the boats. Returning to the ship with the dead whale, the crewmen realized one sailor, James Bartley, was missing. They decided he had been tossed overboard in the fight and had drowned.

Six hours later the crewmen began removing the blubber from the dead whale. By midnight they still were not finished, and the sailors went to bed. In the morning, they resumed their job. Suddenly the sailors were startled by something in the stomach giving spasmodic signs of life. Inside was found the missing sailor, James Bartley, doubled up and unconscious. He was placed on deck and given a bath of seawater which soon revived him, but his mind was not clear so he was placed in the captain's quarters.

Recovering, Bartley recalled being hit by the whale's tail and then encompassed by great darkness, and he felt he was slipping along a smooth passage that seemed to move and carry him forward. His hands came in contact with a yielding, slimy substance, which seemed to shrink from his touch. He could easily breathe, but the heat was terrible. It seemed to open the pores of his skin and draw out his vitality. The next he remembered he was in the captain's cabin.

Except for the fact that his face, neck and hands had been bleached white, Bartley, like Jonah, survived the belly of the monster.

Did You Know?

What's the moral of Jonah's story? (You can't keep a good man down!)

The largest marine mammal is the blue whale, measuring over 100 feet long and weighing 143 tons (286,000 pounds). These are the largest animals that have ever lived — bigger than any known dinosaur!

One of the Greatest Miracles of All Time

3,600,000

people survived in a wilderness for 40 years. No one had a job yet they lacked nothing. They raised no crops yet they didn't starve. They dug no wells yet they didn't go thirsty.
Their clothes and sandals never wore out!

Moses' story of the Exodus of the Hebrews from Egypt and their 40-year journey to their Promised Land is one of the Bible's most amazing accounts. *(Exodus 13 - Numbers 36; Deuteronomy)*

Consider the math of what was needed:

3,600,000 people. There were 600,000 men, their wives and an average of 4 children per family.

3,600,000 animals. A family average of 2 goats, 2 sheep, 1 donkey and 2 families sharing a cow and camel would not be unusual.

3,000,000,000 square feet of camping space. A plot of 50' by 50' per family would require an area 10.5 miles square for the whole nation.

184,000 cubic feet of food daily. God allowed each person 7 pints of manna (food from Heaven) daily but gave extra. At an average of 4,000 cubic feet each, this would require 46 modern boxcars daily to feed the people plus 160 boxcars full for the animals. At today's prices, it would cost over $7,000,000 per day for food.

10,800,000 gallons of water per day. People today use 60-75 gallons per day in the city and 25 gallons per day when camping. Allowing each wilderness wanderer only 1 gallon per day and the animals 2 gallons each would require 1,080 modern railroad tank cars.

1,268 modern rail cars would be needed to haul each day's supply of food and water. This equals a 9.5 mile long train. Or 13 trains of 100 cars each 6 days a week. (God provided double on the day before the Sabbath.)

800 mile long column if the people walked double file with their animals. At an average walking speed of 2.5 miles per hour, even walking 50 abreast would take 49 hours for them all to pass by any point.

3-5 mile gap in the Red Sea. For all to cross through God's opening in one night, they had to walk at least 5,000 abreast.

Miracles in the Bible

The Bible opens with a miracle — the existence of an all-powerful God who creates the heavens and the earth. The Bible closes with a great miracle — the creation of a new heaven and earth. And supernatural events happen all through the Bible.

The Bible miracles mainly center around three periods of time: (1) Moses, (2) Elijah and Elisha, (3) Jesus and the apostles. *Jesus' miracles are on the next page.*

Moses

Moses' shepherd's staff a snake	(Exodus 4:2-4)
Moses' leprosy healed	(Exodus 4:7)
Aaron's staff a snake	(Exodus 7:10-12)
Water to blood	(Exodus 7:19-25)
Frogs	(Exodus 8:5-7)
Dust to lice	(Exodus 8:16, 17)
Flies everywhere except in Goshen	(Exodus 8:20-24)
Deadly cattle disease except Hebrews'	(Exodus 9:1-7)
Ashes to dust causing sores	(Exodus 9:8-12)
Hailstorm with fire	(Exodus 9:22-26)
Swarms of locusts	(Exodus 10:12-20)
Darkness three days except for Hebrews	(Exodus 10:21-23)
Oldest sons died unless blood on their door	(Exodus 12:21-30)
Cloud to hide	(Exodus 14:19, 20)
Red Sea crossing	(Exodus 14:21-28)
Water sweetened by a tree	(Exodus 15:23-25)
Quail to eat	(Exodus 16:11-13)
Manna from heaven	(Exodus 16:14-22)
Water from a rock twice	(Exodus 17:1-6; Numbers 20:1-11)
Fire from heaven three times	(Numbers 11:1, 2; 16:16-18, 35)
Miriam's leprosy healed	(Numbers 12)
Earth opened for rebels	(Numbers 16:28-33)
Plague stopped by incense	(Numbers 16:46-50)
Aaron's shepherd's staff budded	(Numbers 17)
Brass serpent to heal	(Numbers 21:5-9)
Moses talked with Jesus	(Luke 9:28-36)

No rain for three and a half years	(1 Kings 17:1)
Widow's food supply	(1 Kings 17:13-16)
Boy raised from the dead	(1 Kings 17:17-23)
Fire from heaven	(1 Kings 18:17-38)
Rain after prayer	(1 Kings 18:41-46)
Two miraculous meals lasting 40 days	(1 Kings 19:4-8)
Ravens bring food	(1 Kings 17:2-7)
Fire from heaven	(2 Kings 1:10-12)
Jordan River parted	(2 Kings 2:8)
Elijah taken to heaven	(2 Kings 2:11)
Elijah talked with Jesus	(Luke 9:28-36)
Jordan River parted	(2 Kings 2:13, 14)
Water purified with salt	(2 Kings 2:19-22)
Bears defend Elisha	(2 Kings 2:23-25)
Water supplies	(2 Kings 3:14-20)
Widow's oil multiplied	(2 Kings 4:1-7)
Infertile woman healed	(2 Kings 4:14-17)
Boy raised from the dead	(2 Kings 4:32-37)
Poison stew made edible	(2 Kings 4:38-41)
Food multiplied for 100 men	(2 Kings 4:42-44)
Naaman's leprosy healed	(2 Kings 5:1-14)
Iron ax head floated	(2 Kings 6:4-7)
Angelic army made visible	(2 Kings 6:15-17)
Syrian army blinded and healed	(2 Kings 6:18-20)
Man raised from the dead	(2 Kings 13:20, 21)

Peter and Paul

Walking on water	(Matthew 14:28-31)
Instant language ability	(Acts 2:1-3)
Crippled man healed	(Acts 3:1-8)
Recognized deception	(Acts 5:1-11)
Healings from a shadow	(Acts 5:15, 16)
Angel-aided prison escapes	(Acts 5:17-29; 12:1-17)
Visible display of the Holy Spirit	(Acts 8:14-17; 10:34-48)
Paralyzed man healed	(Acts 9:33, 34)
Dorcas raised from the dead	(Acts 9:36-41)
Dramatic conversion	(Acts 9:1-9)
Eyes healed	(Acts 9:10-18)
Sorcerer temporarily blinded	(Acts 13:8-11)
Crippled man healed	(Acts 14:8-10)
Demons cast out	(Acts 16:16-18)
Prison opened by earthquake	(Acts 16:25-33)
Many healings	(Acts 19:11, 12; 28:8, 9)
Eutychus raised from the dead	(Acts 20:9, 10)
Poisonous snakebite nullified	(Acts 28:3-6)

Modern Miracles

According to a Newsweek poll taken recently, more than eight in ten Americans believe God performs miracles, and almost half believe they have experienced or witnessed one. Here's the breakdown:

84% believe in miracles.

79% believe the miracles in the Bible are true.

48% have experienced miracles.

63% know someone who has experienced a miracle.

90% of Christians believe in miracles.

It's a Miracle

The PAX TV series, It's a Miracle reports on true-life accounts of miraculous coincidences and interventions. The show looks at the mystery of that which cannot be explained and how such experiences compassionately touch individual lives.

It's a Miracle is the first show Pax ever produced. It has been so popular that several books featuring favorite stories from the show have been published. Richard Thomas was the show's original host. Roma Downey, who gained fame as the angel, Monica, on TV's Touched by an Angel is currently hosting the program.

Many fans favor the stories that tell of people helping others. Sometimes the help comes from sacrificial and unselfish actions. These stories show the loving and compassionate nature of people. The popularity of this program and others like it show that people are looking for miracles. They are looking for hope.

How Jesus Proved He Is God

It's one thing
for someone to claim to be God. It's another thing to prove it. Jesus claimed to be God, "The Father and I are one" (John 10:30). And He proved it by the miracles He performed.

MIRACLES	Matthew	Mark	Luke	John
Nature Miracles				
Water into wine				2:1-11
Huge catch of fish			5:1-11	
Calming a storm at sea	8:23-27	4:35-41	8:22-25	
Feeding 5,000	14:15-21	6:35-44	9:12-17	6:5-13
Walking on water	14:22-33	6:48-51		6:19-21
Feeding over 4,000 people	15:32-39	8:1-9		
Coin from a fish	17:24-27			
Withered fig tree	21:18-22	11:12-26		
Huge catch of fish				21:1-11
Healing Miracles				
Nobleman's son				4:43-54
Peter's mother-in-law	8:14. 15	1:30, 31	4:38, 39	
Leper	8:1-4	1:40-42	5:12,13	
Paralyzed man	9:1-8	2:1-12	5:18-25	
Crippled man, Bethesda Pool			5:1-15	
Withered hand	12:9-13	3:1-5	6:6-10	
Centurion's servant	8:5-13		7:1-10	
Woman with a hemorrhage	9:20-22	5:25-29	8:43-48	
Two blind men	9:27-31			
Canaanite's daughter	15:21-28	7:24-30		
Deaf-and-dumb man		7:31-37		
Blind man		8:22-26		
Mentally ill child	17:14-21	9:17-29	9:38-43	
Ten lepers			17:11-19	
Man born blind				9:1-7
Bent over woman			13:10-17	
Man with dropsy			14:1-6	
Malchus' ear			22:49-51	
Spiritual Miracles				
Casting out a demon		1:23-26	4:33-35	
Healing demon-possessed man	12:22-37		11:14	
Casting devils out of two men	8:28-34	5:1-15	8:27-35	
Casting out a demon	9:32, 33			
Resurrection Miracles				
Widow's son			7:11-15	
Jairus' daughter	9:18-26	5:22-24	8:41, 42	
Lazarus				11:1-46

The only miracle recorded in all four Gospels is the feeding of the 5,000.
Matthew and Luke are tied in recording the most miracles.
After Jesus healed 10 men of their leprosy, only one thanked Him.
Jesus reattached a soldier's ear after Peter cut it off.
The ultimate proof that Jesus is God is His own resurrection from the dead. Read the fascinating account in Matthew 28 and what it means in 1 Corinthians 15.
A lawyer set out to disprove Jesus' resurrection. Read what happened to Frank Morison in *Who Moved the Stone?* (Zondervan).

Where Kids

1. Afghanistan
2. Algeria
3. Azerbaijan
4. Bhutan
5. Brunei
6. Cambodia
7. Cocos Islands
8. Comoros
9. Djibouti
10. Gambia
11. Guinea
12. Guinea-Bissau
13. Iran

14. Iraq
15. Kirghizia
16. Laos
17. Libya
18. Maldives
19. Mali
20. Mauritania
21. Mayotte
22. Mongolia
23. Morocco
24. Nepal
25. Niger

26. North Korea
27. Oman
28. Pakistan
29. Sahara
30. Senegal
31. Somalia
32. Somaliland
33. Tajikistan
34. Tunisia
35. Turkey
36. Turkmenistan
37. Uzbekistan

Haven't Heard the Good News

In 38 countries, less than half the people have had a chance to hear the Gospel.

Did You Know?

Presently, more than 70% of Christian ministry is directed at people who say they already are Christians. Less than 5% of our total missionary activity is focused on those who have never once had a chance to hear about the good news of the Gospel. For more information, visit www.globalChristianity.org.

Life as a Missionary Kid

Have you ever wondered what it's like to be a missionary kid?
Here's a little info on life as an MK:

What is the best part of being a missionary kid?

It's cool to live in another country and learn another language. MKs get to learn the culture of another nationality and sample their foods! It's fun to take part in the national celebrations and festivals. MKs get to see how kids in any culture can worship God together.

What is the most difficult part of being a MK?

One of the hardest parts is missing family and friends back home. MKs don't get to see their grandparents very often—and cousins can grow up hardly knowing one another. It's frustrating not to be able to communicate easily in another language. Some MKs really miss the climate of their homeland—for example winter! Another kind of hard and kind of good thing is that some MKs live in boarding schools away from their parents. Its can be totally fun—but they don't get to be with their parents every day.

How does being a MK make your life different from that of other kids?

Well, everyone in school is going to speak the language of the country where a MK lives. A MK may not hear his native language spoken very often at all. A MK may only get to visit back home once every two or three years.

What is your favorite hobby, sport or activity?

MKs are just like you! They like to swim or do gymnastics or play baseball. Some play the piano or other instruments or love to sing.

You Know You're a MK* When You...

- Speak two languages, but can't spell either.
- Embarrass yourself by asking what swear words mean.
- Read *National Geographic* and recognize someone.
- Have a time zone map next to your telephone.
- Would rather eat seaweed than cafeteria food.
- Consider a city 500 km away to be "very close."
- Can cut grass with a machete, but can't start a lawn mower.
- Read the international section before the comics.
- Have friends in 29 different countries.
- Have spoken in dozens of churches.
- Have many friends who don't speak English.
- Watch a foreign language film . . . and understand what they're saying.
- Think fitting 15 or more people into a car seems normal.
- Haggle with the checkout clerk for a lower price.
- Don't think that two hours is a long sermon.
- Put five hot sauces on a Taco Bell taco.
- Miss the subtitles when you see the latest movie.
- Surf the Internet looking for fonts that support your "native" language's alphabet.
- Think a "foreign school" conducts classes in English.

MK* means missionary's kid

253

THE LORD'S BOOT CAMP

As the negative influences of this world began affecting children at a younger age, Teen Missions had a burden to start a preteen program in 1989 for 10-13 year olds, and a peanut program in 1994 for 7-9 year olds.

There are exciting projects to choose from: puppet evangelism, clowning and work projects around the world. Everyone trains at the 500-acre Lord's Boot Camp in Merritt Island, Florida. There is a daily obstacle course for fun and team unity. Team members raise their own support the same as an adult missionary would.

What's in It for Me?

The Lord's Boot Camps can help you to:
- Grasp the basics of the Bible.
- Learn why we need to reach people with the Gospel.
- Get acquainted with some open mission fields and jobs available.
- Get "control" of your life so you can stand against peer pressure.
- Learn respect and discipline.
- Develop a regular quiet time with God.
- Learn responsibility in work and witness.
- Get along with others without being self-centered.
- Make lifelong friends.

What the Kids Say

"This was the best summer I have ever had. I enjoyed my trip to Indiana and I was able to lead two people to the Lord." —*Kirsten Graham Austin, 12, Cocoa, Florida, Indiana Clown Puppet Team*

"I have never enjoyed a summer more than this one and no summer has had more of an impact on my life. This summer I had many awesome experiences. I met new friends, I saw much of God's awesome creation in Ecuador." —*Amelia Weaver, 10, Los Alamos, New Mexico, Ecuador Team*

"I had a great time in Sweden and the whole experience taught me not to complain or take things at home for granted." —*Benjamin Bloomer, 12, Minneapolis, Minnesota, Sweden Team*

"This summer was great, God called me to be a missionary!" —*Linda OK, 10 La Canada Flintridge, California, Australia Team*

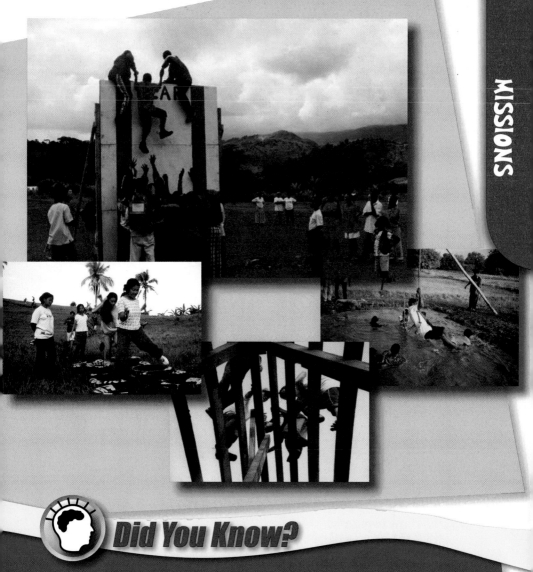

MISSIONS

Did You Know?

Over 35,000 kids have experienced missions firsthand through Teen Missions, assisting with a variety of evangelistic and building projects with over 100 other missions in 60 countries.

Since 1989, an additional 30,000 national teens have been sent out from 25 other Boot Camps held around the world each year.

The timed Obstacle Course includes a mountain of tires, rope swings over a moat, a 30-foot Jacob's ladder, a maze, the Red Sea and finally a 12-foot wall! The Peanut course (just their size) includes a rope swing, a tunnel and smaller wall.

View team video presentations, download the current brochure, send in an application and more online at www.teenmissions.org. Or write to Teen Missions Int'l, 885 E. Hall Rd., Merritt Island, FL 32953 (321-453-0350).

255

Praying For Missionary Kids

Surrendering to God's call to missions calls for sacrifice and adjustment by the children of the missionaries. MKs need prayer support. The following are some things that you can pray for the children of missionaries.

Pray that they will have a growing relationship with Jesus Christ (John 3:15-16, 15:4-5).

Pray for a loving relationship with their parents (Ephesians 6:4).

Ask God to give them good friends (Proverbs 17:17, 27:17).

Pray for their ability to learn the language of the land they are living in (Jeremiah 29).

Ask God to keep them from being lonely or discouraged (Hebrews 13:5).

Pray for them to learn what God's will is for their lives (Psalm 23:3).

Fill in the names of missionary kids you know as you pray these verses for them:

I pray that _____ may grow in the grace and knowledge of our Lord and Savior Jesus Christ (2 Peter 3:18).

I pray that you will create in _____ a hunger for your Word. (Psalm 19:10).

Create in _____ a pure heart, O God, and cause that purity to be shown in his/her actions (Psalm 51:10).

O God, create a servant's heart in _____ that he/she may serve wholeheartedly as if they were serving the Lord and not men (Ephesians 6:7).

I pray that you, the God of hope, would cause hope to overflow in _____'s life (Romans 15:13).

Please cultivate in _____ the ability to have true humility before you and to show true humility before all (Titus 3:2; 1 Peter 5:5).

Enable _____ to always be strong and courageous in his/her character and his/her actions (Deuteronomy 31:6).

Enable _____ to show proper respect to everyone as your Word commands (1 Peter 2:17).

Help _____ to develop a strong sense of self-esteem that is rooted in the righteousness of Jesus and the realization that he/she is your workmanship, created in Christ (Ephesians 2:10).

Chairway to China
Mission Books for Kids

From Arapesh to Zuni: A Book of Bibleless Peoples by Karen Lewis (International Academic Bookstore; age 3-10)

Teaching Kids to Care and Share: 300+ Mission & Service Ideas for Children by Jolene L. Roehlkepartain (Abingdon)

Deserts and Jungles: A Child's Guide to God's Contrasting Climates by Michael W. Carroll (Chariot Victor; age 9-12)

Peanut Butter Friends in a Chop Suey World by Deb Brammer (Bob Jones University Press; age 9-12)

Missions Made Fun for Kids by Elizabeth Whitney Crisci (Accent Books)

Fun Around the World by Mary Branson (Women's Missionary Union)

Children in Crisis by Glenn Myers (OM Publishing)

Reach Around the World by Bob and Sandy Friesen (Gospel Publishing House)

The Third Culture Kid Experience: Growing Up Among Worlds by David C. Pollock and Ruth E. Van Reken (Intercultural Press)

Where in the World Are You Going? by Judith M. Blohm (Intercultural Press)

You Know You're an MK When... by Andy and Deborah Kerr (Watermelon World Publishing)

Children of the Call: Issues Missionaries' Kids Face by Charlene Gray (New Hope)

Being a Christian: A Study Book for Children by David Walters (Good News Fellowship Ministries; age 9-12)

For more great missions resources for kids, visit Multicultural Links for Kids at www.ethnicharvest.org/links/kids.htm.

Movies, TV and Video

Young Artist

The Young Artist Awards (http://www.youngartistawards.yrg/) is a nonprofit organization honoring performers under the age of 18 for their accomplishments in film, television, music and all areas of entertainment. These are the winners of the 24th Annual Young Artist Awards. www.Youngartistawards.org

Best Performance in a Feature Film

Leading Young Actor: Tyler Hoechlin in "Road To Perdition"
Leading Young Actress: Alexa Vega in "Spy Kids 2"
Supporting Young Actor: Marc Donato in "White Oleander"
Supporting Young Actress: Eva Amurri in "The Banger Sisters"
Young Actor Age Ten or Younger: Tyler Patrick Jones in "Red Dragon"
Young Actress Age Ten or Younger: Caitlin E.J. Meyer in "Little Secrets"

Best Performance in a TV Movie, Miniseries or Special

Leading Young Actor: Jeremy Sumpter in "Just A Dream"
Leading Young Actress: Clara Bryant in "True Confessions"
Supporting Young Actor: Ryan Merriman in "Taken"
Supporting Young Actress: Hallee Hirsh in "My Sister's Keeper"

Best Performance in a TV Series (Comedy or Drama)

Leading Young Actor: Gregory Smith in "Everwood"
Leading Young Actress: Masiela Lusha in "The George Lopez Show"
Supporting Young Actor: Steven Anthony Lawrence in "Even Stevens"
Supporting Young Actress: Emily Hart in "Sabrina the Teenage Witch"
Young Actor Age Ten or Younger: Dylan Cash in "General Hospital"
Young Actress Age Ten or Younger: Sasha Pieterse in "Family Affair"

Awards

Best Ensemble in a TV Series (Comedy or Drama)
"Malcolm in the Middle" Frankie Muniz, Justin Berfield, Erik Per Sullivan, Kyle Sullivan, Craig Lamar Traylor

Best Performance in a Voice-Over Role

Thomas Dekker in "The Land Before Time, Part IX"
Age Ten or Younger: Daveigh Chase in "Lilo & Stitch"

Best Performance in a Commercial
Christian Roberts for 7-Up

Best Family Television Movie or Special
"My Sister's Keeper" (CBS)

Best Family Television Series (Comedy or Drama)
"The George Lopez Show" (ABC)

Best Family Feature Film

Animation: "Spirit: Stallion of the Cimarron"
Comedy: "The Crocodile Hunter: Collision Course"
Drama: "The Lord of the Rings: The Two Towers"
Fantasy: "Star Trek: Nemesis"

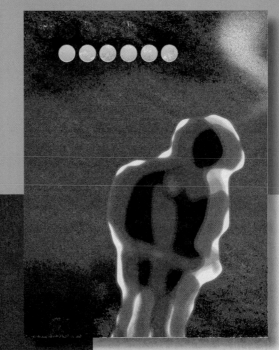

Animal Stars

10 Animals
Who Had Their Own TV Series

1. Lassie, the collie
2. Black Beauty, the horse
3. Rin Tin Tin, the Alsatian
4. Champion, The Wonder Horse
5. Flipper, the dolphin
6. SALTY, the sea lion
7. Fury, the black stallion
8. Skippy, The Bush Kangaroo
9. Gentle Ben, the bear
10. My Friend Flicka, the horse

10 Films
Featuring Pigs

1. Animal Farm (1955)
2. Babe (1995)
3. Big Top Pee Wee (1988)
4. Charlotte's Web (1972)
5. Doc Hollywood (1991)
6. Leon the Pig Farmer (1992)
7. Misery (1990)
8. Pigs (1982)
9. A Private Function (1984)
10. Razorback (1984)

Did You Know?

Lassie was treated like a Hollywood star. She lived in an air-conditioned kennel and was insured for $100,000. On the set, she rested on a mobile bed between takes.

Rin Tin Tin had a valet, a personal chef, a limousine and a chauffeur. He also had a five-room dressing-room complex on the studio lot.

The dolphin who played Flipper beat out 80 other dolphins to win the coveted role.

VeggieTales — A Big Idea

Phil Vischer, like so many other kids his age, was fascinated by the Muppets. He thought Bert and Ernie, Cookie Monster and Oscar the Grouch were cool! He even dreamed about being a puppeteer that got to work those puppets. His dreams led him to a totally cool career!

Today Phil is the voice of Bob the Tomato, one of the stars of VeggieTales, and now kids love his character! Phil also performs other VeggieTales voices and writes many of the stories and songs. In fact, it was Phil who thought up the whole idea of vegetables telling stories in the first place.

Phil thought about lots of different ways to tell stories—even using candy to be characters. But, when a talking cucumber popped into his mind, his first character was born! That cucumber became Larry. Next came Bob the Tomato and soon the whole wacky cast was born.

A little over ten years ago Phil started Big Idea Productions in his spare bedroom. Four people made the first video, including Mike Nawrocki, Phil's friend from Bible college. (Mike's still a Big Idea writer and director—and the voice of Larry.)

It takes more than 150 people working for nine months to create each new Veggie Tale. The process begins with a storyline, the script and songs come next. Then the voices are recorded and the artists get busy sketching each scene. Finally, computer artists and animators bring the ideas to video. And once sound effects and final music are added, ta da—a VeggieTale is born!

How to Make Your Big Idea Come True

Phil Vischer has said, "Draw, write. Daydream. The key to changing the world is picturing it differently, and then thinking up ways to make your dream real.

"In the Bible, the two greatest commandments are to love God and to love our neighbors. Ask these questions about your dream: Will it honor God? Will it help others? If the answers are yes, you can be pretty certain your idea will please God. If that's true—He will help you all the way!"

Live in the Hive

What kind of action goes on inside a beehive?

With close-up photography, *City of the Bees* takes you inside a beehive. But the Moody Institute of Science cameramen will tell you it wasn't easy—hot photographic lights kept melting the honeycombs.

Here are some of the amazing facts this video reveals.

• A beehive has thousands of cells, but bees varnish each one of these after every use.

• Bees create their own air conditioning by distributing water through the hive and then fanning their wings.

• Bees have their own language. One bee can tell another bee everything about a good nectar source a mile or more away. They communicate by using a complicated figure-eight dance.

• The waggle of the dance indicates the sugar content of the food. The angle of the dance in relation to the sun conveys the direction of the food source. And the length of time spent on the waggle and the number of pulses of sound emitted in each buzz are a measure of the distance to the food source.

• The hexagonal pattern of the honeycomb is the ideal and most efficient shape for multi-cell storage, combining maximum space with minimum building material. High-speed aircraft, in their construction, utilize the principle of the honeycomb.

• Bees could live for years, but they literally work themselves to death in five or six weeks!

Did You Know?

Check out some of these videos made by the Moody Institute of Science. www.moodyvideo.org

Dust or Destiny
Empty Cities
Experience with an Eel
Facts of Faith
God of Creation
God of the Atom
Hidden Treasures

Journey of Life
Mystery of the Three Clocks
Of Books and Sloths
Prior Claim
Professor and the Prophets
Red River of Life

Signposts Aloft
Time and Eternity
Ultimate Adventure
Voice of the Deep
Where the Waters Run
Windows of the Soul

Top 10 Kids' Videos and DVDs

How many of these ten favorite Christian videos or DVDs have you seen?

1. The Star of Christmas - VeggieTales
2. Larryboy and the Angry Eyebrow – Larryboy
3. Jonah's Sing-Along Songs – VeggieTales
4. The Toy that Saved Christmas – VeggieTales
5. Leggo My Ego – Larryboy
6. Let Freedom Ring – Bill & Gloria Gaither
7. The Star of Christmas (DVD) – VeggieTales
8. God Bless America – Bill & Gloria Gaither
9. Amazing Carnival of Complaining – 3-2-1 Penguins!
10. Freedom Band

The Climb

Two hotshot mountain climbers become unwilling partners in order to climb one of the world's most dangerous peaks. A daring rescue just earned show-off Derrick Williams the climb of a lifetime, but his dream comes with an unwanted partner. "Safety man" Michael Harris doesn't hot dog, doesn't blaze trails and rarely takes life to the edge.

Training takes a backseat to their stormy relationship. But no amount of training can prepare them for the harsh reality of the Chilean Andes. The Climb escalates into a test of wills, character and sacrifice that pushes both men beyond limits. Their treacherous journey takes them higher—and deeper—than they've ever been before.

Check out this exciting Christian video: The Climb (Worldwide Pictures).

Did You Know?

There are over 50 VeggieTale web sites. Try these for starters:

- http://www.bigidea.com. Home of the Big Idea. Keep up on the latest ways to experience the Veggies in books, videos, DVDs, music and games. Sign up for VeggieGrams.
- http://www.bigideafun.com. Arcade games, e-cards, stories, downloads—cool as a cucumber!
- http://www.bigidea.com/other/fanclub.htm. Official fan club.

Music

Audio A-List for Christian Kids

Have you listened to any of these tapes or CDs? They are all favorites of lots of kids.

On the Road With Bob & Larry   Big Idea (Word)

O Veggie, Where Art Thou?   Big Idea (Word)

Shout to the Lord Kids!   Hillsong/Hosanna!/Integrity (Word)

Jonah: Original Movie Soundtrack   Big Idea (Chordant)

Shout Praises! Kids 3   Integrity Just for Kids (Word)

Action Songs   Cedarmont Kids (Provident)

Toddler Bible Songs   Cedarmont Kids (Provident)

Jonah's Overboard Sing-Along   Big Idea (Word)

Audie Awards

The Audie Awards honor excellence in audio publishing in 27 categories. They are awarded each year in May. The following Christian tapes have been winners in recent years.

- The Christmas Shoes by Donna VanLiere, read by Paul Michael (Audio Renaissance)
- In This Mountain by Jan Karon, read by John McDonough (Recorded Books)
- The Remnant by Tim LaHaye and Jerry B. Jenkins, read by Richard Ferrone (Recorded Books)
- The Youngest Hero by Jenkins, read by Laurie O'Brien and Jack Sondericker (Time Warner AudioBooks)
- Wild & Wacky Collections Vol. 1 by Frank Peretti, read by Peretti (Tommy Nelson)
- Billy Budd, Sailor, adapted from the novel by Herman Melville
- The Silver Chair by C.S. Lewis, both read by full casts (Focus on the Family)

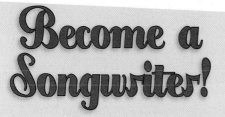

Become a Songwriter!

Did you ever wish you could write songs? Here's your chance at musical stardom, and you don't have to know anything about music. Simply make up new words to fit an existing tune.

Count the number of syllables per line in a familiar song. It's easiest to count on your fingers as you sing. Then make up new lines with the same number of syllables. For example, "Jesus Loves Me" has seven syllables per line. Here's a song some kids composed, using this tune.

Jonah went against God's wish.
So he wound up in a fish!
Nineveh turned to the Lord.
But the worm got that old gourd!

(chorus)
Don't be like Jonah!
Don't be like Jonah!
Don't be like Jonah!
Accept God's perfect will.

You can also copy the original words and put corresponding new words under them. Or simply put one new syllable under each musical note. It's okay to stretch a syllable over several notes, but don't "bunch" two or more syllables under one note. This example by a group of fourth graders uses the tune from "Savior, Like a Shepherd Lead Us."

One day many people came to Jesus,
It was late; they were hungry.
Jesus asked His twelve disciples,
"How much bread and fish have we?"
Jesus blessed it; Jesus broke it:
The five loaves and two fishes.
Fed five thousand, lots left over,
Jesus fed five thousand men.

Have you composed a song or written new lyrics you'd like to send to us?
See page 350.

Dove Awards

The Dove Awards recognize the best in contemporary Christian and gospel music. Here are some of the 2003 winners. Learn more at http://www.doveawards.com.

Short-form Music Video: **"Irene," tobyMac** (ForeFront/Chordant)

Long-form Music Video: **Worship, Michael W. Smith** (Reunion/ Provident)

Children's Album: Jonah: **A Veggie Tales Movie Original Soundtrack** (Big Idea/Chordant)

Contemporary Gospel Album: **The Rebirth of Kirk Franklin;** Kirk Franklin (Gospo Centric/Provident)

Country Album: **Rise And Shine;** Randy Travis (Word)

Inspirational Album: **Legacy...Hymns & Faith;** Amy Grant (Word)

Pop/Contemporary Album: **Woven & Spun;** Nichole Nordeman

Praise & Worship Album: **Worship Again, Michael W. Smith** (Reunion/Provident)

Southern Gospel Album: **A Crabb Collection; The Crabb Family** (Family Music)

Spanish-Language Album: **Navidad; Jaci Velasquez** (Word)

Traditional Gospel Album: **Higher Ground, Blind Boys of Alabama** (Real World/EMI Gospel/Chordant)

Urban Album: (tie) **The Fault Is History; Souljahz** (Warner/Word); **This Is Your Life; Out of Eden** (Gotee/Chordant)

Contemporary Gospel Recorded Song: **"In The Morning," Mary Mary** (Columbia/Integrity/Word)

Country Recorded Song: **"The River's Gonna Keep On Rolling," Amy Grant**

Inspirational Recorded Song: **"Here I Am To Worship," Tim Hughes** (Worship Together/Chordant)

Pop/Contemporary Recorded Song: **"Holy"; Nichole Nordeman**

Southern Gospel Recorded Song: **"Don't You Wanna Go?" The Crabb Family**

Traditional Gospel Recorded Song: **"Holding On," Mississippi Mass Choir** (Malaco)

Urban Recorded Song: **"Meditate," Out of Eden**

Musical: **The Christmas Shoes;** Donna VanLiere, Eddie Carswell, J. Daniel Smith (Brentwood/Provident)

Youth/Children's Musical: **Meet Me At The Manger;** Celeste Clydesdale (Clydesdale & Clydesdale/Word)

266

GOD'S RODS

Kids like to call me the "stick man," because I use "sticks" to teach Bible stories. My real name is Jeff Smith.

My sticks are actually dowel rods—small, round wooden poles, about three feet long and less than a half an inch in diameter. You can hold one or two dowel rods in each hand and make pictures or shapes. You can also create moods by making sounds with the dowel rods. We call our "sticks" the God Rods!

The best part of the God Rods is the story behind them. It started when I was the Director of Creative Arts at a local church in Chester, Virginia. There was a young boy named Josh, who didn't have much natural dramatic ability. But he liked to be involved. One day Josh asked me to help him prepare something for a local talent show. He had chosen a song called "Arise My Love" and he wanted to do something creative with it.

As we prayed for God to show us a way to interpret the song that would bring Him glory, I "heard" a word picture! God showed me a peacock in my "mind's eye." The word picture was that others saw Josh as a gnarly bird. Josh was kind of a small boy, but God saw him as stately and majestic when he "spread his wings" and worshipped. I felt like God wanted me to give Josh his "wings." So I gave him two dowel rods that were in my office and told him to stretch out his arms. We worked for a couple of hours and eventually, I choreographed the movements for "Arise My Love" using the God Rods.

From that humble and innocent beginning, I never imagined how God would take this idea and use it around the world to tell others about His love. We eventually made a training video to teach others how to use the "God Rods." There were six songs on the first video called "Stick It 2 'Em." I continued to teach the ideas at conferences and eventually we made another video called "Stick With Me."

A couple of years later we got a phone call from a youth pastor in Paducah, Kentucky. It was after the first of several high school shootings. One of the girls who died in that terrible incident was Jessica James. It turned out that Jessica liked to perform the choreography to "Arise My Love". The youth pastor called to see if the "Stick Team" at his church could perform that piece at Jessica's funeral. Many people saw that performance and the news about the God Rods started to spread.

Now we have developed more than 15 training videos in a series called "Movement 4 Non-Movers" that teach people creative movement ideas. Whatever happened to Josh? Today, he is a young man who recently graduated from college with a degree in art.

By the way, remember that talent show Josh wanted to enter? He won!
Meet Jeff and his ministry at www.saltandlightmin.org.

MUSIC

Born-again teenagers have musical tastes similar to those of their non-Christian peers, according to data collected by the Barna Research Group.

The only real difference in stylistic preferences was that born-again teens were substantially more likely to list contemporary Christian music (CCM) as their favorite. Even among the born-again group, however, just 1 out of every 14 (7%) identified CCM as his or her preferred style.

Few Christian artists have risen to the level of enduring role model or hero among teens. DC Talk, the rap-turned-rock ensemble, may be the closest thing that today's Christian teens have to a reigning pop idol—and even this star is losing some of its luster in terms of popularity.

For a long time, Christian artists such as Amy Grant and Michael W. Smith were seen by millions as the epitome of the clean-cut, wholesome followers of Christ whose music and lifestyles were worthy of closer examination. For better or worse, kids these days are hard-pressed to identify such icons. Given the constricted nature of stardom these days, even mega-selling artists like Kirk Franklin and Jars of Clay may well be soon forgotten.

TASTES

Here are the musical likes and dislikes of teenagers, according to Barna's 2000 survey:

The Musical Likes and Dislikes of Teenagers

Style of music	Favorite Style	Dislike it
rap/hip-hop	25%	20%
rock	22	12
R&B	13	2
pop	11	8
country	6	33
Christian	3	1
dance/techno	2	1
classical	2	3
Latin	1	1
jazz	1	2

Did You Know...

Most teenagers' parents have no idea what music their kids listen to or the lyrical content of their musical diet.

TOP TEN KIDS' NAMES
(AND MOST COMMON NICKNAMES)

BOYS
Jacob—Jake, Jay
Michael—Mike, Mick, Micky
Matthew—Matt
Joshua—Josh, Jos
Christopher—Chris, Kit
Nicholas—Nick, Claas, Claes
Andrew—Andy, Drew
Joseph—Joe, Joey, Jos, Jody
Daniel—Dan, Danny
Tyler—Ty

GIRLS
Emily—Emmy, Millie, Emma
Hannah—Nan, Nanny, Anna
Madison—Maddie, Maddy, Mattie
Ashley—Lee
Sarah—Sally, Sadie
Alexis—Alex
Samantha—Sam, Sami, Sammy
Jessica—Jessie, Jess
Taylor—Taye
Elizabeth—Beth, Betsy, Betty, Lisa, Liz

TOP TEN KIDS' NAMES
100 YEARS AGO

GIRLS	BOYS
Mary	John
Helen	William
Anna	James
Margaret	George
Ruth	Charles
Elizabeth	Joseph
Marie	Frank
Rose	Henry
Florence	Robert
Bertha	Harry

Did You Know...

Dozens of nicknames exist for Elizabeth. How many can you think of? (for starters: Eliza, Bess, Bessie, Beth, Betsy, Betty, Lib, Libby, Liza, Lisa, Liz, Lizzie)

271

MOST POPULAR NAMES IN THE BIBLE

BOYS	GIRLS
DAVID	SARAH
JESUS	ESTHER
MOSES	MARY
SAUL	RACHEL
JACOB	LEAH
AARON	JUDITH
SOLOMON	REBEKAH
ABRAHAM	TAMAR
JOSEPH	JEZEBEL
JONATHAN	RUTH

Did You Know?

The Old Testament prophet Isaiah had two sons with very unusual names: Shear-Jashub (meaning "a remnant shall return") and Maher-shalal-hash-baz (meaning "the spoil hastens; the prey speeds" Isaiah 7:3, 8:1-4). What nicknames would you give these boys?

There's More to a Name

Names were carefully chosen in Bible times. Parents didn't thumb through baby name books or check the most popular name lists. Sometimes God chose a child's name, as with Jesus (Savior; Matthew 1:21) and John (Jehovah has been gracious; Luke 1:13).

A name was not just a label. It might reveal a person's character, position. calling or his relationship with God or other people. Some names revealed a person's origin, such as Adam (taken out of the red earth) or predicted their destiny, such as Hagar (fugitive).

Some Famous Bible Names and Their Meanings

Aaron — enlightened
Abram — father of height
Abraham — the father of a multitude
David — beloved
Joseph — may God add
Joshua — Jehovah is salvation
Moses — taken out of the river
Luke — light-giving
Noah — rest
Saul — demanded
Solomon — peace
Eve — life
Mary/Miriam — bitterness
Martha — mistress of the house
Naomi — my joy
Ruth — something worth seeing
Rebekah — captivating
Sarai — princess
Sarah — queen

What Does Your Name Mean?

What can your parents tell you about the name they chose for you? Check out the background on your name at www.behindthename.com. Every name's meaning refers to some character quality. What might your name imply? Some are a little less obvious.

Wayne, for example, means "wagon" or "wagon maker." Wayne might be one who bears or eases the burdens of others (Galatians 6:2 KJV).

Did You Know?

There are 17 different men named Jesus in the Bible.

Three Bible men are named Dodo.

There are 188 different Bible characters whose names begin with the letter Z.

Numbers

NUMBERS

The Bible is filled with numbers. It's fun to think of how a number is used in the Bible. Then look it up in a Bible concordance which lists every word in the Bible and where it occurs.

"There is only one God and one Mediator who can reconcile God and people. He is the man Christ Jesus" (1 Timothy 2:5 NLT)

"Two by two they came into the boat" (Genesis 7:15 NLT)

"As Jonah was in the belly of the great fish for three days and three nights, so I, the Son of Man, will be in the heart of the earth for three days and three nights." (Matthew 12:40 NLT)

"I see four men, unbound, walking around in the fire. They aren't even hurt by the flames! And the fourth looks like a divine being." (Daniel 3:25 NLT)

"Five thousand men had eaten from those five loaves!" (Mark 6:44 NLT)

"In six days the Lord made the heavens, the earth, the sea, and everything in them" (Exodus 20:11 NLT)

is More Than a Bible Book!

"Then he rested on the seventh day. That is why the Lord blessed the Sabbath day and set it apart as holy." (Exodus 20:11 NLT)

"Josiah was eight years old when he became king" (2 Chronicles 34:1 NLT)

"It was nine o'clock in the morning when the crucifixion took place." (Mark 15:25 NLT)

"Honor your father and mother. This is the first of the Ten Commandments that ends with a promise." (Ephesians 6:2 NLT)

And so on...

Did You Know?

1. Why are 2, 10, 20, and 613 all correct answers for how many commandments God gave at Mount Sinai?

2. Why did God pick 70 as the number of years for Judah's Babylonian captivity?

3. Why was the number 40 chosen for the years the Hebrews would wander in the wilderness?

Answers on page 341

BIBLE MATH

1. _____ (Methuselah's age at death)
   - _____ (number of books in the Old Testament)
   = _____ (year Rehoboam split the Hebrew kingdom)

2. _____ (days Jesus spent in the wilderness)
   x _____ (number of Noah's sons)
   = _____ (years Moses lived)

3. _____ (years of Judah's Babylonian captivity)
   x _____ (day God rested from His creating)
   = _____ (number of times Jesus said we should forgive one another)

4. _____ (number of faithful spies in the wilderness)
   x _____ (days of God's creation activity)
   = _____ (number of Jacob's sons)

5. _____ (number of minor prophets)
   ÷ _____ (number of Jesus' apostles)
   = _____ (number of apostles who died a natural death)

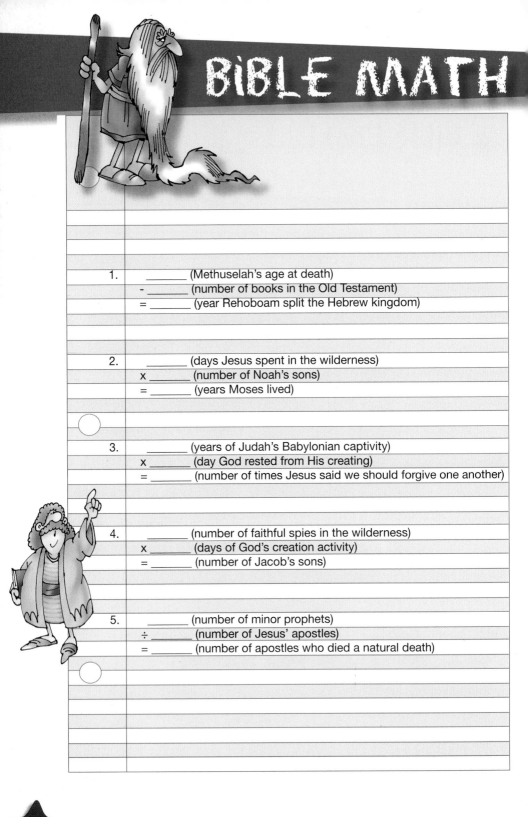

6. _____ (Jesus' approximate age when He began to preach
   + _____ (generations from Adam to Noah)
   = _____ (days the twelve Hebrew spies were in Canaan)

7. _____ (number of Old Testament law books)
   x _____ (number of Jacob's daughters)
   = _____ (number of Bible books written by John)

8. _____ (number of major prophetic books)
   + _____ (number of apostolic helpers appointed in Acts 6)
   = _____ (number of tribes in Israel)

9. _____ (number of known New Testament authors)
   - _____ (number of persons in the Trinity)
   = _____ (number of loaves Jesus used to feed the five thousand)

10. _____ (years Hebrews were in desert after leaving Egypt)
    - _____ (number of Jacob's children)
    = _____ (number of books in the New Testament)

How America
Between

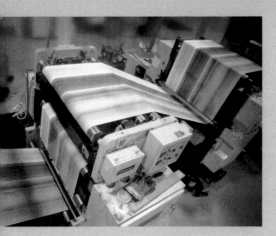

Teens completing high school:
Average annual income:
Average size of household:
Average work week:
Cancer deaths:
Cars produced in the US:
City with the most millionaires per capita:
Daily newspapers:
Deaths in childbirth:
Defense expenditures (in 1999 dollars):
Divorced men:
Divorced women:
Farm population:
Federal budget outlay:
Highway fatalities:
Homes with electricity:
Immigrant population:
Life expectancy for men:
Life expectancy for women:
Median age:
Miles of paved road:
National debt (in 1999 dollars):
Number of bison:
Number of farms:
Number of millionaires:
Passenger cars registered in the US:
Patents granted:
Population of Los Angeles:
US population:
Urban vs. rural populations:
Voter turnout:

Changed
1900 and 2000

15%	83%
$8,620	$23,812
4.76 persons	2.62 persons
60 hours	44 hours
64 per 100,000	200 per 100,000
5,000	5,500,000
Buffalo NY	Seattle WA
2,226	1,489
9 in 1,000	1 in 10,000
$4 billion	$268 billion
0.3%	8.2%
0.5%	10.3%
29,875,000	4,600,000
$10.3 billion	$1.7 trillion
36 / 100 MIL miles	1.64 / 100 MIL miles
8%	99.9%
14.7%	7.9%
46.3 yrs	73.6 yrs
48.3 yrs	79.7 yrs
22.9 yrs old	35.7 yrs old
10 miles	4,000,000 miles
$24.8 billion	$5 trillion
400	200,000
5,740,000	2,191,510
3,000	3,500,000
8,000	130,000,000
24,656	147,500
102,479	3,800,000
75,994,575	273,482,000
40% / 60%	75% / 25%
73.7%	48.9%

People

Over Six Billion and Counting

Currently the world's population is 6,312,694,437. But this figure is outdated before I finish typing this sentence because the world population is growing by 200,000 people a day!

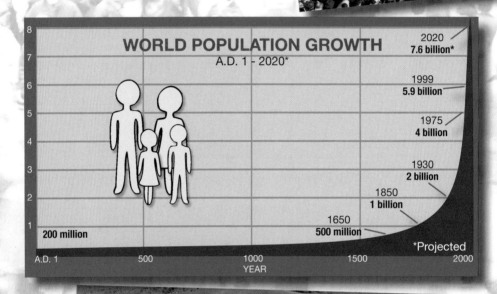

WORLD POPULATION GROWTH
A.D. 1 - 2020*

- 2020 7.6 billion*
- 1999 5.9 billion
- 1975 4 billion
- 1930 2 billion
- 1850 1 billion
- 1650 500 million
- 200 million

*Projected

YEAR: A.D. 1, 500, 1000, 1500, 2000

10 Countries Where Sheep Outnumber People

1. Falkland Islands
2. New Zealand
3. Australia
4. Uruguay
5. Mongolia
6. Syria
7. Namibia
8. Iceland
9. Mauritania
10. Somalia

Did You Know?

If you have a java-enabled browser, you can watch the USA and world population estimates dynamically updated at every tick of the clock at www.census.gov/main/www/popclock.html.

Who Knew Whom in the Beginning

Did you know Adam (the world's first man) was still alive when Noah's dad lived?

This chart shows the people who were contemporaries in the first 20 generations of mankind. The family tree is listed across the top: father, son, grandson, etc. beginning with Adam. The same names are listed twice on the left—when each was born and died. Everyone listed between a person's "B" and "D" were alive at the same time.

It's fun to look at ages, too. For example, Noah was 502 years old when his son Shem was born! How many people can you find who lived over 900 years? Who is the oldest?

		Adam	Seth	Enos	Cainan	Mahalaleel	Jared	Enoch	Methuselah	Lamech	Noah	Shem	Arphaxad	Selah	Eber	Peleg	Reu	Serug	Nahor	Terah	Abram	Isaac	Jacob
										A	G	E											
Adam	Cr																						
Seth	B	130																					
Enos	B	235	105																				
Cainan	B	325	195	90																			
Mahalaleel	B	395	265	160	70																		
Jared	B	460	330	225	135	65																	
Enoch	B	622	492	387	297	227	162																
Methuselah	B	687	557	452	362	292	227	65															
Lamech	B	874	744	639	549	479	414	252	187														
Adam	D	930	800	695	605	535	470	308	243	56													
Enoch	Tr		857	752	662	592	527	365	300	113													
Seth	D		912	807	717	647	582		355	168													
Noah	B			821	731	661	596		369	182													
Enos	D			905	815	745	680		453	266	84												
Cainan	D				910	840	775		548	361	179												
Mahalaleel	D					895	830		603	416	234												
Jared	D						962		735	548	366												
Shem	B								869	682	502												
Lamech	D								964	777	595	93											
Methuselah	D								969		600	98											
The Deluge											600	98											
Arphaxad	B										602	100											
Selah	B										637	135	35										
Eber	B										667	165	65	30									
Peleg	B										701	199	99	64	34								
Reu	B										731	229	129	94	64	30							
Serug	B										763	261	161	126	96	62	32						
Nahor	B										793	291	191	156	126	92	62	30					
Terah	B										822	320	220	185	155	121	91	59	29				
Peleg	D										940	438	338	303	273	239	209	177	147	118			
Nahor	D										941	439	339	304	274		210	178	148	119			
Noah	D										950	448	348	313	283		219	187		128			
Abram	B											450	350	315	285		221	189		130			
Reu	D											468	368	333	303		239	207		148	18		
Serug	D											491	391	356	326			230		171	41		
Terah	D											525	425	390	360					205	75		
Arphaxad	D											538	438	403	373						88		
Isaac	B											550		415	385						100		
Selah	D											568		433	403						118	18	
Shem	D											600			435						150	50	
Jacob	B														445						160	60	
Abraham	D														460						175	75	15
Eber	D														464							79	19
Isaac	D																					180	120
Jacob	D																						147

KEY: Cr=Creation
B = Born
D = Died
Tr=Translated

Fascinating Facts about Bible People

Methuselah, the oldest person in the Bible, lived to the ripe old age of 969 years. He fathered his first son, Lamech, when he was 187 years old.

Naomi lost her husband and two sons. Her name means "pleasant," but she told people to call her Mara, which means "bitter," because of her misfortune.

Ahilud, who lived during the time of the book of Judges, must have been kind of short. Supporting pillars for roof beams in his house were only five feet three inches tall.

Several good Bible characters had troubled sons: Aaron's two sons offered unsanctioned sacrifices (Leviticus 10); Eli's two sons were not too nice (1 Samuel 2); and Samuel's two sons took bribes (1 Samuel 8).

The Edomites, descended from Esau, often clashed with the Israelites. They celebrated when Israel was defeated, and the prophet Obadiah condemned them for this (Psalm 137:7).

Onesiphorus was a friend to Paul. When Paul was imprisoned in Rome, Onesiphorus went to Rome and searched until he found the apostle, then he stayed around and encouraged Paul. Paul compared this friend's actions with that of Phygelus and Hermogenes, who abandoned him and the Gospel he preached (2 Timothy 1:15—18; 2:17—18).

Did You Know?

Top-notch illustrations, maps, timelines and photos, combined with short text makes *Who's Who in the Bible: An Illustrated Guide* by Stephen Motyer (DK Publishing) one of the best books about Bible people.

Bible Record Holders

First: Adam, the world's first human being (Genesis 2:7)

Oldest: Methuselah, who lived to be 969 (Genesis 5:27)

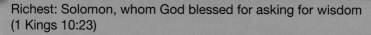

Strongest: Samson, who carried away a city's iron gates (Judges 16:3)

Wisest: Solomon, whom God made wiser than anyone (1 Kings 3:12)

Richest: Solomon, whom God blessed for asking for wisdom (1 Kings 10:23)

Tallest: Goliath, who stood over nine feet tall (1 Samuel 17:4)

Shortest: Zacchaeus, who climbed a sycamore tree to see Jesus (Luke 19:3-4)

Fastest: Asahel, who could run like a deer (2 Samuel 2:18)

Greatest of the prophets: John the Baptist (Matthew 11:11)

Guiltiest: Judas, who betrayed Jesus (Matthew 27:3-5)

Vainest: Nebuchadnezzar, who set up a gold statue of himself to be worshipped (Daniel 3:5)

Most Beautiful: Esther, who won the Miss Persia contest (Esther 2:7, 17)

Most Traveled: Paul, who went on many long missionary journeys (Acts 13:4; 15:36; 18:23)

Most Persecuted: Job, attacked by Satan, who took everything but his life (Job 1-2)

Most lovestruck: Jacob, who worked 14 years to be able to marry Rachel (Genesis 29:18-28)

Most Frightened: Belshazzar, whose knees knocked as the hand wrote on the wall (Daniel 5:6)

Most Impetuous: Jephthah, who promised to offer a sacrifice, which turned out to be his daughter (Judges 11:30)

Most Doubtful: Thomas, who wouldn't believe Jesus was alive until he touched His wounds (John 20:24-29)

PEOPLE

283

Most-Mentioned

10 Most Mentioned Men in the New Testament

1. Jesus — The Son of God (983)

2. Paul — Apostle to the Gentiles (162)

3. Peter — Chief apostle (162)

4. John the Baptist — Jesus' cousin and forerunner (86)

5. Pontius Pilate — Roman ruler who sentenced Jesus (56)

6. John — Jesus' apostle (35)

7. Herod — The villainous tetrarch (30)

8. Timothy — Paul's co-worker (28)

9. Judas Iscariot is mentioned 23 times.

10. Philip — Church deacon and evangelist (16)

10 Most Mentioned Men in the Old Testament

1. David — Second King of Israel (1080)

2. Moses — Author of the first five books of the Bible (768)

3. Saul — First king of Israel (399)

4. Jacob — Patriarch of the 12 Hebrew tribes (350)

5. Aaron — Moses' brother and high priest (345)

People in the Bible*

10 Most Mentioned **Women** in the Bible

1. Sarah — the wife of Abraham who had a child when she was 90 years old. (56*)

2. Rachel — one of Jacob's wives. Jacob loved her the most and worked 14 years for her father so that he could marry her (47)

3. Leah — Jacob's first wife, whom he was tricked into marrying (34)

4. Rebekah — Isaac's wife and the mother of Esau and Jacob (31)

5. Jezebel — An infamous person (23)

6. Mary — Mother of Jesus (19)

7. Abigail — Wife of Nabal, and later of King David (15)

8. Miriam — Moses' sister (15)

9. Mary Magdalene — She received deliverance and forgiveness from Jesus (14)

10. Hagar — Abraham's concubine and the mother of Ishmael (14)

Eve, the mother of the human race, is mentioned only four times in the whole Bible!

6. Solomon — Third king of Israel (294)

7. Abraham — God's friend and Sarah's husband (237)

8. Joshua — Moses' successor (216)

9. Joseph — Interpreter of dreams (215)

10. Jeremiah — The weeping prophet (147)

PEOPLE

Plants

Every Bloomin' Thing

There are over 250,000 different kinds of plants in the world. God made them all. The Bible mentions 80 kinds of plants, starting with all but eight letters of the alphabet. Fifty-four of them are pictured on these two pages. How many can you name? (Answers are on page 341)

33.

7.

12.

18.

51.

30.

26.

4.

13.

2.

50.

24.

15.

48.

6.

49.

29.

44.

40.

32.

34.

22.

17.

23.

43.

19.

1.

54.

20.

41.

28.

31.

46.

52.

8.

42.

9.

10.

11.

53.

38.

14.

47.

21.

39.

3.

45.

16.

35.

5.

27.

RECORD HOLDERS

Deadliest — castor bean plant

Fastest-growing on land — bamboo (12 inches/day)

Largest flower — rafflesia (36-inch diameter flower)

Largest fruit — pumpkin (1,061 pounds).
Next largest is a 50-pound watermelon.

Largest leaves — raffia palm (65 feet long)

Largest seed — coco de mer (12 inches long)

Largest vegetable — yam (150 pounds).
Next largest is a 124-pound cabbage.

Most apples grown — state of Washington
(6 billion tons/year)

Most coffee consumed — Finland
(25 pounds/person/year)

Most expensive — saffron
(spice from purple crocus. $2,000 per oz.)

Most massive tree — giant sequoia
(trunk diameter up to 30 feet)

Most nutritious fruit — avocado
(741 calories/pound; lots of vitamins A, C, E)

Most peanuts produced — state of Georgia
(1.3 billion pounds/year)

Most poisonous mushroom — death cap

Most rice grown — China (190 million tons/year)

Most sugar consumed — Belize (135 pounds/person/year)

Most-harvested plant — rice (599 million tons/year)

Oldest coral reef — Isle La Motte, Vermont

Oldest living tree — bristlecone pine
(nicknamed Methuselah; 4,700 years old)

Smallest vegetable — snow pea (average length 1/4 inch)

Slowest flowering — Bolivian herb, puya raimondii
(80 to 150 years to bloom once)

Tallest cactus — saguaro (50-75 feet average height)

Tallest tree — California redwood (up to 385 feet tall)

Prayer

Kids' prayers

Dear GOD,
Maybe Cain and Abel would not kill each other so much if they had their own rooms. It works with my brother. —Larry

Dear GOD,
Instead of letting people die and having to make new ones, why don't You just keep the ones You have? —Jane

Dear GOD,
I read the Bible. What does "begat" mean? Nobody will tell me. Love, Alison

Dear GOD,
Are You really invisible or is it just a trick? —Lucy

Dear GOD,
Did You mean for the giraffe to look like that or was it an accident? —Norma

Dear GOD,
What does it mean You are a jealous God? I thought You had everything. —Jane

Dear GOD,
Thank You for the baby brother, but what I prayed for was a puppy. —Joyce

Dear GOD,
Please send me a pony. I never asked for anything before. You can look it up. —Bruce

Dear GOD,
I think about You sometimes even when I'm not praying. —Elliott

Dear GOD,
Of all the people who work for You I like Noah and David the best. —Rob

Dear GOD,
I would like to live 900 years like the guy in the Bible. —Love, Chris

Dear GOD,
We read Thomas Edison made light. But in Sunday school they said You did it. So I bet he stole Your idea. —Sincerely, Donna

Dear GOD,
The bad people laughed at Noah. "You made an ark on dry land, you fool." But he was smart, he stuck with You. That's what I would do, too. —Eddie

Dear GOD,
I do not think anybody could be a better God. Well, I just want You to know but I am not just saying that because You are GOD already. —Charles

Dear GOD,
I didn't think orange went with purple until I saw the sunset You made on Tuesday. That was cool. —Eugene

Do you have a prayer you'd like to submit for the next edition? See page 350.

Personal Prayers

There are over 600 prayers in the Bible. Many of them can be read as personal prayers. Here are two examples:

"I pray for you constantly, asking God, the glorious Father of our Lord Jesus Christ, to give you spiritual wisdom and understanding, so that you might grow in your knowledge of God. I pray that your hearts will be flooded with light so that you can understand the wonderful future He has promised to those He called. I want you to realize what a rich and glorious inheritance He has given to His people. I pray that you will begin to understand the incredible greatness of His power for us who believe Him. This is the same mighty power that raised Christ from the dead and seated Him in the place of honor at God's right hand in the heavenly realms." (Ephesians 1:16-20)

"I fall to my knees and pray to the Father, the Creator of everything in heaven and on earth. I pray that from his glorious, unlimited resources he will give you mighty inner strength through his Holy Spirit. And I pray that Christ will be more and more at home in your hearts as you trust in him. May your roots go down deep into the soil of God's marvelous love. And may you have the power to understand, as all God's people should, how wide, how long, how high, and how deep his love really is. May you experience the love of Christ, though it is so great you will never fully understand it. Then you will be filled with the fullness of life and power that comes from God." (Ephesians 3:14-19)

The "Lord's Prayer" Is Like a Letter

Addressee: Our Father

Address: in heaven

Greeting: may your name be honored

Body: May your Kingdom come soon. May your will be done here on earth, just as it is in heaven. Give us our food for today, and forgive us our sins, just as we have forgiven those who have sinned against us. And don't let us yield to temptation, but deliver us from the evil one.

Closing: For yours is the kingdom and the power and the glory forever.

Seal: Amen

(Matthew 6:9-13)

Famous Bible Prayers
(With Some Dramatic Answers!)

Many of the prayers in the Bible have specific results that can only be explained as God's answers. Here's where to find these and some other well-known prayers in His book.

Abraham's prayer for an heir (Genesis 15:2-3)
Abraham's prayer for Sodom (Genesis 18:23-33)
Anna and Simeon thank God for Christ (Luke 2:25-38)
Christians' prayer for Peter's safety (Acts 12:5)
Church's prayer for missionaries (Acts 13:3)
Daniel's prayer to interpret a dream (Daniel 4:18)
David thanks God for His great mercy (Psalm 136)
David's prayer for forgiveness (Psalm 32, 51)
David's prayers of praise (Psalms 100, 103, 106, 107)
Elijah's prayer for a dead boy (1 Kings 17:20-21)
Elijah's prayer for fire (1 Kings 18:36, 37)
Elisha's prayer for a dead son (2 Kings 4:33-35)
Gideon's prayer for a sign from God (Judges 6:36-40)
Hannah's prayer for a son (1 Samuel 1:9-11)
Hannah's prayer of praise for the birth of Samuel (1 Samuel 2:1-10)
Isaac's prayer for Jacob and Esau (Genesis 25:21-23)
Job's prayer because of his suffering (Job 3:3-12; 10:18-22)
Jonah's prayer because God spared Nineveh (Jonah 4)
Joshua's prayer for more sunlight (Joshua 10:12)
Mary's prayer of thanks for being God's servant (Luke 1:46-55)
Peter's prayer for Dorcas (Acts 9:36-43)
Prayer of praise for the Red Sea deliverance (Exodus 15)
Samson's prayer for strength (Judges 16:28-31)
Solomon's prayer for wisdom (1 Kings 3:5-9)
Stephen's prayer on behalf of his killers (Acts 7:59, 60)
Thanking God for salvation (Revelation 5:8-14; 7:9-12)

Kids Praying for Kids

Samaritan's Purse is an organization that helps people all around the world – much like the Good Samaritan in the Bible did. Read that story in Luke 10:25-37.

Samaritan's Purse offers a colorful spiral 12-month prayer journal that features photos of children from different countries. *Kids Praying for Kids* tells about their country, and how you can pray specifically for their needs. The journal also includes fun crafts you can make and a monthly Bible verse to memorize. Call Samaritan's Purse at 1-800-345-6111 to get your free copy. (Ask your parent first if it's okay to make this call.)

Franklin Graham of Samaritan's Purse says, "Can you imagine the great ways God can use us if we just ask Him? My mother taught me that prayer was simply talking and listening to God. You know that God created the universe, our world, and each one of us. But did you know that God loves for us to talk to Him, and He loves to answer us? And no matter where you are, your prayers can reach around the world. Now that's an adventure!"

Remember that prayer doesn't just change the world. It changes you, too! Spend time talking with God and see how much He loves you and pray for children all around the world who need to know that, too.

Did You Know?

Franklin Graham is the son of the famous evangelist Billy Graham. Learn more about Franklin at www.grahamfestival.org/franklin.html

WHO AND WHAT TO PRAY FOR

Keeping a log of prayer requests and answers is very encouraging. Specific prayers with names and places are best. Some people and items to add to a prayer list include:

Christian workers (Matthew 9:37-38)
Effective proclamation of the Gospel (Ephesians 6:18-19)
Enemies (Matthew 5:44)
Giving thanks (1 Thessalonians 5:17, 18)
God to be glorified (John 14:13)
Love and spiritual growth (Philippians 1:9)
One another (1 Samuel 12:23)
President, kings and all civil leaders (1 Timothy 2:1-4)
Protection and peace (Psalm 127:1)
Salvation of others (Romans 10:1)
Sick people (James 5:14-16)
Spiritual strength (Matthew 26:41)
Victory over sin (2 Corinthians 13:7)
Wisdom to know and do what God wants (Colossians 1:9)

PROMISES TO CLAIM
Thank the Lord for what He promises His kids.

Abundant life (John 10:10)
Answered prayer (1 John 5:14)
Assurances for the future (2 Timothy 1:12)
Cleansing (John 15:3)
Comfort (Isaiah 51:3)
Crown of life (Revelation 2:10)
Deliverance (2 Timothy 4:18)
Everlasting life (John 3:16)
Gifts of the Spirit (1 Corinthians 12)
God's care (1 Peter 5:6, 7)
God's guidance (Isaiah 42:16)
Growth in the Christian life (Ephesians 4:11-15)
Home in heaven (John 14:1-3)
Hope (Hebrews 6:18, 19)
Inheritance (1 Peter 1:3, 4)
Joy (Isaiah 35:10)
Peace (John 14:27)
Rest (Hebrews 4:9, 11)
Resurrection (Romans 8:11)
Spiritual healing (Hosea 6:1)
Spiritual light (John 12:46)
Strength (Philippians 4:13)
Understanding (Psalm 119:104)
Victory (1 John 5:4)
Wisdom (James 1:5)

Did You Know?

In America the first Thursday of May is the National Day of Prayer. To learn more, go to http://www.nationaldayofprayer.org.

Window on the World by Daphne Spraggett with Jill Johnstone uses stunning graphics and interesting facts to encourage prayer for the many countries and kids of the world. Check it out at http://www.gmi.org/ow/resources.

Write a Letter TO GOD

The Bible is a personal letter from God to us. If someone so important has written such a loving and thoughtful letter as the Bible, we ought to write back.

To write a letter to God, begin paragraphs with:

- **Thank You, Lord**
- **Help me, Lord**
- **I confess, Lord**

Everyone likes to receive thank-you notes. God is no exception. Start your letter by thanking the Lord for what you have learned from the Bible about Him, yourself, and your relationship. Think about God's characteristics, and thank Him for who He is. Then thank the Lord for what He has done for you, is doing this week, and has promised to do in the future.

Ask Him to help you with your responsibilities. The Christian life is often not doing what comes naturally, but what comes supernaturally. None of us can handle this life apart from God's help. His power and resources are available by asking.

Next, confess to the Lord anything standing between you and Him. To confess means to agree with what God says. You can ask Him for forgiveness just as you would a friend whom you have wronged.

Now send your letter to God by reading it to Him as a personal prayer. Keep your letters so you can look back and see how God answers you. If you have brothers or sisters, you may need a secure hiding place for your letters. :-)

Or simply copy a Bible prayer, personalizing it as your own. For example, Philippians 1:9-10: "Dear God, I pray that my love for others will overflow more and more and that I will keep on growing in your knowledge and understanding. For I want to understand what really matters, so that I may live a pure and blameless life until Christ returns."

Just like any friendship, a growing friendship with God is a two-way street. Make time for God in your life.

295

10 Things I Can Pray About Today Are...

1.

2.

3.

4.

5.

6.

7.

8.

9.

10.

God Gave Me Answers to my Prayers (write in the date)

1.

2.

3.

4.

5.

6.

7.

8.

9.

10.

Radio

Radio Theatre

It used to be a part of everyday life. In the days before television and video games families would gather around their radios in the evening for the latest installments of their favorite daily serial. Focus on the Family Radio Theatre brings back that tradition! Focusing on the values of the Christian faith, these fictional stories and biographical sketches entertain and educate adults and children alike.

Billy Budd, Sailor

Adaptation by Philip Glassborow from the novel by Herman Melville

Good and evil go head-to-head in this seafaring tale set on a British warship in the 1700s. Billy Budd, Sailor, pits a cold-blooded, evil superior officer against the innocent goodness of a young sailor. Caught between the two men is Captain Vere—who must enforce justice for a crime committed on the high seas.

The Silver Chair

By C.S. Lewis, adaptation by Paul McCusker

In the fantastic land of Narnia, ordinary children do extraordinary things. Eustace and Jill never imagined that escaping from a gang of school bullies would lead them to Narnia—and an encounter with the Great Lion, Aslan. When Aslan sends them to search for the long-lost Prince Rillian, they begin an amazing journey of adventure and danger.

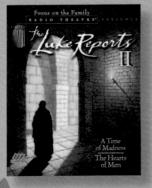

The Luke Reports II

By Paul McCusker

Driven to save the life of his friend Paul, Luke the Physician searches rebel-torn Judea to record the life and ministry of Jesus. But it's A Time of Madness, and before Luke realizes it, he is drawn into in a game of political intrigue and double crosses between Romans and Zealots.

Other titles available include:

- Ben-Hur
- Bonhoeffer: The Cost of Freedom
- Child of Promise: The First Chapter of the Luke Reports
- A Christmas Carol
- Chronicles of Narnia
- The Magician's Nephew
- The Lion, the Witch, and the Wardrobe
- The Horse and His Boy
- Prince Caspian
- The Voyage of the Dawn Treader
- Father Gilbert Mysteries
- The Legend of Squanto
- Les Miserables
- The Secret Garden
- Silas Marner

Did You Know?

You can go backstage and meet all the Focus on the Family Radio Theatre actors and producers at www.radiotheatre.org.

All of these titles are available on cassette at www.tyndale.com.

Adventures in Odyssey

Whit's End – An Actual
"Ice Cream Parlor and Discovery Emporium"

Are you a fan of the Adventures in Odyssey program? Have you ever wished you could enter the world of Odyssey—step through the front door of Whit's End itself? When Focus on the Family opened their Welcome Center in Colorado Springs, they devoted almost the entire basement to kids. They call it "Kids Korner." It is a great re-creation of Whit's End. Though it's not exactly the same as the place described in the radio show or seen in the videos, it is a truly unique place to visit.

There is the hustle and bustle of the kitchen crew, the sounds and smells of food being prepared, and an awesome example of great architecture and artwork. It's not tough to decide what to order at Whit's End—a WodFamChocSod, of course! That's World Famous Chocolate Soda, from the Odyssey episode "Our Best Vacation Ever." New on the menu: "Raspberry Ripple" right from the AIO episode "With a Little Help from My Friends." There were also a couple other items on the menu from the radio series.

One main attraction at Whit's End is a 3-story tube slide. Appropriately named "A-Bend-A-Go", it is described as "76-Feet of twisting, turning, bumpy fun!" Part of Kid's Korner is a re-creation of the diner and B-17 bomber from the "Last Chance Detectives" videos.

In the main lobby of the Welcome Center is an interactive multimedia gallery. There are many pictures, videos and displays. One of the displays runs a short clip of AIO Video 3: "A Fine Feathered Frenzy," and you can push buttons to add your own sound effects, then play back the clip, with your own sound effects added! Sometimes it's pretty hilarious. There's also a display of all the "McGee and Me" videos.

Whit's End – A Virtual
Visit to Adventures in Odyssey

There's wholesome entertainment, lots of fun, and always something to learn at Whit's End, the official Adventures in Odyssey web site. Get background information on the series, scripts and behind-the-scenes glimpses, and interactive activities.

You can listen to today's show on the internet, too. There's also a large collection of past episodes for online listening. Search by characters, writers, albums, original air date or key words. It's all at www.whitsend.org.

Tuning In

His Kids Radio
A Christian station for the young at heart 24/7.

His Kids Radio, sponsored by the Children's Sonshine Network, is available live, via Web audio stream. Enjoy your favorite programs such as "Adventure Time," "Keys for Kids," "Adventures in Odyssey," "Critter Country," "The Children's Bible Hour" and more. Kids may also subscribe to a newsletter. Tune in for family fun and faith—age doesn't matter here!

Check out the radio schedule at www.HisKidsRadio.net, then tune in live at any time and listen through your computer. The programming is also rebroadcast in some areas or beamed from the SkyAngel satellite system.

Down Gilead Lane

This popular kids' dramatic series comes from CBH Ministries (formerly known as Children's Bible Hour). Go behind the scenes, meet all the characters, listen in and more at www. cbh.gospelcom.net. You can also check out the coolest places in Coleraine. Be sure to visit The Zone for fun, games and community.

Every day is your chance to learn more about God's love by hearing Keys for Kids. Read a fun story and hide His Word in your heart with the Key of the day. Check out today's Key! Or, look for your favorite story in the archives! http://cbh.gospelcom.net/keys

American Inspirations Radio

These one-minute radio broadcasts feature a daily story of a different American hero, revealing his or her dependence on God and prayer as a source of strength, wisdom and peace. Find a station airing them near you or listen to a selection as MP3 files. http://pptkids.org/radio.php

Recreation

PLAY AROUND THE WORLD

Want some new games to play? Try out these games from around the world. Some will be brand-new to you. Others are probably a lot like games you've played before.

JERUSALEM OR JERICHO (COSTA RICA)

Everyone gets in a big circle and someone starts by shouting either "Jerusalem" or "Jericho." If they shout "Jerusalem," everyone remains standing, but if they yell "Jericho," everyone falls down. If you make a mistake, you're out of the circle.

O QUE VOA (BRAZIL)

Everyone gets in a circle and someone begins by asking a question such as, "Do birds fly?" If the answer is yes, everyone raises their arms and waves them around. But if the answer is no, they keep their arms tightly at their sides. If a player responds incorrectly, he or she is out.

PANJ SANG OR OJAMI (IRAN AND JAPAN)

Panj Sang, or Five Stones, is played with pebbles. You toss the pebbles up and then try to catch them on the back of your hand. You flip them again, trying to catch them in your palm. Then you toss a pebble in the air, and while it's still in the air, try to scoop another one up from the ground. In Japan, kids play Ojami, the same game using little beanbags instead of stones.

JEGEECHAGEE (SOUTH KOREA)

Boys especially like to play Jegeechagee (jay Gee cha Gee), Kick the Feather. They used to use real feathers with a small weight on the end. Now they use a special lightweight plastic toy. Kick the feather in the air and then just keep on kicking. If it hits the ground, you lose your turn.

FUN AND GAMES

Check out these fun games – have you played any of them?

The Book. Build character while brushing up on Bible trivia.

House Rules. In a fast-paced team game full of spills, upsets and unexpected twists, teams race against the clock to answer family-related questions and head up through the house.

Sticky Situations. Join McGee & Me to reinforce positive values and good decisions through surprise, laughter and exciting board game play.

WWJD? Kids constantly face situations where they must decide what Jesus would do. To win, they must make the right choices and gain Christian virtue.

The Great Adventure Game. Have fun building a foundation of faith playing this exciting, colorful game with a jungle adventure theme.
Link to all of the above at www.tyndale.com.

Settlers of Canaan is a biblically-based game that takes place in the territory of Canaan (Israel today). Each player represents a tribe of Israel seeking to settle the land of Canaan and build Jerusalem.
http://www.cactusgamedesign.com/board_games_settlers.htm)

One of the best-selling games in America is Timestream. They hold an annual tournament with Focus on the Family's *Breakaway* Magazine. Find out how to be part of a year-long tournament and more at www.cahabaproductions.com.

Things Kids Collect

Do you have a collection of some favorite thing? Here's a list of some of the most popular things kids your age collect.

Action figures
Autographs of famous people
Barbie dolls
Baseball cards
Beanie Babies
Birds' nests
Bottle caps
Buttons, badges, patches and pins
Butterflies
Chess sets
Comic books
Dolls and dollhouses
Dried flowers
Horse figurines
Hot Wheels cars
Insects
Keys
Leaves
Marbles
Matchbox cars
Models
Paper dolls
Postcards
Posters
Quarters from each of the 50 states
Rocks
Seashells
Snow globes
Stamps
Stickers
Teddy bears

Toy Trivia

1. The teddy bear, which was first made in 1902, was named after President Theodore Roosevelt.

2. The Raggedy Ann doll was named after the comic-strip character Little Orphan Annie.

3. Roller skates, which were first patented in 1863 by James Plimpton, became popular in the 1860s.

4. Silly Putty was first created by General Electric as a substitute for rubber, but it was found to have no industrial uses, so it was marketed as a toy instead.

5. The Frisbee flying disc was named after the Frisbee Company of Bridgeport, Connecticut, which manufactured pie plates. (The flying disc got its start as a toy when someone noticed that college kids liked tossing the plates to one another for fun.)

6. Mattel produced the first Barbie doll in 1958. By 1980 she had become so popular that her clothes were designed by a top New York fashion designer.

7. The hula hoop is known to be the greatest toy fad in history. When it was first made in the 1950s, it sold twenty million in the first year.

8. The yo-yo got its start as a weapon used by Philippine Island warriors in the sixteenth century. Their yo-yo was a four-pound sphere with a twenty-foot cord. The first toy version appeared in the United States in 1929.

9. Dominos were created by French monks. They named it after the first line of Psalm 110, which in Latin reads, "Dixit Dom-inus meo" ("The Lord said to my Lord").

10. Each year the Parker Brothers Company prints more play money for their Monopoly game than the U.S. Mint prints real money.

MAKE A GAME OF IT

o or more kids can have fun learning Bible concepts or verses by adding
estions to an existing game. Before each turn, take a question card.

ad a Bible portion together, and discuss its meaning. Then two "teams" make
questions to ask of each other. For more fun, include some statements such
, "Extra move for right answer," or, "Back to home for wrong answer." Mix in a
good and bad "wild cards."

ake about 20 new questions for each game, and include Bible references. When
layer misses, he must look up the answer and read it aloud. Shuffling used
rds into the playing pile gives motivation to remember the answer.

ese examples of students' games will give you some idea starters.

- Using Jeopardy, let the category and amount chosen determine the difficulty of questions.

- Guess what product Jonopoly adapted, converting money to biblical terms and allocating portions of the playing board to Scripture passages?

- Using Twister, provide two dials, one to select a Bible question, the other to designate what part of one's anatomy goes on the mat.

- Proverbs Parcheesi arranges the book of Proverbs into 10 categories of questions, selectable by spinner. A correct answer allows the player's piece to be moved that many spaces. Leviticus Parcheesi's board is designed after the Old Testament Tabernacle layout.

- John-O adapts Rack-o to learn the words of a verse or Bible event in order.

- Make new cards with Bible terms for Password by putting red highlight or Xs over black letters. The red window of the game sleeve masks the red overmarking.

- Assign a topic or number to each of the nine squares of Tick-Tack-Toe with corresponding questions to answer before placing an X or 0.

- Make questions for each chess piece.

- As questions are asked of the whole group, Saved players may only cover a square if it contains the answer. (Adapted from Bingo)

Most electronic or computer games designed for more than one player can be adapted to a fun Bible learning activity by adding questions.

Bibletime Kids Played, Too

The Bible doesn't say much about what children played in those times. But, a few references give brief insights into the subject, and verify the fact that even in biblical times children had fun times, as well as work times.

Job said, "they send forth their children as a flock—their little ones dance about" (Job 21:11, 12). Zechariah said that boys and girls will play in the "city streets" (Zechariah 8:5).

Jesus remarked on children's games of imitation in the marketplaces in which they first playacted a wedding and then quickly changed to playact a funeral (Matthew 11:16-17; Luke 7:32).

Because of the agricultural economy in which they lived, most Israeli children soon developed skills relating to outdoor life, including hunting, fishing and using the slingshot and bow and arrows. David illustrates his skill with a sling against Goliath (1 Samuel 17). And his friend Jonathan was good at archery (1 Samuel 20:20). The fact that David's skillful warriors could shoot arrows or toss stones from a sling with either the right hand or the left (1 Chronicles 12:2) meant they had developed those skills earlier, perhaps as young boys.

Some children and young people also developed musical skills. The children who Jesus said acted out weddings in their playtime "played the flute" (Matthew 11:17 NIV). David's

skill on the harp helped him sooth King Saul (1 Samuel 16:23 NIV). That young people played musical instruments is clear from Lamentations 5:14, which speaks of the young men stopping their music.

Some kids had pets in those days. In a parable told to David, Nathan spoke of a poor man who bought a little ewe lamb that "grew up with him and his children" (2 Samuel 12:3). A Canaanite woman talking with Jesus referred to dogs eating crumbs from a table (Matthew 15:27).

Toys used by young children in Mesopotamia, Egypt and in the Greco-Roman Empire may also have been played with by Israelite children. Rattles, whistles, toys, teeter-totters, hoops, clay animals, dolls, toy dishes, knucklebones (a game something like jacks), kites, pull toys, a form of checkers, chess (played in Babylon before 2000 B.C.), swings, marbles, dice, yo-yos, balls, a stick with two small wheels and even small chariots drawn by a donkey or a goat have been found by archaeologists. Models of furniture were perhaps used in ancient dollhouses.

In ancient Athens, children played "hide-and-seek, tug-of-war, blindman's bluff, trick or treat, ducks and drakes, and jackstones." Boys learned archery, horseback riding, swimming, boating, disc throwing, javelin throwing, boxing, wrestling and fencing.

Religions

RELIGIONS AROUND THE WORLD
The Big 5

Christianity has the most followers among the world's major religions (so-called because of their size). Of course, not all who profess to hold certain religious beliefs actually practice that religion.

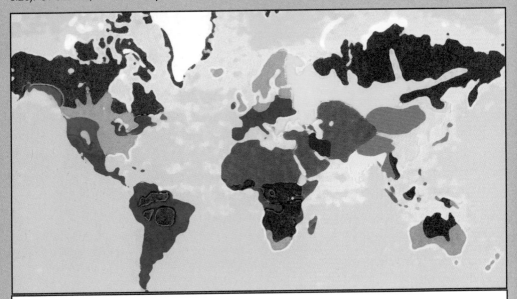

Religion	Members	Center	Leader	Sacred book(s)
Christianity	1.9 billion	Jerusalem, Israel	Jesus Christ	The Bible
Roman Catholic	1 billion	Vatican City, Italy	Pope	The Bible
Protestant	383 million		Jesus Christ	The Bible
Other (mixed)	343 million		Jesus Christ	The Bible
Eastern Orthodox	174 million	Istanbul, Turkey	Patriarch	The Bible
Islam	1.1 billion	Mecca, Saudi Arabia	Muhammad	The Koran
Hinduism	752 million	India (7 sacred cities)		The Vedas
Judaism	18 million	Jerusalem, Israel	Abraham, Moses	The Old Testament
(Native)				

THE APOSTLE'S CREED

A creed summarizes basic beliefs. The Apostles' Creed is one of the oldest.

I believe in God, the Father Almighty, the Creator of heaven and earth, and in Jesus Christ, His only Son, our Lord: Who was conceived of the Holy Spirit, born of the Virgin Mary, suffered under Pontius Pilate, was crucified, died, and was buried. He descended into hell. The third day He arose again from the dead. He ascended into heaven and sits at the right hand of God the Father Almighty, whence He shall come to judge the living and the dead. I believe in the Holy Spirit, the holy catholic church, the communion of saints, the forgiveness of sins, the resurrection of the body, and life everlasting. Amen.
(The word "catholic" refers to the universal church, not to the Roman Catholic Church.)

THE NICENE CREED

The Church Council at Nicea in A.D. 325 adopted a more complete statement of doctrine known as the Nicene Creed.

I believe in one God, the Father Almighty, maker of heaven and earth, and of all things visible and invisible; And in one Lord Jesus Christ, the only begotten Son of God, begotten of his Father before all worlds, God of God, Light of Light, very God of very God, begotten, not made, being of one substance with the Father; by whom all things were made; who for us men and for our salvation came down from heaven, and was incarnate by the Holy Ghost of the Virgin Mary, and was made man; and was crucified also for us under Pontius Pilate; he suffered and was buried; and the third day he rose again according to the Scriptures, and ascended into heaven, and sitteth on the right hand of the Father; and he shall come again, with glory, to judge both the quick and the dead; whose kingdom shall have no end. And I believe in the Holy Ghost the Lord, and Giver of Life, who proceedeth from the Father [and the Son]; who with the Father and the Son together is worshipped and glorified; who spake by the Prophets. And I believe one holy Catholic and Apostolic Church; I acknowledge one baptism for the remission of sins; and I look for the resurrection of the dead, and the life of the world to come. AMEN.

SATURDAY, SUNDAY, SABBATH

Jewish kids don't have to do any chores on Saturday. God said so.

The fourth of the Ten Commandments says, "Remember to observe the Sabbath day by keeping it holy" (Exodus 20:8 NLT). This weekly holiday began at sundown each Friday and ended at sundown on Saturday. It was a day of physical and spiritual renewal. Shops were closed; trade was forbidden.

This command got the longest explanation of the top 10. "Six days a week are set apart for your daily duties and regular work, but the seventh day is a day of rest dedicated to the Lord your God. On that day no one in your household may do any kind of work.... For in six days the Lord made the heavens, the earth, the sea, and everything in them; then he rested on the seventh day. That is why the Lord blessed the Sabbath day and set it apart as holy" (Exodus 20:9-11 NLT).

Sabbath Do's and Don't's

• DO use Friday afternoon to finish up your week's work. Women, do your cleaning, refill your lamps, prepare your meals in advance, do your laundry.

• DON'T do any kind of work on the Sabbath. Cooking, baking, beating with a hammer, lighting a fire, writing two letters, tying certain kinds of knots, or even helping injured persons, unless their lives are in danger, is NOT allowed.

• DON'T forget Friday evening prayer. Three sharp blasts of a ram's horn will signal the start of the Sabbath and prayer.

• DO have a special meal with your family after the service (prepared the night before). Recite the Kiddush—a special blessing said over the wine.

• DO attend a special service Saturday morning—more prayer and Scripture readings.

Sabbath Setbacks

In 168 BC 1,000 Jewish soldiers were killed because they wouldn't defile the Sabbath defending themselves in combat. Later, they decided that defensive action (only) was acceptable.

In 63 BC the Romans conquered Jerusalem because Jews were not permitted to destroy siege works on the Sabbath.

By the time Jesus came, the Jews had hundreds of laws about the Sabbath.

A Sabbath Day's journey was 2,000 paces or less than half a mile—the maximum distance Jews were allowed to travel on the Sabbath. But they could set out provisions every 1/2 mile ahead of time. Then they were allowed to go from one "home" to another on the Sabbath.

FROM GOD TO US

GOD

REVELATION
God makes Himself known in many ways
He spoke directly with Adam and Eve. Creation is God's handiwork. He also made Himself known through angels, prophets and miracles.

INSPIRATION
Bible portions are written with God's authority
God guided the Bible writers to record his words. "All Scripture is inspired by God" (2 Timothy 3:16 NLT) "It was the Holy Spirit who moved the prophets to speak from God" (2 Peter 1:21 NLT)

RECOGNITION
Scripture is accepted by people as divine
Individual Bible books were treasured and protected as sacred. They were read aloud as God's words.

COLLECTION
Bible books are collected into one volume
As new books were written, they were accepted as inspired and added to the Bible.

PRESERVATION
Scripture is faithfully copied for distribution
Since there were no printing presses, computers or Internet, the Bible was carefully copied by hand.

TRANSLATION
The Bible is put into other languages
Originally written in Hebrew, Greek and Aramaic, Scripture is still being translated into all the languages of the world.

MEDITATION
We read and study the Bible
"Be a good worker...one who correctly explains the word of truth" (2 Timothy 2:15 NLT)

ILLUMINATION
The Holy Spirit helps us understand the Bible
"When the Spirit of truth comes, he will guide you into all truth" (John 16:13).

APPLICATION TO US
We base our beliefs and behavior on the Bible
"All Scripture...is useful to teach us what is true and to make us realize what is wrong in our lives. It straightens us out and teaches us to do what is right" (2 Timothy 3:16).

Sports

First Presidential Little Leaguer

President George W. Bush is the first Little League graduate to win election to the highest office in the land.

As a young boy, George played on the Midland (Texas) Cubs team for several years in the 1950s. His parents, George and Barbara Bush, were volunteers in the league during those years. President Bush once told Oprah Winfrey that playing in Little League was his fondest childhood memory.

In 1955. his father wrote in a letter, "Georgie aggravates me at times. I am sure that I do the same to him. But then at times I am so proud of him I could die. He is out for Little League, so eager. He tries so very hard. He has good, fast hands and even seems to be able to hit a little."

In a letter to the Little League Association, the former president said: "Little League has, indeed, been a big part of (George W.'s) life. To say we are proud of George W. is the classic understatement of the year."

Frank Ittner, young George's coach from 1955 until 1958, once reminisced that "He was a good catcher, and you could always rely on him to be there for every game and every practice. He was very dependable."

Before being elected Governor of Texas, Mr. Bush was a managing partner for a Major League baseball team, the Texas Rangers.

President Bush has continued a tradition begun by President William Howard Taft on April 14, 1910—throwing out the first pitch of the Major League season.

On August 26, 2001, President Bush was enshrined in the Little League Museum Hall of Excellence during a ceremony at the Little League Baseball World Series in Williamsport, Pennsylvania.

In keeping with his life long love of baseball, Mr. Bush began a tradition of holding Tee Ball games on the South Lawn of the White House. Every player on both teams plays on defense and bats once. The one-inning game is followed by a picnic for players and families. A baseball autographed by President George W. Bush is presented to each player.

Did You Know?

Over 30 million kids have played in Little League since Carl Stotz began the program in Williamsport, Pennsylvania, in June, 1939.

National Little League Week is always the second week of June.

For more about baseball at the White House, see www.whitehouse.gov/kids/baseball.

Little League's interesting site is www.littleleague.org.

The Amazing Blake and His Brother Tyler

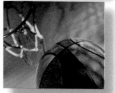

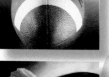
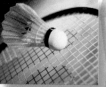

"Having a younger brother with Downs Syndrome has taught me to accept and appreciate the differences in people," says young Tyler Peacock. "Everyone has value. People with disabilities are awesome. I've been around them all my life and I've enjoyed volunteering for Special Olympics since I was eight years old."

Ever since they were in elementary school, Tyler has been a great older brother, protecting his young brother, Blake, from anyone who tried to torment him. One day a group of kids, who didn't know Blake, started picking on him. Tyler happened to come along, and no one in the group knew that Blake was his brother.

"I told them to cut it out," Tyler says. "Then I told them how cool Blake is, that even though he has Downs Syndrome he can do a lot of things and is pretty much like everybody else. When I told them that he plays in the high school band, does gymnastics, performs in theater productions, is a student helper at church and on and on, they were amazed."

The amazing Blake even competed in snowshoeing at the 2001 Special Olympics World Winter Games in Anchorage, Alaska. The whole family showed up to cheer him on. And Blake, a big fan of Tyler's, always shows up at Tyler's hockey and baseball games.

"We shouldn't label or segregate people just because they look or talk differently," says Tyler. "People with disabilities can accomplish great things if they have the chance, and we can learn from them, too."

Did You Know?

Special Olympics offers kids with mental retardation year-round training and competition in 26 Olympic-type summer and winter sports. There is no charge to participate.

Over a million persons in 150 countries are currently involved in Special Olympics programs. That number is expected to double by 2005.

To meet other special olympians or find a program near you, visit www. specialolympics.org.

SPORTS SPECTRUM

Get a Christian perspective on sports from the Sports Spectrum trifecta.

SPORTS SPECTRUM IN PRINT

Each colorful bi-monthly issue of *Sports Spectrum* Magazine tells you about the good guys in sports. Included is a pull-out 16-page weekday sports devotional guide called Power Up!

SPORTS SPECTRUM ON THE RADIO

Every Saturday for 55 minutes (beginning at noon Eastern time) Sports Spectrum sponsors an interactive radio program hosted by Chuck Swirsky, the radio play-by-play voice of the Toronto Raptors. You can call in and talk sports, or just sit back and listen to Chuck and his impressive array of sports-related guests. A station locator is on their web site, or listen live online. www.sport.org.

SPORTS SPECTRUM ON THE INTERNET

The Sports Spectrum site in cyberspace is a great way to get up-to-date info on the day in sports. Hot Corner comments on the day's happenings. You'll also get the Verse of the Day, Quote of the Day, a daily devotional, articles from the magazine and lots of new stuff. Log on at www.sport.org! Sign up for the daily update, "Hot Corner."

 Did You Know?

Other sports sites to visit:
Athletes in Action www.athletesinaction.org
CBS Sportsline for Kids cbs.sportsline.com/u/kidszone
Fellowship of Christian Athletes www.fca.org
Special Olympics www.specialolympics.org

Current Christian Athletes

Did you ever hear someone say that Christians aren't tough enough to make it in the "big leagues"? Mention some of these famous CHRISTIAN athletes.

Garret Anderson
(World Series champion, 2002)

Barb Lindquist
(top American triathlete, 2002)

Lance Berkman
(NL Leader, RBI, 2002)

David Carr
(No. 1 NFL draft pick, 2002)

John Smoltz
(National League, Rolaids Relief Award, 2002)

Krissie Wendell
(USA Hockey Women's Player of the Year, 2001)

Rich Gannon
(NFL MVP, 2002)

Markus Naslund
(leading goal scorer, NHL, 2002-2003)

David Robinson
(NBA MVP, 1995; NBA champion, 1999)

Kurt Warner
(NFL MVP, 1999)

To read more about the lives and legacies of any of these greats, enter his or her name into the Site Search at http://www.christianitytoday.com/sports

Angkor, Cambodia

The sprawling temples of Angkor remain "the largest ruins in Southeast Asia and one of the great wonders of the world."

Historic Center of Prague, Czech Republic

Loaded with 600 years of "incredibly beautiful architecture," this vibrant city center is one of the few in Europe undamaged by war. "It's an almost fairy-tale kind of place."

Everglades National Park, Florida

This famous "river of grass" is still a "magical place" providing sanctuary for birds, reptiles and the endangered manatee. The largest subtropical wilderness in North America, it's also quite accessible.

Maya Site of Copan, Honduras

These ruins of one of the largest Mayan cities "mesmerize anyone who visits," in part because "we don't know what happened. The (people) just disappeared." The site includes a citadel and three "absolutely beautiful" public squares.

Meteora, Greece

Perched on rock formations 1,000 feet above the plains of northern Greece, this 700-year-old monastic community is a little-known gem in one of the world's most visited countries. "You have to climb a lot of steps."

Belize Barrier Reef Reserve System, Belize

The largest barrier reef in the Northern Hemisphere explodes with "colors so remarkable you want to rub your eyes." The system's seven sites include offshore atolls, sand cays, mangrove forests, coastal lagoons and estuaries.

Be Awed Heritage

THE SUN TEMPLE, KONARAK, INDIA

In one of India's most famous sanctuaries, the sun god's chariot "leaves people stammering when they talk about it." Built in the 13th century, the chariot has 24 decorated wheels and is led by a team of six sculpted horses.

GALAPAGOS ISLANDS, PACIFIC OCEAN

Six hundred miles from Latin America, it's a "living museum" where each of 19 islands offers something different. "You'll see animals you won't see anywhere else," such as the land iguana and the giant tortoise.

MONT-SAINT-MICHEL, FRANCE

Perched on a rocky islet off the French shoreline, this Gothic-style Benedictine abbey "is the perfect example of art coexisting with nature." Built between the 11th and 16th centuries, "it's just beautiful," a technological and artistic tour de force.

NGORONGORO CONSERVATION AREA, UNITED REPUBLIC OF TANZANIA

The conservation area, including an extinct volcanic crater, is home to 25,000 large animals, including zebras, wildebeest, black rhino and lions. "It's one of the great places to see game on an African safari." The area also is an archeological gold mine.

Did You Know?

The United Nations' World Heritage List of 730 sites records the world's most important natural and cultural places. "They're the best of the best," says Bernard Ohanian, an editor at *National Geographic*. http://whc.unesco.org/heritage.htm

Turning Leaps into Bounds

Hayes Paschal, 16, stops traffic when he jogs through his neighborhood.

He covers ground the way a deer would, leaping half a car length at a time, overtaking pedestrians and disappearing down a street so quickly that breathless onlookers can't be sure what just passed by.

Paschal's super-powered athleticism comes via a pair of Powerisers that are strapped to his feet. Described as jumping stilts, they're made of fiberglass springs shaped as long, narrow arcs. Each spring is attached to the body with foot straps and an aluminum leg brace with knee pads.

With his Powerisers on, Paschal stands 18 inches taller than usual and can jump as high as six feet and leap as far as nine feet. Paschal first saw Powerisers advertised on TV. "Ten or 15 people were running across a stage flipping and jumping high, and I liked it right off," he said. "It seemed like the coolest thing in the world."

He bought a pair and takes them out two or three times a week for trips around his Memphis neighborhood. "It feels close to flying," he said. "You're going pretty fast, and you're off the ground a lot." Walking on them is "not at all like walking regularly. They're like stilts on a trampoline—real springy."

See more user stories and photos at www.superdairyboy.com.

Segway Scooter

People looking for an easier way to travel short distances are thrilled about the Segway Human Transporter. Invented by millionaire Dean Kamon, the scooter is a two-wheeler that travels up to 17 miles an hour. It weighs 65 to 80 pounds and costs up to $8,000. Kamon says it will change the way we travel. The Segway has no pedals, gears or motor. "It acts as an extension of your body," Kamon says. The Segway's sensors can tell which way its rider wants to go just by the way the rider leans. Riders can't fall off! So how does it work? All the details are at www.segway.com.

Skittle's Saga

"Skittles" skedaddled. The 2-year-old orange tabby cat disappeared while his family was on summer vacation in southern Wisconsin.

"We called him and called him," said 16-year-old Jason Sampson. "We just couldn't find him." The Sampsons reluctantly returned home to Minnesota just before Labor Day, minus Skittles.

But on January 14 came a surprise. Skittles just strolled up to the front door of the Sampson's home with raw paws and protruding ribs—140 days later! The cat came back—traveling 350 miles home from one state to another.

Jason told The Associated Press that after his long journey, Skittles now seems to be fully recovered. He is back to snoozing in the living-room armchair and playing with his feline friend, Yum-Yum.

Operation Migration

Whooping cranes are one of America's best-known and rarest endangered species. These five-foot-tall birds are white with black wing tips and a red patch on top of their heads. There are only about 400 left, and too many breed in the same place in winter. To avoid disease and other dangers they needed to have another breeding place.

Half the group of 2003 Whoop... return journey - Cranes 1. 3.

A group called Operation Migration tried an experiment to help cranes breed. They used an ultralight aircraft to guide 11 sandhill cranes from Wisconsin to a wildlife refuge in Florida for the winter. The pilot wore a crane disguise, and the birds learned to follow the aircraft as they would follow their own parents. The plan worked. In October 2001, seven whooping cranes made the same trip. Forty-eight days and 1,218 miles later, they got to Florida. In April 2002, the five birds who survived flew back to Wisconsin. Operation Migration's goal is to have 125 birds in this flock by the year 2020. Read more about this project at www.operationmigration.org.

Did You Know?

Did Operation Migration get the concept of using an ultralight from a 13-year-old girl? Anna Paquin starred in the soaring adventure film Fly Away Home (Sony Pictures 1996). She and her estranged father adopted an orphaned flock of geese and taught them to fly! The adventure is available on VHS/DVD. www.sonypictures.com

Vacation

Best Parks

Top Fourteen Amusement Parks

Epcot, Lake Buena Vista, Florida
www.disneyworld.com

Disney-MGM Studios, Lake Buena Vista, Florida
www.disneyworld.com

Magic Kingdom, Lake Buena Vista, Florida
www.disneyworld.com

Sea World, Orlando, Florida
www.seaworld.com

Universal's Islands of Adventure, Orlando, Florida
www.universalstudios.com

SeaWorld, San Diego, California
www.seaworld.com

Disney's Animal Kingdom, Lake Buena Vista, Florida
www.disneyworld.com

Disneyland, Anaheim, California
www.disneyland.com

Cedar Point, Sandusky, Ohio
www.cedarpoint.com

Busch Gardens, Tampa Bay, Florida
www.buschgardens.com

Universal Studios, Orlando, Florida
www.universalstudios.com

Knott's Berry Farm, Buena Park, California
www.knottsberryfarm.com

Universal Studios Hollywood, Universal City, California
www.universalstudios.com

Disney's California Adventure, Anaheim, California
www.disneyland.com

for Kids

Top Ten National Parks

Glacier National Park, Montana
www.nps.gov/glac

Carlsbad Caverns National Park, New Mexico
www.nps.gov/cave

Yellowstone National Park, Wyoming
www.nps.gov/yell/

Sequoia & Kings Canyon National Park, California
www.nps.gov/seki

Hawaii Volcanoes National Park
www.nps.gov/havo/

Grand Canyon National Park, Arizona
www.nps.gov/grca

Everglades National Park, Florida
www.nps.gov/ever

Rocky Mountain National Park, Colorado
www.nps.gov/romo

Olympic National Park, Washington
www.nps.gov/olym

Mesa Verde National Park, Colorado
www.nps.gov/meve

Did You Know?

Link to all the national parks at www.nps.gov.

One of the most unusual and fascinating national parks is an isolated prison—Alcatraz Island in the middle of the San Francisco Bay. Check out the Rock at www.nps.gov.

Top Ten Cruises for KIDS

One professional cruise critic picked the best cruises for kids based on activities and facilities.

1. Disney Magic/Wonder (Disney)
Number one in a league of its own. www.disneycruise.com

As you might expect, the Disney fleet has the most creative play space on any cruise ship. Only Disney can take kid cruisers on a daily voyage to a world devoted to fun and fantasy. Your magical cruise on one of the largest, best-equipped-for-kids ships afloat will be four or seven of the fastest, most fun days of your life. Guaranteed!

Mix with all your favorite Disney characters. Eat in a restaurant with animated walls and ceilings. Enjoy pool and deck games with kids your age. Catch all the Disney flicks and be awed by the live full-scale theater productions.

The day spent on Disney's private island, Castaway Cay (pronounced "key") gets raves from tween snorkelers, surfers and sunners. Walk off your floating castle onto your private beach with everything you could possibly want.

On board, Disney's Oceaneer Lab offers age-specific activities guaranteed to transport young minds to the edge of their imagination. Choose from dozens of activities such as making your own "Flubber-like Goo," learning how to draw and animate Disney characters, or playing a role in producing TV spots. The results are hilarious!

See 360-degree onboard photos you can zoom and rotate or watch a QuickTime movie at www.disneycruise.com.

Read more about the other nine top choices at www.cruisecritic.com.

2. Voyager/Explorer/Adventure of the Seas (Royal Caribbean) www.royalcaribbean.com

3. Golden/Grand Princess (Princess) www.princesscruises.com

4. Carnival Triumph, Destiny and Carnival Victory (Carnival) www.carnival.com

5. Ocean/Sun/Dawn/Sea Princess (Princess)

6. Paradise (Carnival)

7. Radiance of the Seas (Royal Caribbean)

8. Maasdam (Holland America) www.hollandamerica.com

Did You Know?

A family cruise is an incredible bargain compared to what it would cost for similar entertainment, food, lodging and transportation on land.

Nearly 1 million children cruised in 2002, twice the 1998 number.

The Largest Zoos In America

San Diego Wild Animal Park, San Diego, California
(2,200 acres) www.sandiegozoo.org

Minnesota Zoo, Apple Valley, Minnesota
(500 acres) www.mnzoo.com

Columbus Zoo and Aquarium, Powell, Ohio
(404 acres) www.colszoo.org

Miami Metrozoo, Miami, Florida
(300 acres) www.zsf.org

Bronx Zoo, New York City
(265 acres) www.bronxzoo.com

The Most-Visited Zoos In America

San Diego Zoo, San Diego, California
(3.5 million*) www.sandiegozoo.org

National Zoo, Washington, D.C.
(3 million) www.natzoo.si.edu

Lincoln Park Zoo, Chicago, Illinois
(3 million) free admission! www.lpzoo.com

St. Louis Zoo, St. Louis, Missouri
(2.9 million) www.stlzoo.org

Bronx Zoo, New York City
(2.2 million) www.bronxzoo.com

Denver Zoo, Denver, Colorado
(1.7 million) www.denverzoo.org

(*annual attendance)

Did You Know?

A virtual visit to any of these zoos is fun. Link to all the zoos in America at www.aza.org or to great zoos around the world at www.zooish.com.

There are currently over 1,500 zoos worldwide. Based on the most animals housed in a zoo, the largest zoos in the world are the Berlin Zoo (13,000), the New York Bronx Zoo (6,000), the San Diego Zoo (4,000) and the Pretoria Zoo (3,500).

The Vienna Zoo is the oldest zoo in the world (from 1752) and has kept over 35 elephants since 1772. The next oldest zoos are the London Zoo (1828) and the Berlin Zoo (1841). The oldest zoo in the United States is the Philadelphia Zoo, which was opened on July 1, 1874. The Cincinnati Zoo opened in 1875 and the Bronx Zoo opened in 1889.

SUPERCROC IN DINOSPHERE

As long as a city bus and weighing in at about 10 tons, "SuperCroc" lives up to its nickname. Sarcosuchus imperator, or "flesh crocodile emperor." Sarcosuchus didn't walk with the dinosaurs; it ate them for dinner!

Imagine walking through a forest during the Cretaceous period. You brush aside prehistoric plants that block your path. The air is humid and smells of rain. Suddenly, the ground trembles beneath your feet and you hear an ear-splitting roar. And find yourself face-to-face with SuperCroc!!

This is just one of the experiences you may have at the $25 million Dinosphere exhibit at The Children's Museum of Indianapolis. The museum's most thrilling and dramatic exhibit to date, Dinosphere provides an incredible experience as you explore the Cretaceous world of dinosaurs. The exhibit features the largest collection of real juvenile dinosaur fossils in the United States.

Get a sneak preview of the dinos and see how their bones are preserved at www.childrensmuseum.org/dinosphere/index.htm. SuperCroc is currently on display and will be moved to his new Dinosphere home. The PaleoPrep Lab is also open.

The Children's Museum of Indianapolis is a giant, 356,000-square-foot facility on 13 acres that houses 10 major galleries. Every year approximately 1.2 million people come to experience the wide variety of kid-friendly exhibits.

Some permanent exhibits include SpaceQuest Planetarium, Passport to the World, Indianapolis 500 Mile Race Car and Mysteries in History. The 310-seat CineDome theater features a 76-foot-high domed screen. The games and activities on their web site are excellent. Don't miss the Arts Workshop and Birthdays Around the World online. www.childrensmuseum.org

Tripping with Words

How many of these winning words could you spell correctly after hearing them pronounced? These are all the championship words in the National Spelling Bee from 1925 to 2003. (How many of these words can you define?)

To play during travel, give this list to a quizmaster. And take a dictionary along. How many Spelling Bees would you have won? Each correct spelling is worth a $12,000 scholarship. Double the score for any you can also define. What are your total winnings?

abalone	fibranne	psoriasis
abrogate	foulard	psychiatry
albumen	fracas	Purim
antediluvian	gladiolus	ratoon
antipyretic	hydrophyte	sacrilegious
asceticism	incisor	sanitarium
canonical	initials	sarcophagus
catamaran	insouciant	semaphore
chiaroscurist	intelligible	shalloon
Chihuahua	interlocutory	smaragdine
chlorophyll	interning	soubrette
condominium	kamikaze	spoliator
croissant	knack	staphylococci
crustaceology	logorrhea	succedaneum
deification	luge	sycophant
demarche	luxuriance	syllepsis
deteriorating	lyceum	therapy
dulcimer	macerate	torsion
eczema	maculature	transept
elegiacal	meticulosity	vignette
elucubrate	milieu	vivisepulture
equipage	narcolepsy	vouchsafe
eudaemonic	prospicience	xanthosis

Did You Know?

Boredom Blasters by Susan Todd (E F Communications) gives you a lot of reasons to stop asking, "When will we get there?" It's packed with hours and miles of games to make time fly on a trip. The 77 travel games, creativity games, word and language skills, and thinking games are all designed to be used in confined spaces. There's jokes and riddles, too. ("Why didn't the boy get hurt when the bottle of root beer fell on his head? It was a soft drink").

327

10 Great Places to Watch Stuff Being Made

Harley-Davidson Motor Co., York, PA
Watch the assembly of these legendary motorcycles as you travel overhead by conveyor. Free. Freebies: fan magazine and catalog. 877-746-7937; www.harley-davidson.com

Basic Brown Bear Factory, San Francisco, CA
See how teddy bears are born and learn how to stuff your own bear with air and polyester. Free (optional stuffing activity: $12 to $300). No freebies. 800-554-1910; www.basicbrownbear.com

Jelly Belly Candy Co., Fairfield, CA
"See a sea of jelly bean colors along with Jelly Belly mosaic portraits of famous faces and figures, such as Ronald Reagan and the Statue of Liberty, each made of 14,000 of the famous candies." Free. Freebies: Bag of Jelly Belly beans with color menu. 800-522-3267; www.jellybelly.com

Toyota, Georgetown, KY
At the largest Toyota plant outside of Japan, "ride on a tram to get a close-up view of flying sparks as computer-controlled robots weld vehicles' body shells." Free. Freebies: Toyota vehicle magnet. 800-866-4485; www.toyotageorgetown.com

Boeing, Everett, WA
"From a third-story walkway, visitors can oversee the airplane assembly areas in the world's largest building (11 stories high, covering 98 acres)." Small charge. Freebies: brochure. 800-464-1476; www.boeing.com

Fenton Art Glass, Williamstown, WV
"Walk onto the factory floor as glassblowers perform their art. The tour takes you from the extreme heat and speed of the glassmaking shops to the decorating area's quiet calm." Free. Freebies: glassmaking brochure. 800-319-7793; www.fentongiftshop.com

Celestial Seasonings, Boulder, CO

"At the corner of Sleepytime Drive and Zinger Street (the company's two best-selling teas) is America's largest herbal tea manufacturer." Learn about the origins of tea, see how it's put into little bags and smell the intense aroma in the mint room." Free. Freebies: samples of any or all iced or hot flavors at the tea bar. 303-581-1202; www.celestialseasonings.com

Herr's Snack Factory, Nottingham, PA

Herr's produces tens of thousands of snack foods daily. See smart machines sense and discard discolored potato chips). Savor warm potato chips right off the production line. Free. Freebies: warm chips during the tour and sample bag. 800-637-6225; www.herrs.com

Hillerich & Bradsby, Louisville, KY

See Northern white ash billets turned into the famous Louisville Slugger bats. "Watch the sizzle and smoke as the famous oval trademark is seared into the wood bat." At the Louisville Slugger Museum, see the world's biggest baseball bat, 120 feet tall weighing 68,000 pounds. Small charge. Freebies: 16-inch miniature wood bat. 502-588-7228; www.sluggermuseum.org

Ben & Jerry's, Waterbury, VT

"Learn how Ben Cohen and Jerry Greenfield started this offbeat, successful company with a social mission from a $5 correspondence course on ice-cream making." Small charge. Freebies: two ice cream samples and a button. 866-258-6877; www.benjerry.com

Did You Know?

Great factory tours are available from hundreds of companies in many states. Find out where in Watch It Made in the U.S.A.: A Visitor's Guide to the Companies That Make Your Favorite Products (Avalon Travel).

Bat photo By Sam Upshaw,
The Courier Journal

5 Places I Would Like to go on Vacation

1.

2.

3.

4.

5.

My Favorite Vacation was...

_____
_____
_____
_____
_____
_____
_____
_____

Vacation Memories

_____
_____
_____
_____
_____
_____
_____

ANSWERS

Angels

Page 20: They Saw Angels

Angel dust, Angel Falls, angelfish, angel food cake, angel hair, angelica, angel of death, angel shark, angel's-trumpet, archangel, California Angels, guardian angels, Los Angeles (Spanish for "city of angels")

Animals

Page 24: Animal Alphabet

ant	68	elephant	50
antelope	30	falcon	18
ape	87	ferret	69
badger	19	fish	63
bear	23	fly	47
beaver	28	fox	86
bee	24	frog	10
beetle	34	giraffe	3
buffalo	25	goat	66
butterfly	71	goldfish	77
camel	13	goose	76
cat	73	grasshopper	35
caterpillar	85	hare	79
cattle	75	hawk	37
chicken	36	hippopotamus	17
crocodile	33	horse	26
deer	65	ibex	64
dog	74	ibis	14
donkey	12	iguana	20
dove	4	jackal	89
dragon	5	ladybug	41
dragonfly	16	lamb	72
duck	46	lapwing	58
eagle	39	leopard	55

lion 9	ram 8
lizard 61	rhinoceros 53
locust 29	seagull 44
mole 88	sheep 7
monkey 54	skunk 81
moose 51	snail 59
mosquito 31	snake 49
mountain goat 57	spider 27
mouse 15	squirrel 80
mule 70	stork 43
nighthawk 52	swallow 38
opossum 2	swan 48
ostrich 56	turtle 82
owl 48	unicorn 60
partridge 11	vulture 45
peacock 83	whale 6
pelican 78	wolf 32
pig 67	worm 21
quail 11	yellowbird 62
rabbit 22	zebra 1

Page 29: Missing Creatures

1. lion (Revelation 5:5-6; Proverbs 28:1; 1 Peter 5:8; Ezekiel 22:25).
2. fox (Luke 13:31-32).
3. lamb or goat (Exodus 12:5, 7).
4. wolves, sheep (Matthew 7:15).
5. locusts (Matthew 3:4).
6. ant (Proverbs 6:6-8).
7. bear (1 Samuel 17:34-37).
8. snakes, doves (Matthew 10:16).
9. hen (Matthew 23:37).
10. livestock (horses, donkeys, camels, cattle, sheep, goats; Exodus 9:3, 6).
11. sheep (Psalm 100:3).
12. serpent (Genesis 3:1).
13. quail (Exodus 16:12-13).
14. camel (Matthew 19:24).

Bible in Life

Page 51: Matching Truth to Life

1. E. Haggai (Haggai 1:2-4). **2.** J. John the Baptist (John 1:26-27, 35-37). **3.** A. Achan (Joshua 7:1, 4-5, 11-12). **4.** F. Hosea (Hosea 3:1). **5.** N. Peter (Matthew 26:75; John 21:15). **6.** L. King Saul (1 Samuel 18:8-9; 19:9-10). **7.** C. David (2 Samuel 12:7-19). **8.** I. Job (Job 2:11; 11:13-16; 42:7). **9.** G. Jacob (Genesis 27:19-24; 29:15-27). **10.** H. Jeremiah (Jeremiah 7:1; 9:1).

Page 51: Does the Bible Really Say That?

Read the King James Version to find:

2. Numbers 32:23
4. 1 John 4:8
6. Luke 6:39
8. Mark 3:25

Body

Page 58: Your Portable Personal Computer

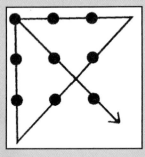

Page 65: For Fun

The lines in #1 and #2 are the same length. The bars in #3 are perfectly straight.

Books of the Bible

Page 75: Search 66

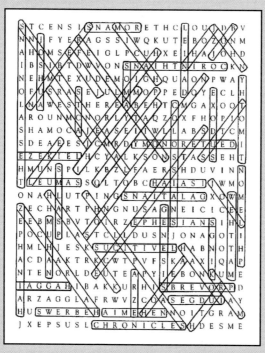

Christmas

Page 100: What's Wrong with This Picture?

Christmas

Page 106: From Saint to Santa Claus

1. his new tomb
2. life (out of death)
3. Sarah, his wife
4. a beautiful robe (or coat of many colors, KJV)
5. the widow who gave two copper coins, all she had
6. the queen of Sheba
7. his only Son
8. from above, from the Father
9. a beautiful jar of expensive perfume
10. Jacob

Computers

Page 124: Net Lingo

:-)))	very happy	:-e	disappointed
:-\	undecided	:-"	whistling
:-)	smile	:-V	shouting
:---)	Pinocchio	X:-)	propeller head
X-(	mad	:`-(	crying
:")	embarrassed	(:-D	blabbermouth
:3-]	dog	8(:-)	Mickey Mouse
=8-0	yikes!	:-!	foot in mouth
:-(0)	yelling	:-t	pouting
'-)	winking	:-C	real unhappy
:-&	tongue-tied		
*<l:-)	Santa Claus		
:-#	my lips are sealed		
:-S	confused		
}:-X	cat		
:~-(	bawling		
0:-)	angel		
(((H)))	big hug		
;-(	chin up		

Education

Page 140: Bee Contests

1920s
gladiolus
abrogate
luxuriance
albumen
asceticism

1930s
fracas
foulard
knack
torsion
deteriorating
intelligible
interning
promiscuous
sanitarium
canonical

1940s
therapy
initials
sacrilegious
semaphore
chlorophyll
psychiatry
dulcimer

1950s
meticulosity
insouciant
vignette

soubrette
transept
crustaceology
condominium
schappe
syllepsis
catamaran

1960s
eudaemonic
smaragdine
esquamulose
equipage
sycophant
eczema
ratoon
chihuahua
abalone
interlocutory

1970s
croissant
shalloon
macerate
vouchsafe
hydrophyte
incisor
narcolepsy
cambist
deification
maculature

1980s
elucubrate
sarcophagus
psoriasis
Purim
luge
milieu
odontalgia
staphylococci
elegiacal
spoliator

1990s
fibranne
antipyretic
lyceum
kamikaze
antediluvian
xanthosis
vivisepulture
euonym
chiaroscurist
logorrhea

2000s
demarche
succedaneum
prospicience
pococurante

Future

Page 173: Prophets in the News

1. Nathan (2 Samuel 12:1, 9). **2.** Jeremiah (Jeremiah 36:4). **3.** Jesus (Matthew 27:35; 28:8-10). **4.** Isaiah (Isaiah 8:3). **5.** Lamentations (Lamentations 2:13, 16—17). **6.** Malachi (Malachi 3:10). **7.** John (John, 1 John, 2 John, 3 John, Revelation; see a Bible dictionary). **8.** Jonah (Jonah 1:17). **9.** Micah (Micah 5:2). **10.** Samuel (1 Samuel 28:15). Secret message in boxed letters: "Trust in Him."

Holidays

Page 198: The Great Turkeyhunt

1. Indians
2. one (Luke 17:12-18)
3. Jonah (Jonah 2:1, 9)
4. Massachusetts
5. 367 years (was in 1621)
6. Daniel (Daniel 6:10-17)
7. Plymouth Rock
8. William Bradford
9. Psalms
10. good (Psalm 136:1)

Humor

Page 199: A Bible Riddle

A great fish, such as swallowed Jonah

Page 200: Bible Crossword

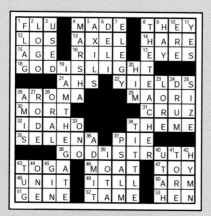

Page 202: Picture Books

1. Matthew; **2.** Chronicles; **3.** Isaiah; **4.** Numbers; **5.** Titus; **6.** Acts;
7. 1 Peter; **8.** Mark

Languages
Page 235: How Well Can You Read English?

1. A watched pot never boils; **2.** Haste makes waste; **3.** Beggars can't be
choosers; **4.** Don't cry over spilled milk; **5.** All that glitters is not gold;
6. Don't count your eggs before they're hatched; **7.** People who live in
glass houses shouldn't throw stones; **8.** A bird in the hand is better than
two in the bush; **9.** Make hay while the sun shines; **10.** You can lead a
horse to water but you can't make him drink.

Numbers

Pages 276 Bible Math

1) 969 (Genesis 5:27)
    - 39 (Bible table of contents)
  = 930 (Bible dictionary)

2)   40 (Matthew 4:1-2)
    x 3 (Genesis 5:32)
  = 120 (Deuteronomy 34:7)

3)   70 (2 Chronicles 36:9-10, 20-2 1)
    x 7 (Genesis 2:2)
  = 490 (Matthew 18:21-22, margin)

4)   2 (Numbers 14:6-9)
    x 6 (Exodus 20:11)
    = 12 (Genesis 49:1-3, 5, 8, 13-14, 16, 19-22, 27)

5)   12 (Bible table of contents; Bible dictionary)
    / 12 (Mark 3:13-19)
    = 1 (John; John 21:18-24; Christian tradition)

6)   30 (Luke 3:23)
    + 10 (Luke 3:36-38)
    = 40 (Numbers 13:1-17, 25)

7)   5 (Genesis-Deuteronomy; Joshua 23:6; Bible dictionary)
    x 1 (Dinah; Genesis 30:21)
    = 5 (John; 1-3 John; Revelation; Bible dictionary)

8)   5 (Isaiah-Daniel; Bible dictionary)
    + 7 (Acts 6:5, 6)
    = 12 (Genesis 49:28)

9)   8 (Bible dictionary)
    - 3 (Matthew 28:19; 1 John 5:7, KJV)
    = 5 (Mark 6:38-44)

10) 40 (Numbers 14:33-34)
    - 13 (Genesis 30:19, 21; 49:1-28)
    = 27 (Bible table of contents)

Page 275: Numbers Is More than a Bible Book

1. They all relate to Commandments. Jesus summarized them all in 2 categories. God wrote the first 10 on tablets; Moses broke the tablets and received them again making 20. There were a total of 613 commands issued at Mount Sinai.

2. By the number of sabbatical years His people had robbed during the 820 years they lived in the Promised Land (2 Chronicles 36:20-21)

3. One year for each day the spies had spent checking out the land of Canaan in unbelief (Numbers 14:32-35)

Plants
Page 286-287: Every Bloomin' Thing

Answers

1. Acacia
2. Almond
3. Aloe
4. Apple
5. Balm of Gilead (prune)
6. Barley
7. Beans
8. Blight (fungus)
9. Bramble
10. Broom
11. Caper
12. Cassia (cinnamon)
13. Cattail
14. Cedar
15. Coriander
16. Cotton
17. Cumin
18. Cypress
19. Dill
20. Fig
21. Flax
22. Flowers of the field
23. Gall
24. Garlic
25. Gourd
26. Grapes
27. Laurel
28. Leeks
29. Lentil
30. Lilies
31. Melon
32. Mildew
33. Mint
34. Mustard
35. Oak
36. Olives
37. Onion
38. Palm
39. Papyrus
40. Pines
41. Pistachio
42. Pomegranate
43. Poplar
44. Reed
45. Rose of Sharon
46. Rush
47. Saffron
48. Sorghum (millet)
49. Sycamore fig tree
50. Thistle
51. Thorn
52. Walnut
53. Wheat
54. Willow

INDEX

INDEX

343

If you have any ideas, suggestions or submissions for the next edition of *The Bible Almanac for Kids*, please send them to:

Educational Publishing Concepts, Inc.
PO Box 665
Wheaton, IL 60189

If you wish to contact Media Ministries, the address is:

Media Ministries
516 East Wakeman
Wheaton, IL 60187

WHITE STONE BOOKS
LAKELAND, FLORIDA